OKLAHOMA STATESMAN

PUBLICATION MADE POSSIBLE BY:

James & Judy Adams
Jean-Paul Audas
Clay & Louise Bennett
Thomas R. Brett
Michael Burrage
ConocoPhillips
James & Joan Ellison
Jim & Christy Everest
Barry & Kathryn Galt
Ike & Mary Beth Glass
Harold Hamm
The Helmerich Foundation
Joel & Carol Jankowsky
Simon A. Levit
Mabrey Bancorporation, Inc.
Paul & Judy Kaye Massad
Eugene McDermott Foundation
Melvin & Jasmine Moran
Larry & Polly Nichols
Perot Foundation
H. E. & Jeannine Rainbolt
Nancy & George Records
Richard L. Sandor
Charles and Lynn Schusterman Family Foundation
Lee & Mary West
The Anne and Henry Zarrow Foundation

OKLAHOMA *TRACKMAKER* SERIES

Oklahoma STATESMAN

THE LIFE OF DAVID BOREN

BY **BOB BURKE**
AND **VON RUSSELL CREEL**

FOREWORD BY **ALEX ADWAN**

SERIES EDITOR: **GINI MOORE CAMPBELL**
ASSOCIATE EDITOR: **ERIC DABNEY**

 OKLAHOMA HERITAGE | Association

OKLAHOMA CITY, OKLAHOMA

OKLAHOMA HERITAGE ASSOCIATION

Contents

Acknowledgments

WE GRATEFULLY ACKNOWLEDGE the assistance of many people who helped complete this intense project. David Boren's life has touched hundreds of thousands of people, and each has his or her story. The mountains of research necessary could not have been completed without the help of Blake Rambo, Dr. Shad Satterthwaite, and Kathy Morley.

The list of those who helped is substantial—Molly Boren, Carrie Boren, and Dan Boren; at the University of Oklahoma, Sherry Evans, Paul Massad, Tripp Hall, Carol Burr, Dean Sul Lee, Jon Lovett, and Carolyn Hanneman; at the Oklahoma Publishing Company, Linda Lynn, Melissa Hayer, Mary Phillips, Robin Davison, and Billie Harry; at Oklahoma Baptist University, Interim President John W. Parrish; and at the Oklahoma Historical Society, Michael Dean, William Welge, Rodger Harris, and Bill Moore.

We also thank two dozen former Boren staff members who have dredged their memory banks for funny and exciting stories about their association with him as governor, United States Senator, or president of OU.

Our research and writing has been guided by Gini Moore

Campbell, our superb editor. She was assisted by proofreaders Alex Adwan, Justice Steven Taylor, and Eric Dabney. Sandi Welch has performed her magic in designing the cover and contents of the book.

We only wish that President Boren's parents were still alive to read this book. They were incredible, supportive parents whose pride in his accomplishments has never faded with the passage of time.

—Bob Burke

—Von Russell Creel

2008

Foreword

BY **ALEX ADWAN**

THE BOOK IS RIGHTLY ENTITLED "Oklahoma Statesman." But the story of David Boren's public service career could just as well be labeled "Oklahoma Teacher."

From his days as a maverick Democratic state legislator through his 16 years in the United States Senate, Boren seemed to regard public office as a means to educate—hopefully to enlighten—as well as to legislate. His transformation from politician to full-time educator as president of a great state university was, in hindsight, preordained.

Of all the threads running through the David Boren story, his passion for education might be the most consistent. He appears to see the world as a classroom, a place to teach and, first of all, to learn. He sees both as essential to representative government.

"Shockingly," he wrote recently, "we as citizens are becoming incapable of protecting our rights and democratic institutions because we do not even know our own history."

But David Boren, the teacher at heart, was, and still is, a natural-born politician. He has been involved directly—often in important ways—in many of the most notable events in Oklahoma and national public life since the 1960s. His record is to a biographer what a 20-point lead is to a basketball coach.

An Oklahoma example is Boren's successful 1974 "Broom Brigade" campaign for governor. An underdog contender, Boren passed out hundreds of brooms as symbols of his intention to sweep out graft and corruption and a vaguely-defined "Old Guard." The campaign is still talked about wherever Oklahoma political junkies gather.

In the United States Senate, Boren was chairman of the Intelligence Committee for six years. The Cold War ended during that time. The struggle for a new world order began. Boren's role as chairman found him involved at one point in an unpublicized visit with the head of the Soviet Union's KGB.

Boren, like many southern and border state Democrats in the House and Senate, was seen as a moderate or conservative. He took pride in working across party lines. Despite some sharp differences on policy, his dealings with Presidents Ronald Reagan and George H.W. Bush were businesslike, even cordial. The details of Boren's help and advice to Reagan during the Iran-Contra blow-up will surprise you. Read all about it.

In March, 2008, Boren worked with New York Mayor Michael Bloomberg, former Georgia Senator Sam Nunn, and other independents and moderates of both parties to arrange a sort of political seminar at the University of Oklahoma. Their goal was to find ways to tone down the acrimony and excessive partisanship that they believe is now crippling the American political system.

One of the problems of telling the David Boren story is that it is not finished. The urge to teach and to make a difference is still at work.

ONE

A Remarkable Career

THE INDELIBLE MARK LEFT BY DAVID L. BOREN on Oklahoma and the nation is well known, especially to the people of Oklahoma. Without his efforts, there might not have been the Oklahoma Arts Institute to promote arts education for gifted high school students or the Oklahoma Foundation for Excellence, a private foundation formed to recognize teachers and honor students for achievement in education. His efforts also led to the creation of more than 200 local private foundations to promote academic excellence, making Oklahoma a national leader in this field.

Without Boren, there would not have been 4,000 Boren scholars and fellows studying at universities in scores of countries, including the developing countries. Their studies are funded by the National Security Education Act which Boren authored as a United States Senator. There might not be state-supported classes for gifted and talented students or medical school scholarships for doctors who promise to practice in rural areas and underserved urban areas. The oppressive inheritance tax for Oklahoma wives and husbands might not have ended. Prison reform might never have taken place.

Boren's contributions to the enhanced academic stature of the University of Oklahoma (OU) are well known. Boren helped bring

OU to lead the nation in the number of National Merit Scholars at public institutions. He established the Honors College to fully challenge top students. He also led OU as one of the first 20 public institutions of higher learning to reach $1 billion in private endowment. In his first decade at OU, he quadrupled the number of endowed family donations and doubled the number of scholarships for undergraduate and graduate students.

It is well known that Boren played a leadership role in bringing the National Weather Research Center to Oklahoma and in establishing a new comprehensive Cancer and Diabetes Treatment and Research Center in the state.

But few people realize that Boren played a major role in some of the nation's most sensitive and often secret projects and negotiations in the 1980s and 1990s. Few know of Boren's secret trip to Baghdad, Iraq, following the first Gulf War to obtain the release of a kidnapped Oklahoma oil field worker or of Boren's meeting with resistance leaders in Afghanistan and his help in getting Afghan rebels armed. Not many know of his secret meeting with anti-communist rebels in Nicaragua.

Outside his staff and close friends, Boren's trip to the Philippines and his meeting with a Catholic cardinal before President Ferdinand Marcos left power, his relay of a personal message from the President to Congolese leaders, and his private meeting with Russian leader Boris Yeltsin remained a secret. There were no public reports of Boren bringing back to President George H.W. Bush reports of a meeting with the head of the Russian KGB which led to Boren's prediction to President Bush that a coup would be attempted against Soviet President Mikhail Gorbachev.

Few people know of the role Boren played in arranging Nelson Mandela's first visit to the United States after his release from years in a South African prison or of Boren's participation in secret negotiations in assisting President Bill Clinton in formulating American policy toward China.

It was never revealed publicly, until the publication of this book, that Boren was the first person to inform the President of a missed opportunity to capture Panamanian President Manuel Noriega without having to launch a massive military operation to remove Noriega from power.

To be complete, the story of Boren's career must include all of these unusual senatorial missions as well as his childhood in Washington, D. C. and Seminole, Oklahoma, his college years at Yale University, Oxford University, and the University of Oklahoma, his term as governor of Oklahoma, and his coming home to OU to become president of that institution.

Some would argue that David Boren has had a greater impact upon Oklahoma than any other person in history. Virtually all would agree that his legacy is significant. During the course of his political career Boren made history by winning his United States Senate seat with the highest winning percentage in the nation, 83 percent, in 1990. When he left the Senate, his approval rating was a remarkable 90 percent.

However, Boren's great potential may never have been realized without the influence of his family, his friends, and the path of life that led him to public service.

Thank you for the letter.

PRESIDENT RONALD REAGAN

TWO

The Letter

TEARS WELLED UP IN THE EYES of arguably the most powerful man in the world. Ronald Reagan, President of the United States, spoke softly as he embraced David L. Boren, Oklahoma's senior United States Senator, with "a bear-hug."[1]

Reagan and Boren were standing alone in the Oval Office of the White House in Washington, D.C., on a day in early August, 1987. Reagan put his arm around Boren's shoulder as he said, "Thank you for the letter."

A few days before, Boren had handwritten a heart-felt letter to the President, expressing his personal support of Reagan who was struggling in the midst of a critical time in his presidency and in the history of the nation. According to his top aides, Reagan was "very depressed"[2] over public reaction to his administration's involvement in what became known as the Iran-Contra Affair.

The political controversy began the previous November when a Lebanese magazine, *Ash-Shiraa,* reported that the United States had illegally sold arms to Iran to attempt to influence the release of American hostages. The matter was further complicated by the fact that profits made from the arms sale to a recognized enemy of the United States were being used to finance the Contras, a right-wing guerilla organization engaged in an open insurgency against the leftist Sandinista government of Nicaragua. Such action was in violation of a law passed by Congress.

After the Lebanese report and the downing of an airlift of guns in Nicaragua, the American press began questioning White House officials about the validity of the allegations. At first President Reagan denied American involvement, but later had to admit that the American government, without his knowledge, had indeed sold arms to Iran, and that the money had been funneled to the Contras in Nicaragua.

For months, Iran-Contra was the lead story on the nightly news and was front-page material in major newspapers. Boren was in the middle of the fray as a member of the congressional panel that conducted an investigation of the matter. The congressional hearings were parallel to the Tower Commission, a high-level presidential commission appointed by Reagan to assess the weaknesses of the structure of the National Security Council that allowed a lieutenant colonel, Oliver North, to manage what, in Boren's opinion, was an obvious unconstitutional and illegal sale of arms to Iran. The Tower Commission was headed by former United States Senator John Tower of Texas. Members of the presidential commission included former Secretary of State Edmund Muskie and former National Security Advisor Brent Scowcroft.[3]

Boren asked hard and pointed questions of members of the administration who appeared before the Iran-Contra congressional committee. How could something like this happen? The Congress had passed legislation making it illegal to sell arms to Iran. Iran was engaged in a war with Iraq. Helping Iran in the war also was against the stated policy of the Reagan administration.

Even though Boren supported the cause of the Contras in trying to overthrow what he believed to be a corrupt and

Communist government in Nicaragua, he in no way supported the unconstitutional actions of a lieutenant colonel being able to sidestep the laws of his own government to carry out a clandestine operation, approved at the highest levels of the American power structure. "It is dangerous," he said, "to have a system in which a relatively low-ranking military officer can control obviously illegal activities."[4]

Boren deeply believed that under the American system, the President and military leaders were constitutionally required to obey the laws passed by Congress, whether they agreed with them or not. Boren was not hesitant to label North's activities a "clear violation of the constitution." He also said that some of the people responsible "ought to go to jail."[5]

Boren's public statements about Iran-Contra brought concern to his own life. Back home in Seminole, Oklahoma, Boren's wife, Molly, was frightened one night when an unknown person, apparently upset over Boren's harsh words about the scandal, drove up in front of the Boren home and hurled a rock through a porch light. The police chief of Seminole sent officers to watch the home and even left a police department pistol with Molly.[6]

At the heart of the investigation of Congress and the Tower Commission was the extent of the President's involvement in the illegal activity. If Reagan had approved Colonel North's plans, the President could be impeached for violating the constitution. The nation was split. Many believed Reagan knew about North and his operation. Reagan, who had enjoyed incredible popularity as president, had seen his approval rating drop to 46 percent, nearly 20 points below the level of support after he had been overwhelmingly elected to a second term in 1984.[7]

The stress on the President heightened when the Tower Commission report was delivered to the White House on February 26, 1987. The report found the sale of arms to Iran was contrary to the federal constitution and statutes. The document criticized the actions of North, Secretary of Defense Caspar Weinberger, and National Security Advisor Admiral John Poindexter. Even though the Tower Commission report did not determine that President Reagan had any knowledge of the arms sale, the conclusion of the commission members was that Reagan was culpable for not properly supervising his subordinates and being aware of their actions.[8]

Pressure mounted even more on the President as the Joint House-Senate Congressional Investigation Committee concluded its hearings. Its role had been expanded and a new report could prove more critical of Reagan. There was even talk of impeachment.

Boren was firm in his criticism of Colonel North and others, but did not believe Reagan knew of their actions. "He was a man whose style of leadership was looking at the big picture. Reagan was an effective leader because he focused on the big picture and not minute, day-to-day details," Boren later reflected. Boren had met with Reagan on numerous occasions and knew of the President's genuine desire to end the Cold War and bring pressure on the government of the Soviet Union when the Russians tried to exert their influence in other parts of the world. Boren agreed with Reagan's doctrine of enhanced containment—contain the Russian influence within that country's own borders and make the Russians pay a high price when they tried to further expand their influence.[9]

During the days that followed the conclusion of the congressional hearings, Boren talked frequently with White House Chief of Staff Howard Baker and other White House aides who were concerned with the President's deep depression. Clearly, the public expected the President to share with the nation his reaction to events that came to light during the hearings.

There were rumors that Reagan might resign, return to his home in California, and forego the final 17 months of his presidency. As Reagan announced plans to speak to the nation, Baker and Vice President George H.W. Bush confided in Boren that Reagan was torn on what direction his speech to the American people should take.

At one meeting in the Oval Office, Reagan proposed being apologetic to the nation's citizens. However, in a subsequent meeting, Reagan was defiant and wanted a speech written that would challenge the idea that the arms-for-hostage deal was unconstitutional. Aides were concerned that if the President appeared defiant, congressional leaders might launch impeachment proceedings.[10]

After conversations with Baker and Vice President Bush, Boren wrote Reagan a personal letter. After expressing the hope that the President would see the letter, Boren wrote, "I truly believe that the decisions you make as the Iran-Contra hearings come to a close will have a profound influence on the future of this country for decades to come. We are in a crucial period."[11]

Boren spent much of the letter focusing on Reagan's opportunity to bring the Cold War to a conclusion. He talked about how he applauded the President for strongly frightening the Russians with his missile defense system and harsh criticism for Russian involvement outside its sovereign territory.[12]

In the three-page, hand-written letter, Boren laid out support for Reagan's efforts to make the world a safer place by negotiating arms control treaties. Warmly, Boren told the President of his personal admiration and how he would stand as a Democrat to help Reagan achieve worthy goals in the best interest of the country. Boren believed that it was absolutely necessary for Reagan to stand tall as America's leader. Boren wrote, "The rest of the world has observed our lack of unity…The failure of the United

States to speak to the rest of the world with a single voice has been devastating to our national interests."[13]

Boren promised his personal support, writing, "As a Democrat and as chairman of the Senate Intelligence Committee, I pledge to you that I will walk the extra mile to try to make it work. In the year and a half remaining in your term, you have a chance to make a great and positive mark on our future in areas like arms control and Central American policy. As an American, without regard to party, I pray that you will succeed."[14]

Boren observed, "Twenty years of growing mistrust and divisiveness cannot be overcome in a few days or weeks, but we have a rare opportunity to start moving in the right direction."[15]

Boren strongly suggested that the President be candid with the American people, admit that mistakes had been made, and avoid any appearance of being defiant to the Congress or other critics of the administration's involvement in the controversy.

Boren completed the letter and delivered it to Chief of Staff Baker at the White House. Boren and Baker had worked closely in the United States Senate in a bipartisan fashion, so Boren was comfortable in handing the letter to him.

The following day, Boren and several other United States senators were invited to meet with the President in the Cabinet Room at the White House. Just before the meeting, Baker whispered to Boren, "When every one else leaves, stay behind. Don't tell anyone or make it appear you are staying, but the President wants to see you alone in the Oval Office."[16]

Boren had no knowledge that President Reagan had read the letter and wondered why the President wanted to see him. However, the letter soon became the topic of a private conversation. Boren was seated at the meeting table next to Vice President Bush, who leaned over to him and quietly said, "Thank you for your letter to the President!" Boren was surprised and responded,

"Oh, you know about the letter?" Vice President Bush replied, "Oh, yes! The President called several of us into the Oval Office last night and read the entire letter to us."[17]

When the brief meeting ended, and Boren quietly delayed his departure, Baker motioned Boren to follow him through a small hallway that connects the Cabinet Room to the Oval Office. Boren was ushered into the Oval Office where Reagan stood alone.

When the door closed behind Boren, Reagan walked toward him and pulled from his inside coat pocket Boren's hand-written letter. The President said, "David, I received your letter and I read it over and over again. I have been struggling with my speech. I didn't know what to tell the country about Iran-Contra."[18]

Reagan became emotional as he drew Boren close in a "bear-hug." Reagan told Boren, "I can't tell you how much your letter meant to me. It convinced me that we can go on! We can accomplish things!"[19]

Tears welled in Boren's eyes as he told Reagan, "Mr. President, of course we can! You can do so much, and I will help you in any way I can!" Reagan ended the emotional conversation by saying, "Thank you and God bless you! You've really helped me see things differently." Boren replied, "Just share your heart with the American people and tell them how much more we can still do together and how much you want to do just that! Everybody makes mistakes. Admit your mistakes and the American people will forgive you and move on."

The two men hugged again and Boren left. Baker was waiting for Boren outside the Oval Office and said, "I want to thank you again for the letter. It made a real difference."

Boren left through the back door of the White House and went back to his Senate office. On August 12, the President spoke to the nation with an apology and a plan to make the world safer by emphasizing arms control negotiations. The President, taking the advice contained in Boren's letter, took the opportunity to call for a renewal of trust between the White House and Congress. Reagan said, "The biggest lesson we can draw from the hearings is that the executive and legislative branches of government need to regain trust in each other. We've seen the results of the mistrust in the forms of lies, leaks, divisions, and mistakes. We need to find a way to cooperate while realizing foreign policy."[20]

With a new determination, Reagan said, "My fellow Americans...I'm not about to let the dust and cobwebs settle on the furniture in this office or on me. I have things I intend to do, and with your help, we can do them."[21]

After the speech, Boren quickly responded with a statement to the press that he still strongly believed in Reagan's integrity and his ability to accomplish much during his remaining time in office. As the Democratic chairman of the Senate Intelligence Committee, Boren promised bipartisan support to further arms control negotiations and end the Cold War that had created disharmony among the nation's super powers since the end of World War II.

Boren also promised to help the President draft an executive order that would prevent the actions that had resulted in the national controversy. Boren and United States Senator William Cohen met with Howard Baker and National Security Advisor General Colin Powell to finalize an executive order that was issued by Reagan to expand congressional oversight of secret operations.

This story is but one of dozens of examples of the impact Boren made upon national and international affairs, demonstrating a deep commitment to bipartisanship, especially in foreign affairs, that had defined Boren's public career.

His constituents in Oklahoma were well aware of Boren's contributions as a member of the Oklahoma House of Representatives and as the nation's youngest governor when he was elected in 1974. However, this grandson of a tenant farmer acted far beyond the borders of Oklahoma. Shortly before he left Congress, *The Almanac of American Politics* ranked Boren as one of the Senate's most influential members.

David Boren's service to Oklahoma and the nation is an extension of the support of his family and community.

Judge Robert Henry

THREE

A Proud Heritage

THE ANCESTRAL FAMILY TREE of David Lyle Boren is marked with chapters of adventure, difficult circumstances, pioneering, hard work, and integrity.

The story of his paternal Boren ancestors began in the middle of the seventeenth century amidst internal struggles in the beautiful and gentle countryside of County Clare in Ireland. Four Boren brothers were leaders in the town of Ennis, founded in 1600.[1]

In the early eighteenth century, the Borens left Ireland and settled in North Carolina, continuing the family tradition of farming and horse breeding.

After decades in North Carolina, three of the brothers followed others to the advancing frontier of the American colonies. By the early nineteenth century, Borens were farming and raising horses in Kentucky where they became acquainted with Daniel Boone. The Borens accompanied Boone to Missouri where the famous frontiersman died in 1820.[2]

Still looking for new adventure and more elbow room, the Borens made friends in Missouri with Moses Austin, a banker, who had convinced the Spanish government to give him authority to establish a colony in Texas. However, before Austin could interest enough people in the colonization idea, he died.

His son, Stephen F. Austin, took up the cause and led 300 families to Texas. Austin's deal with the Spanish government was that heads of families would be granted a league, 4,428 acres, and a labor, 177 acres, in exchange for a promise to farm the land, raise livestock, and become Mexican citizens.[3]

Michael Boren, the son of James and Nancy Boren, followed the lure of a new life in Texas in 1827. Michael was 21 when he arrived. Soon he met and married Elizabeth "Bitty" Morrow. In 1829, Bitty gave birth to their first son, William M. Boren.

Michael became self-sufficient by growing corn, king of the Texas crops. Corn was an incredibly versatile commodity. It could be ground into meal and baked for food, distilled into liquor for drink, or stored in hastily-constructed cribs to feed animals in the winter.

Michael and his family lived in Texas during tumultuous times. General Santa Anna overthrew the constitutional government of Mexico in 1835 and proclaimed himself dictator. Santa Anna's actions resulted in a revolt by American colonists. Michael became a colonel in Sam Houston's army that overcame the fall of the Alamo in 1836 and defeated Santa Anna in the Battle of San Jacinto. Texas was independent and would remain a sovereign nation for the next decade.[4]

In 1841, Michael joined Peters Colony, the largest and most successful colony ever established in Texas. From the area encompassed by the colony came the present-day Texas counties of Dallas, Ellis, Collin, Denton, Grayson, Wise, and Tarrant. Michael received a huge parcel of rich farmland near the Trinity River. The nearby settlement later was called Ennis, named for an early official of the Houston and Texas Central Railroad that extended a line to the area.[5] In the same year Michael began homesteading his league and labor, Major General William Worth settled to his north and called his settlement Fort Worth. Michael was to become the first county commissioner of Ellis County after statehood.[6]

During the years of the Texas Republic, President Sam Houston often visited the Boren home, located on the road between Austin and Indian Territory. Houston did business with Indian tribes that had relocated to Indian Territory from their ancestral homes in the southeastern United States.

Houston never wanted to be considered a freeloader. He paid the Borens for supplies and lodging with Republic of Texas money, which the Boren heirs still possess. Young William Boren was honored to sit with President Houston in front of the Boren fireplace at night and whittle toys and hear stories about the defeat of Santa Anna.

William lost his first wife, Eliza Pettit, in 1858, only two years after they were married. A year later, he married Martha Cooke and settled in Reagor Springs in Ellis County. William, at age 32, enlisted in the Confederate Army during the Civil War and rose to the rank of captain. His job was to provide meat for Confederate forces. He commanded a small group of soldiers who drove cattle from Texas to the battlefields of the South.

During the war and in the years following the conflict, William and Martha had nine children, including David Boren's grandfather, Mark Latimer, born at Reagor Springs on November 22, 1868. When Mark Latimer was 26 he married Nannie Mae Wetherall at Bardwell in Ellis County in 1895. Her father was well educated and had established one of the first schools in the area. Mark was a well-respected leader in the community and his church, the Disciples of Christ.

David's father, Lyle Hagler Boren, was born on May 11, 1910. He was fortunate to survive beyond his first few days. He was born as a "blue baby," a victim of cyanosis. The doctor assessed that Lyle had a hole in the wall of the lower chamber of his heart.

Medical textbooks of the time called cyanosis an "extremely grave" condition. Dr. William Pepper, a leading author on the subject, insisted that if a blue baby lived for more than a few days, the infant should be sheltered from unnecessary exertion and be protected from any mental disturbances.[7] As Lyle grew he stayed indoors much of the time with his mother. From her example, he developed a lifelong love of reading which led to his accumulation of a personal library of several thousand books.

Flooding of the rich farmland along the Trinity River ultimately doomed Mark Latimer Boren's farming. Facing bankruptcy in 1915, he sold his land for $13 an acre, property that decades before sold for $1,200 an acre. He bought a small farm in Haskell County, in West Texas, and moved his family there.

A drought hit West Texas in 1916 and 1917 and devastated the cattle industry. The Borens had to haul drinking water for a year. A 350-foot well on their farm went completely dry, in part because Mark was a generous man. He often shared his sparse supply of water with his neighbors. In November, 1917, faced with little prospect for success in West Texas, Mark led his family in a covered wagon caravan that left Haskell County for Oklahoma.[8]

The Borens had two wagons filled with their belongings as they traveled along powder-dry roads toward Oklahoma with visions of fresh water and green grass. Young Lyle, who had recovered his health, rode a stick horse behind the second wagon. Every hour he looked toward the horizon and asked his father, "Is that Oklahoma?"[9]

In 1917, Oklahoma was ten years old and offered the Borens more opportunity for a better life than they had seen in several years. They camped at Randlett in Cotton County and picked cotton for money to buy food and water. They spent Thanksgiving camped in a wagon yard near Comanche, Oklahoma, and then settled in a small house in nearby Lawton.

Mark led his family to tenant farms in Fletcher, Oklahoma, and eventually to Choctaw in central Oklahoma. It was there that Lyle completed high school with seven other seniors in 1927. On the night of his graduation, he stuffed his worn-out shoes with cardboard. However, they were ruined when the toes were run over by a car. Fortunately, his brother, James, arrived for the ceremony in time to rush to town and buy a new pair of shoes.[10]

Lyle sold a cow for $40 to finance his first year of college at East Central State College in Ada, Oklahoma. In speeches in later years, talking about the value of a college education, Lyle jokingly said by the time he graduated, he had spent almost the entire $40.

During his last semester at East Central, Lyle completed his practice teaching assignment by teaching library science to students of the Horace Mann High School, located on the college campus. A pretty young woman, Christine McKown, the daughter of a Maud, Oklahoma, pharmacist, caught his eye. The young teacher fell in love with his student, but it took a long time to convince her to marry him.

Christine was the granddaughter of T. F. Villines, one of the founders of Maud. Both of Christine's parents came from pioneer families. Her paternal grandparents, the Estes family, left Missouri and went to Colorado where they helped found Estes Park. Her maternal grandfather had come to Maud from Berryville, Arkansas, where he ran a store on the town square. Family members were among the early pioneer settlers in northeast Arkansas.

In 1930 Lyle graduated with a degree in history and government and took a job for $150 a month as a teacher at Wolf, an oil boom town in Seminole County. Within a short time, at age 20, Lyle became the principal of the school. Wolf had grown from a spot in the road to a virtual oil field metropolis with more than 2,000 students in the school system.[11]

Lyle pursued Christine. When she graduated from high school he appeared at her home with a diamond ring. Christine refused the ring, instead announcing her intentions to never marry until she completed her college education. She enrolled at Oklahoma A & M College, now Oklahoma State University, in Stillwater. Lyle thought Christine was the most beautiful girl in the state. She was the Pi Phi Homecoming Queen and active in campus life.[12]

While waiting on Christine, Lyle continued as principal at Wolf School. One night his automobile was stolen, reportedly by the infamous Oklahoma outlaw, Pretty Boy Floyd. When word spread that Boren was struggling financially without transportation, his car mysteriously was returned.

Lyle was active in politics, a continuation of his involvement in the art during college days at East Central. There he had founded the Oklahoma Democrat Fraternity in 1932 and had been elected president of his junior and senior classes.

In 1934, with Oklahoma in the clutches of the Great Depression, Lyle decided to run for Congress from Oklahoma's Fourth Congressional District. He saw how badly Oklahomans had suffered from the effects of the worst economic downturn in modern history.[13]

Lyle lost his first race for Congress and returned to the classroom. Frankly, it was good that he lost because had he won, a legal problem would have arisen. He did not have a birth certificate because the courthouse in Waxahachie, Texas, where he was born, had burned. His mother had incorrectly recorded his birth year in the family Bible, making him 25 years old, the minimum age for a congressman. She later discovered that mistake. Had Lyle been elected, he could not have served in Congress because he was only 24 years old.

Lyle threw his hat into the ring for the Fourth District position two years later in 1936. With the economy still a major issue, Lyle beat incumbent P. L. Gassaway in the primary and became the Democratic nominee for Congress in the district that was comprised of nine counties in eastern and south central Oklahoma.[14]

While waiting for the general election, Lyle was called into action to campaign for the reelection of President Franklin D. Roosevelt. A convincing speaker, Lyle traveled on trains with Roosevelt and spoke to many gatherings in several states.

After Lyle's election in November, 1936, he turned his full attention to Christine. She had graduated from Oklahoma A & M and had taken a $75-a-month teaching position at Hominy, Oklahoma.

Lyle and Christine were married in late December in Stillwater by Reverend Willmoore Kendall, a blind Methodist minister who Lyle knew from the Oklahoma Democrat Fraternity. As the newest member of Congress from Oklahoma, and with his new wife at his side, Lyle headed for Washington, D.C., a place he had never been. He was anxious to represent the people of Oklahoma's Fourth Congressional District.

*You can always learn something
from every single person you meet.*

LYLE H. BOREN

FOUR

Childhood

L YLE BECAME A REBEL IN CONGRESS. He was fiercely independent and voted his conscience on any issue. Even though he revered his good friend, President Franklin D. Roosevelt, he often voted against Roosevelt's programs when he believed the interests of the Fourth District of Oklahoma were contrary to the president's ideas.[1]

House Speaker Sam Rayburn took Lyle under his wing and granted choice committee assignments during his first years in Congress. Lyle became involved in many congressional battles that divided friends and partisans. However, one of his first law-making efforts united both parties. With fresh knowledge of the death from cancer of Joe Ellis, a Shawnee, Oklahoma businessman, Lyle and a fellow congressman pushed a bill that created the National Cancer Institute to coordinate cancer research in the nation. The institute was a forerunner to what became the National Institutes of Health.[2]

Rayburn and two other Texans, Lyndon Baines Johnson and John Nance Garner, played pivotal roles in Lyle's training. Garner was vice president and Johnson was a newly-elected member of Congress from Texas. Even though he was elected after Lyle, Johnson, later elected President of the United States, had been a congressional aide and knew the landscape on Capitol Hill.

While Christine set up housekeeping in the nation's capital, Lyle organized the First Monday Night Poker Club, a group of friends that met at a member's apartment each month. It was a distinguished group. The young senator from Missouri, Harry Truman, was possibly the best story teller of the group. Other members included future House Speaker John McCormack of Massachusetts and Congressman Clinton Anderson of New Mexico. When Truman became president, the poker club was given one choice for naming a member of the president's cabinet. Anderson was tabbed as Truman's Secretary of Agriculture. Anderson was also a United States Senator after being in the cabinet.[3]

Christine made lifelong friends with wives of Lyle's colleagues. Two of her friends were Claudia "Lady Bird" Johnson, the wife of Congressman Lyndon B. Johnson, and Margaret Chase Smith, wife of a Maine congressman who herself later became a United States Senator. Christine entertained their friends and hoped for the day to begin a family.

Lyle was reelected to Congress in 1938 and 1940. During the 1940 campaign, Christine announced to Lyle that she was pregnant. Lyle often kidded prospective voters about the forthcoming child. He once told an audience, "You need to send me back to Washington! In the spring we're going to have a baby, and I need a good job!"[4]

David Lyle Boren was born at Colombia Hospital for Women on the edge of Georgetown in Washington, D.C., on April 21, 1941. It was San Jacinto Day, certainly appropriate because of the Boren family history involving the Republic of Texas. Oklahoma Congressman Victor Wickersham heard about David's birth and rushed to the hospital. He claimed to have recognized David among dozens of babies in a viewing window.[5]

David was born during tumultuous times in the nation's capital. Daily, there was talk of war. Lyle was an early supporter of efforts to help Great Britain in the war and brought Lord Halifax, Edward Frederick Lindley Wood, the British Ambassador, to Oklahoma to help promote voluntary shipments of scrap metal to that country. The effort was known as the "Iron for Britain" campaign.

On December 7, 1941, Lyle, Christine, and seven-month-old David were traveling by car in Tennessee on their way from Washington, D.C., to Oklahoma when a radio news report announced the Japanese attack on Pearl Harbor. Lyle sent Christine and David on to Oklahoma and he returned to Washington by airplane. The following day Congress declared war on the Empire of Japan. Within hours, Lyle offered himself for active military duty, but Speaker Rayburn convinced him his talents were needed more as a member of Congress. Boren did, however, go on duty with the United States Navy with the rank of lieutenant commander when Congress was not in session. As congressman, he also visited Oklahoma soldiers on the front lines in Europe.[6]

David spent his first five years living between the Boren home on Hoover Street in Seminole and in the Westchester Apartments on Cathedral Avenue in the nation's capital. The trips between Oklahoma and Washington, D.C., were made by car or by train. The apartments were located near the National Cathedral. At first, David had few playmates on the apartment playground. In fact, in his imagination he created an alter-ego in order to have a playmate.[7] Soon young David made friends with children in adjacent apartments and played with children from many nations. His father claimed David spent so much play time with a young boy from Brooklyn that he developed a Brooklyn accent.[8]

Times were simpler in Washington, D.C. Street cars provided quick and efficient transportation from the Borens' apartment to the Capitol and other government buildings. When it snowed, the police department blocked off the street in front of the apartment to allow David and his playmates to ride their sleds down the long hill. During the war years, David has vague memories of being afraid of enemy attacks on Washington, D.C., and pulling black shades over the windows at night.[9]

The Borens walked to church on Sundays. David attended Sunday School at Saint Alban's Church and joined his parents for services at the adjacent National Cathedral. From his earliest recollection, David was inspired by the beauty and splendor of the gothic structure.[10]

Because his father was a member of Congress, young David was surrounded by famous leaders. A close friend of the family was House Speaker Sam Rayburn of Texas. Rayburn was unmarried and often came to the Boren apartment for dinner. After the meal, Rayburn helped David drape blankets over chairs in the living room. Speaker Rayburn got down on his hands and knees and pretended to be camping with his young friend in the wilderness. Rayburn charmed David with his stories.

When David was three, his father took him to see President Roosevelt in the Oval Office at the White House. David remembered him as a man with a wonderful laugh who bounced him on his knee and "had a big smile and a wonderful voice that was so warm." Roosevelt was at ease with children and had charisma with young visitors, just as he had with adults.[11]

Largely because of opposition from labor unions, Lyle was defeated by Glen Johnson, Sr., in the congressional election in 1946. Military service also was a major issue. Lyle had followed Speaker Rayburn's advice to not enter active military duty during World War II. Johnson was a returning veteran and defeated Lyle in the Democratic runoff.

David was introduced to political campaigning in 1946. He had accompanied his father on the campaign trail two years before, but he played a more visible role in Lyle's unsuccessful bid for reelection in 1948. At age five, David made a short radio speech for his father.

At that early age, David already seemed destined for public service. He saw politics as a way to serve people. Often, strangers waited in their cars in front of the Boren home, wanting to talk to Lyle. Frequently, Christine kept warming up dinner because Lyle took as much time as his constituents needed.

From those early experiences, David learned from his father the gift of listening to people. Lyle would lie down on the garage floor to talk to a mechanic working under a car or visit the kitchen of a restaurant to speak with the cooks. Lyle stopped at the side of a field where he saw a farmer plowing his ground or a rancher building fence. Lyle told David, "Remember, you can always learn something from every single person you meet!"[12]

At the end of each conversation, Lyle took the time to teach his son that every person was worthy of respect and every person had a different life experience. Lyle also stressed the importance of moral courage, saying, "People who hold public offices should have their bags mentally packed." Lyle meant that an elected official should always vote his conscience and be prepared to be defeated in the next election. From Lyle, David learned valuable life lessons.[13]

In January, 1947, Lyle took his wife and son back to Hoover Street in Seminole to live fulltime. They said goodbye to Washington, D.C., at least for a few years. Lyle bought a herd of Hereford cattle and began ranching. On July 5, 1948, Christine gave birth to her second child, a daughter, Susan.

David was not overjoyed at beginning his formal education in the fall of 1947. When his mother drove to the entrance of Roosevelt Grade School on College Street in Seminole, David hovered in the floor in front of the rear seat and refused to enter the building. It took David's first-grade teacher, Ruth Robinson, principal, Janie Ross Adair, and Christine to physically pry David from the car. However, Mrs. Robinson was such a kind and interesting teacher that David loved school within two or three days.

Mrs. Robinson became a second mother to David. She deeply cared for each of her students. She lost her husband in World War II and never remarried. She tutored children free after school each day and bought school supplies, gloves, and coats for her students whose families were struggling to make ends meet. Mrs. Robinson, who loved politics, remained a great influence on David's life long after first grade. Until her death, David kept in regular contact with her. He always valued her opinion on the issues of the day. He purchased a chair on the South Oval of the OU campus in Norman in her memory. She was the first of several teachers who greatly influenced his life and led him to believe that there was no more important life's work than teaching.[14]

Because his father had served in Congress, David continued to be exposed to great American leaders. In 1948, President Harry S. Truman came through Seminole on a whistle-stop train tour. Lyle was asked to introduce the President who made a brief speech to thousands of people lined up around the Rock Island Railroad depot. After the speech in Seminole, Lyle and David were invited to ride the presidential train for other stops eastward toward McAlester. Between stops, President Truman came back to the car in which the Borens were riding and struck up a conversation with David, the only youngster on the train.[15]

David had other experiences in public life. He often traveled around the state with his father to organizational meetings of the Oklahoma Cattlemen's Association, of which Lyle was a founder. On occasion, Lyle took David to the ranch where he learned to build fence and do other chores. David said, "It was Dad's way of building character and teaching me the value of hard work."[16]

Lyle and Christine were loving parents. David walked to and from school and very often came home for lunch. Christine prepared three full meals each day and was waiting for her children when they arrived after the school day. If something had gone wrong that day, Christine was ready with words of encouragement. David remembered, "My parents made me realize how much it means to any child to be unconditionally loved and supported."[17]

Christine also faithfully took David and Susan to Sunday School and church. Lyle was a member of the Church of Christ and Christine was Methodist. Most of the time, David went to church at First Methodist Church in Seminole, but he sometimes attended church with his father. Religion often was discussed at home and David heard the views of both his parents.

David spent a lot of time with his maternal grandparents, Cliff and Alice McKown, in nearby Maud. David's mother was an only child so David was the only grandchild, a special bond he enjoyed until his sister was born. David often spent the night and weekends with the McKowns. Mr. McKown was the Maud postmaster and a pharmacist. One of Mrs. McKown's sisters had married the only physician in Maud, Dr. Roland Culbertson. Wherever David went in Maud, he usually was surrounded by relatives. Almost every Sunday after church, Lyle, Christine, David, and Susan drove to Maud for Sunday dinner with the McKowns. Even after his parents moved back to Washington, D.C., David continued to drive to Maud each Sunday during his years in law school to have Sunday dinner with his grandparents.

While his mother's family was small, David's father's family was huge. After spending time in Maud with the McKowns, the Borens often drove to Wewoka where David's paternal grandparents lived. He recalled, "Going to Grandmother and Granddad Boren's house was like going to a three-ring circus. There were usually several of my uncles and aunts there." David grew especially close to his Aunt

Juno Boren, the city librarian in Wewoka. He remained close to her for the remainder of her life.[18]

As many as 40 people stayed for dinner at the Boren house in Wewoka. David enjoyed lively discussions on a variety of topics. Three of his Boren uncles were ministers—two Church of Christ and one Methodist. Spirited debates about religion and politics spiced up the late afternoon family gatherings.

David also was close to his father's only sister, Mae Boren Axton, the writer of "Heartbreak Hotel," Elvis Presley's first hit song. Aunt Mae and her son, David's cousin, Hoyt Axton, came by their musical talent honestly. The Boren grandparents loved to put on old shoes and perform Irish folk dances. David was delighted when his grandparents, accompanied by a fiddle, performed for the grandchildren.[19]

The Boren family gatherings also gave David a love of art. Several members of the extended Boren family excelled in painting. David's cousin, Jodie Boren, excelled in water color. Another cousin, James Boren, was the first art director for the National Cowboy Hall of Fame, now the National Cowboy and Western Heritage Museum in Oklahoma City, and James' daughter, Nancy, was an accomplished painter.

Later in life, David often spoke about the high social price of geographic mobility in later generations chasing economic efficiency. Family members followed their jobs all over the country. No longer are most children in the United States growing up under constant influence of an extended family such as the one David had in Seminole. He was appreciative of growing up in a small town where an enormous effort was made to create a sense of family and community.

School and learning became an integral part of David's life. He was blessed with teachers who served as mentors. His principal, Janie Adair, of Cherokee Indian descent, had been a childhood sweetheart of Oklahoma humorist Will Rogers and was a fascinating storyteller, especially about the history of Oklahoma.

Lucille Dacus, David's third-grade teacher at Roosevelt School, fostered his intellectual curiosity. Mrs. Dacus had known Lyle and Christine before they were married. Lyle had set up the blind date between Mrs. Dacus and her future husband, Foy.

Well into her nineties, Mrs. Dacus remembered David in a 2006 interview. She said, "Even in the third grade, his goal was excellence in every academic effort. He was always dressed up and very studious. At recess, he had rather watch, than play. He was friendly and all the kids liked him." Later, when David was teaching at Oklahoma Baptist University, Mrs. Dacus wrote him with a prophetic wish, "My wish for you is that would become president of a university and live in a big house with a picket fence."[20]

Another observer of David's pre-teen years is Alex Adwan, longtime editorial page editor of the *Tulsa World,* whose family has known the Borens for four generations. Adwan remembers, "When we visited Lyle and Christine, David was always talking with the adults. He was obviously brilliant and was aware of the happenings in the world around us."[21]

David's favorite childhood game was playing school. One of his best playmates in Seminole was Linda Sue Gipson. Her parents, Fred and Leola Gipson, were close friends with the Borens and often visited each other's homes. David and Linda would sit in front of a small chalkboard and take turns being the "teacher" in their make-believe school. When they were not playing school, they climbed trees in the backyard.[22]

Gipson, now Linda Sue Stone, was in David's class each year of elementary school. She remembered she had a crush on David that began in the first grade. "He was the cutest and nicest little boy," she remembered, "He set the standard in each class and was always the consummate student."[23]

David's early training in social graces, especially in dancing, came from time spent at the Martha C. Mitchell School of Dance. Linda and David regularly attended weekly sessions where Mrs. Mitchell, a striking woman who "dressed and maintained the persona of a Bohemian existence," taught the boys and girls the fox trot, waltzes, sambas, tangos, and the jitter bug.[24]

Mrs. Mitchell taught David to dance with all the girls and how to properly "cut in" on other dancers. "There were no wall flowers allowed," remembered Linda, "although at the formal dance at the end of the year, David and I danced the first and last dance together. In my nine-year-old heart, David was the handsomest and smoothest dancer of the lot."[25]

David's sixth-grade teacher, Sarah Wright, was responsible for David thinking ahead to college. Mrs. Wright would pretend to be a college professor and had her students take notes as they would be required to do six years later as college freshmen. Mrs. Wright encouraged all her students to begin planning to attend college.

David and Linda Sue Gipson "claimed" each other from an early age. At box suppers at the First Methodist Church, David always bought Linda her meal, although she was never sure whether it was because he liked her so much or because he liked her mother's fried chicken. Much of David's early non-school activities revolved around the church with parties and meetings of the Methodist Youth Fellowship.[26]

David was the first boy Linda kissed. They both were in band—he played the saxophone and she played the flute. At a party at the home of the band director, Mr. McCoy, David and Linda slipped off and sat in an old row boat. As they held hands, David leaned over and kissed her.[27]

It was in the eighth grade that David suffered his only election defeat in his lifetime. Mike Knowles narrowly defeated David in the race for eighth grade class president. Knowles won with the slogan, "Go to the polls and vote for Knowles."[28]

David cherishes his childhood years in Seminole. "It was a special town," he remembered, "When you grow up in a small town, you know everyone. That helps later when you move to a college campus and continue to think you ought to know everyone there." Growing up in Seminole was like having an extended family. He was fortunate to be nurtured by teachers and family friends. He was blessed to be able to sit in the back yard and hear stories of his family's past, to be mentored by so many people, and to be loved by a "whole range of people in the community." David said, "It provided the kind of security and the sense of possibility in my life that all too many children are not receiving today in a rootless society."[29]

*I am the luckiest person in the world to grow up
in Seminole, Oklahoma. I was surrounded by people
who molded and changed my life.*

DAVID L. BOREN

FIVE

Preparing For the Future

AVID WAS FORTUNATE TO BEGIN HIS EDUCATION in an excellent small town Oklahoma school system headed by School Superintendent O.D. Johns. Seminole's excellence in education perhaps began in the 1930s when John G. Mitchell was superintendent of schools. Before he took the Seminole job, Mitchell had been fired by Oklahoma Governor William H. "Alfalfa Bill" Murray as president of Central State Teachers College in Edmond because he had not supported Murray for governor.

That firing gave Seminole an extraordinary school administrator. Mitchell also brought with him several teachers with master's and doctorate degrees. Mitchell demanded excellence from his teachers and students. He started a small community college and set high standards for everyone involved with the school system.

Superintendent Mitchell's nephew, H. B. Mitchell, was one of David's high school teachers. He made a lasting impact upon David's life. Mitchell is legendary for teaching speech and debate. In fact, the national high school trophy awarded by the National Forensic League is named for Mitchell, perhaps because the Seminole teacher won more national championships in debate than any other high school coach in history.[1]

In addition to David, Mitchell taught other debate students who made a mark on history. His former students include Jim Wright, former Speaker of the United States House of Representatives, and Frank McGee, an early news anchor for NBC Radio and Television.

When David began his debate training, he was so nervous he could not stand and speak to a group of fellow students. Mitchell had to force David to overcome his fear of public speaking by threatening to flunk him in the class until he stood and spoke. Finally, David found inner strength and stood before his classmates and spoke. Thanks to his debate coach, who spent hours teaching him about public speaking and about communicating with other people, public speaking became an important tool in his ability to convince and lead others.[2]

Mitchell took David and other members of the debate team to competitions all over the nation, including Washington, D.C. and New Orleans, Louisiana. The competitions instilled great confidence in young David. He remembered, "It made me realize that even though I was from a small town in Oklahoma, I could take on anyone from any place in the world and have a fair chance to defeat them in open competition."[3]

Before David became proficient at debating, his first debate competition was in Neosho, Missouri. He was teamed with Linda Sue Gipson. Her brother, Fred Gipson, a college freshman, was a chaperone for the debate trip. David and Linda's topic was free trade. David was totally prepared, but Linda admittedly was "becoming spacey" as a teenage girl. Their team lost all four rounds in the competition. Linda said, "I may have cost David his first loss, but, boy, did he do well after that!"

For years David carried a scar that resulted from a collision with a tree outside Linda's home. David was riding with a friend, Eddie Ramey, and spying on Linda who was sitting with another boy in a car in front of her home. As Eddie and David sped by, trying to see what was going on, Eddie lost control of the car and slammed into a tree. David was thrown into the windshield, cutting the middle of his forehead. Blood flowed freely, causing Linda's mother to send David to the hospital with the young man who was visiting her daughter while she telephoned David's mother with the news.[4] David later said his pride was wounded more seriously than his forehead.

In addition to having great leaders in education, Seminole also provided leadership in other areas of life in the community. Fred Adwan was the town's mayor. They spent a lot of time talking about political issues. Adwan encouraged David to follow his father's footsteps in public service.

Milt Phillips, publisher of the *Seminole Producer,* was a strong local leader who influenced David's life. The newspaper had a wide circulation and Phillips wielded considerable power in statewide politics. During many conversations at the newspaper office or at Phillips' home around the corner from the Boren home, Phillips also encouraged David to be active in community affairs and pursue a career in public service. Phillips was well informed about state and national issues and his columns were unusually broad in their subject matter for a small town newspaper. He and David discussed issues, policy, and philosophy for long hours in the Phillips' home and backyard.[5]

Even though he was a teenager, adults talked to David like an adult. If he was having a Coke at Cecil Stanfield's downtown drugstore, Stanfield would sit down at David's table and strike up an adult-level conversation. "He taught me so much about the values of living in a community," David said, "He taught me to be realistic about people. He taught me that even the best people are imperfect and that learning how to forgive others and forget about their failings was critical to building lasting friendships and relationships with other people." [6]

Lessons learned at the drugstore from Cecil Stanfield have served David well throughout his public career. As a teacher, he recognized that all humans will make mistakes and that young people are going through a lot of changes and having difficulty finding themselves. As a public servant and college president, David often has remembered Stanfield's admonition to be tolerant, understanding, and forgiving of others' mistakes. Stanfield's advice also helped David to forgive himself when he made mistakes.[7]

Seminole County was filled with other remarkable people who positively influenced David's life. Allen G. Nichols was a distinguished and long-time state senator from the area. Attorney Hicks Epton founded Law Day, now celebrated on May 1 each year by lawyers across the nation. Juanita Kidd Stout, an outstanding attorney, became a Supreme Court justice in Pennsylvania.[8]

Occasionally, Lyle took his family back to Washington, D.C. for visits. When David was a teenager, House Speaker Sam Rayburn would leave Lyle talking with staff members in the lobby while he and David had special, private conversations in his office about the Nation's well-being and about David's future.

The fact that Rayburn took time from one of the busiest jobs in the federal government to talk to him impacted David for the rest of his life. When he served as governor and United States Senator, he was widely known for taking time for others. He said it was his way of repaying Rayburn and later Speaker Carl Albert for the time they spent talking with and encouraging him.[9]

Lyle and Christine were not only good parents, they were great teachers. On automobile trips across the country, Lyle gave David and Susan history lessons, always stopping at historical markers along the highway. Lyle and Christine tried to take their children to each of the 50 states on vacations so they would learn about their home country.

David continued his academic excellence his sophomore year in high school. He was elected president of the Seminole High School sophomore class and was honored to get to kiss the sophomore queen, his girlfriend, Linda Sue Gipson.[10]

David also experienced the desegregation of Seminole public schools. That experience led him to have a deep and lasting commitment to equal rights as a public official. Following the United States Supreme Court's decision in *Brown v. Board of Education,* Oklahoma became one of the first states to desegregate its schools. Seminole quickly followed the state's policy under Superintendent Mitchell's leadership. Governor Raymond Gary took the unpopular position that Oklahoma would not thwart the law of the land. David later developed a close friendship with Gary, who became his early supporter in races for governor and the United States Senate. David long admired Gary's moral courage in supporting desegregation of schools.

Mitchell led his debate team into the first desegregated high school debate in state history the next year at East Central State College in Ada. Mitchell volunteered his team to compete with the African American team from Muskogee Manual High School. The debate ended with handshakes. David remembered, "I was thankful to have a father and school officials who taught me that this huge societal change would be beneficial to the country." Both Lyle and Mitchell told David and other students that they should go out of their way to assist African American students who would naturally be frightened in attending strange schools for the first time.[11]

David also was a member of the first All-State band in Oklahoma to be integrated. "Playing music with and debating with African American students," David said, "allowed barriers to be broken and friendships formed." That experience led David, during his first year as president of OU, to change regulations that would encourage diversity in university housing. It was the influence of an earlier time that guided David to want OU students to make lasting friendships with students of different races and backgrounds.

During the summer before David's junior year in high school, his father took a job as the Washington, D.C. representative of the Association of Western Railways (AWR). During his years in Congress, Lyle had supported legislation to strengthen the nation's railway system, so he was a logical choice to represent dozens of both small and large railways that made up the AWR. Lyle also found it hard to support his family as a rancher during difficult times in the cattle business. Financial necessity forced him to accept the job in the nation's capital.

It was a tough time for David. Leaving his friends and teachers at age 16 was difficult. He was so involved in school and community activities, he felt he could never adjust to a large city. The Borens moved to the Maryland suburbs in Montgomery County adjacent to the District of Colombia. Bethesda, now a large, sprawling city, still had a small-town charm. There were no buildings in the downtown area more than four stories tall.

David was enrolled in Bethesda-Chevy Chase High School. Although he soon found the school to be outstanding, the initial shock was the size of classes. In Seminole, he was accustomed to his sophomore class of approximately 100 students. At Bethesda-Chevy Chase, his junior class was made up of more than 500 students.[12]

There were students from several countries at David's new high school. The educational standards were high because many parents worked at the National Institutes of Health and other government institutions in the area.

After a short time David was able to form a circle of friends at Bethesda-Chevy Chase. As he had done in Seminole, he played in the school band and orchestra. He also joined the debate team and he and a colleague won the Maryland State High School Debate Championship.[13]

David began writing for the high school newspaper, *The Tattler.* He enjoyed writing about student activities and spotlighting teachers and programs. There was quite a bit of freedom of the press on campus and David occasionally wrote controversial editorials about the student government's performance. He eventually became editor of the newspaper and thought for awhile about pursuing journalism as a career.

It was quite an adventure to publish *The Tattler.* The newspaper was printed at a plant in Baltimore. David, as editor, was charged with the responsibility of placing the draft of the latest edition on a bus headed for the printing plant. He and other students on the newspaper staff had to wait for the return of the bus, often until 2:00 a.m., make necessary corrections, and send the proofs back to the printing plant. The central bus station in Washington, D.C. was an exotic place at night for a high school student who had grown up in Seminole, Oklahoma.

At Bethesda-Chevy Chase David found yet another mentor in the classroom. Benjamin Allnutt was his journalism teacher who made learning about that field exciting and interesting. Later, when David was governor of Oklahoma, Allnutt was recognized as the outstanding high school journalism teacher in the nation. The national convention was held in Oklahoma City. It was a special moment for David, as governor, to present the award to his former teacher.[14]

David's high school journalism experience formed the basis for later decisions about the importance of communicating important issues to the people so they could truly and meaningfully participate in the political process. He insisted his press secretary be one of the top members of his staff. Often governors and United States senators relegate press duties to a junior member of his or her staff who played a purely public relations role. However, as governor and United States Senator, David believed the press secretary should be a member of the top staff that helped him make policy decisions. He said, "I always believed that the person translating what I was attempting to do should have been involved in formulating the decision and therefore would fully understand it."[15]

David had other outstanding teachers at Bethesda-Chevy Chase. Norman Taylor, who had been a history professor at Princeton University, had chosen to teach at the high school level because he was writing a high school history textbook. When Taylor assigned his students a class paper, he required them to look at several sources, not just a single book, when writing on a topic. David found the diversity of opinion on any historical event caused him to think and analyze. He never forgot Taylor's lesson to always study and analyze competing points of view.

One of the most remarkable teachers in David's schooling was Margaret Casey, his high school English teacher. She was an extraordinary woman with a doctor of philosophy degree from Oxford University. Highly regarded as a teacher of composition and English literature, she had written the Advanced Placement Test in English for the Princeton Educational Testing Service.[16]

David was one of only 16 or 17 students in Miss Casey's class. In learning about the works of various authors, students were required to write essays in the style of the author they were studying. For example, when studying Ernest Hemingway, David's essay had to be written in the simple, crisp, and lean Hemingway style. Students read their essays aloud in the classroom and much of their grade depended upon the criticism of fellow students. David remembered, "We learned in the intense program out of fear because her standards were so high we did not want to be embarrassed in class." Miss Casey was never unkind in her criticism, but she never accepted anything less than excellence.[17]

Often Miss Casey required students to rewrite their essays four or five times. The high school class left a permanent impression upon David. Decades later, as president of the University of Oklahoma, David insisted that writing be emphasized as part of the curriculum at OU. University students also have an option called the Harvard Expository Writing Program, a series of courses very similar to Miss Casey's class. OU students work with professors in small classes, requiring long essays that are written and rewritten until they gain the professor's approval.

Miss Casey's influence also has resulted in OU freshman English classes being limited to 19 students. David said, "Success in higher education is built upon the ability to write, to analyze, to think clearly, and express those thoughts in a way that can be easily understood."

David kept in close contact with Miss Casey during his higher education at Yale University, Oxford University, and the University of Oklahoma. Every time he wrote her a letter, he read it over and over to make certain it contained no grammatical errors. After he became president of OU, Miss Casey, in her eighties, made a cross country trip to Norman and surprised him. It was on the first day of classes and President Boren asked his former teacher to accompany him as he addressed incoming freshman. He remembered, "It was a tense moment for me because my mentor was in the audience and I was frightened that I might use a wrong word." Before Miss Casey's death, she continued to relay her ideas about excellence in education to David.[18]

During his years at Bethesda-Chevy Chase, David had chance encounters with two other people he always will remember. As editor of *The Tattler,* David invited a young United States Senator from Massachusetts, John F. Kennedy, to be commencement speaker for his high school graduation.

Another well-known person David encountered was poet Robert Frost who was in Washington, D.C., as the National Poet Laureate and Poet in Residence at the Library of Congress during David's final two years in high school. David learned Frost's works in Miss Casey's class and attended every public lecture and reading Frost scheduled at the Library of Congress.

David did not know exactly where Frost lived, but he had been observed taking daily walks on Massachusetts Avenue between American University and the National Cathedral. One day David noticed Frost walking, so he parked his car and just "happened" to begin walking alongside the great poet. Not wanting to interrupt Frost's train of thought, David asked Frost if he minded him walking the rest of the way with him. Frost was welcoming and struck up a conversation with him.[19]

For the next few months, David traveled to Massachusetts Avenue on Saturday mornings and walked with Frost. It was a unique experience. David remembered, "He treated me like a grandson and was tolerant of my questions." David sometimes asked Frost, during the private walks and in public appearances, to recite one of his poems. When Frost would forget the words, he would say, "Did I write that one?" David often reminded him of the next words and Frost continued with his recitation. They often discussed what Frost was trying to convey in a particular poem.

David's classmates asked him to invite Frost to speak at the baccalaureate service for his graduating class. Frost agreed. What a year it was for the class of 1959. One of America's great poets, Frost, spoke at the baccalaureate service, and the next president of the United States, John F. Kennedy, gave the commencement address.[20]

As David began thinking about college, his first thoughts turned to the University of Oklahoma. He always considered himself an Oklahoman and had often visited his old friends and family back in Seminole and other cities in Oklahoma. However, Miss Casey and his parents asked David to consider higher education at other schools, possibly Ivy League institutions. Although David's father was a champion of higher education, he still thought in the back of his mind that David someday might end up as a cattle rancher in Seminole County.[21]

David visited Yale University and Dartmouth College. He especially liked Dartmouth because of its location in a small New Hampshire town. In the end, Miss Casey and a friend of David's father, a retired District of Colombia lawyer and judge, convinced David to attend Yale, at least for one year. Both believed that Yale offered unlimited opportunities for David. In his own mind, David fully intended to return to the University of Oklahoma at the end of one year.[22]

David scored well on his college entrance examinations and was accepted at both Yale and Dartmouth. He graduated high school in May, 1959, at the top of his class and his grades made acceptance at the Ivy League schools possible.

In September, Lyle and Christine took David to the Yale University campus in New Haven, Connecticut. As soon as they left him at his new station in life, David was incredibly homesick. "I was away from people I knew, foods I liked, and people that spoke to me on the sidewalk," David remembered.

Many times at Yale, hearing some of the people who disagreed with me did not change my mind, but it helped me better understand where I stood and what I believed.

DAVID L. BOREN

SIX

The Yale Experience

THE ROOTS OF YALE UNIVERSITY can be traced to the 1640s when Colonial ministers led an effort to establish a college in New Haven to preserve the idea of European liberal education in the New World. Their vision was realized in 1701 when the charter was granted for a school "wherein Youth may be instructed in the Arts and Sciences through the blessing of Almighty God may be fitted for Publick employment both in the Church and Civil State."[1]

The school was renamed "Yale College" in 1718 for Elihu Yale who helped the infant college survive by donating the proceeds from the sale of nine bales of goods, 417 books, and a portrait of King George I.[2]

Yale is the third-oldest institution of higher learning in the United States. Particularly well known are its undergraduate school and law school, each of which has produced a number of American presidents and foreign heads of state. In 1861, Yale became the first university in the nation to award a Ph.D. degree.[3]

By the time David arrived in 1959, Yale had matured into one of the world's great universities. He was one of 1,007 entering freshmen in a total student body, including the undergraduate and graduate schools, of 7,773. At the time, Yale admitted only male undergraduate students.[4]

It took David several days to become familiar with the campus that stretched from the School of Medicine in downtown New Haven to tree-shaded residential neighborhoods around the Divinity School. David was in awe of the architecture of the more than 200 buildings and the lawns, courtyards, walkways, gates, and arches. The town of New Haven, with its quaint commercial districts, serene residential streets, the famous New Haven Green, and historical landmarks, was uniquely New England.

Yale uses a residential college housing system that is modeled after those at Oxford and Cambridge universities in England. The idea is that students from all walks of life and background and hometowns would be thrown into the mix. However, David was not prepared for the social atmosphere.

The first thing David discovered about Connecticut was that the people were not as outgoing as he had grown accustomed to with his friends and neighbors in Oklahoma and Maryland. As a freshman, his two roommates were chosen for him. Thankfully, his new roommates became both friends and colleagues and helped him transition into his new life at Yale.[5]

Lee Buckwalter was a freshman from New Jersey, but was nice and friendly. David's other roommate was Beverly Head, III, a military school graduate from Birmingham, Alabama. David identified with Beverly who appreciated Southern foods and humor. David discovered that less than half the students at Yale were graduates of public schools.

There was a social clique at the school that was dominated by graduates of prestigious preparatory schools in New England. David even ran into several people who would not get acquainted with fellow students unless they were listed on the New York Social Register.[6]

The transition to life for David as a "Yalie" was softened by several of his professors. Charles Scott, a professor of philosophy and religion, had grown up in Seminole County, in Wewoka, where his father owned a small grocery store. Scott and his wife frequently invited David to their home to help with his homesickness.[7]

Boren formed a close circle of friends shortly after his arrival at Yale. They included his roommate, Beverly Head, III, later a business leader, Dale Hershey of Pittsburgh, Pennsylvania, who later practiced law in his hometown, and Steve Billings of Cape Cod, Massachusetts. Billings became an Episcopalian priest.

Many of David's friends at Yale came from the South and Southwest including Chip Siegel of Georgia, Harvey Gleason of New Orleans, Louisiana, and Peter Maffit of Houston, Texas. Three others who became lifelong friends were Jonathan Rose, Tom Rowe, and Guy Miller Struve.

Although he was a moderate conservative, Boren was a Democrat always, and enjoyed verbal sparring with Rose, a staunch Republican. Rose was in David's Skull and Bones class. Tom Rowe, a campus liberal, also often debated David on the political issues of the day. Rowe followed David a year later into Skull and Bones and was a year behind David later at Oxford as a Rhodes Scholar from Michigan. Rose was editor of the *Yale Daily News* and later worked on the staff of Presidents Richard Nixon and George H.W. Bush.

Struve became a leading lawyer in New York City and served as a top legal staff member with Judge Lawrence Walsh in investigating the Iran-Contra scandal. Struve was an arch-conservative and served as president of the Yale Political Union when David served as Speaker. Reflecting on the debates of his college years, David said, "I always seemed to be caught in the middle of those left of me, and friends on the right of me."

Professor Howard Lamar, who became David's faculty advisor, was originally from Alabama and was a nationally-recognized expert in the history of the American West. Lamar and his wife, Shirley, also invited David to their home for genuine Southern cooking and conversation about life, values, and regional differences. Howard and Shirley became David's lifelong friends.

Another professor to whom David grew close was Rollin Osterweis, his debate coach and professor of American Oratory. Osterweis was from a pioneer Jewish family in New Haven who had settled in the area well before the American Revolution. He and his wife were charming people who entertained David and other students in their home on Sunday afternoons.[8]

At the Osterweis home David was introduced to prominent scholars of the day. Professor Osterweis made certain his debate students were exposed to the authors of famous text books and scholarly works. David remembered, "It was a wonderful experience for a small town boy from Oklahoma to mix and mingle with that crowd."[9]

Osterweis was intentionally and generously giving his students a great gift. David said, "It was on these Sunday afternoons that I met and became associated with Dr. William Clyde DeVane, dean of Yale College and national president of Phi Beta Kappa. He and Yale President A.W. Griswold instilled in me a commitment to academic freedom and the desire for the broadest possible education in the liberal arts."

David remained close to Osterweis until the professor's death. David was intrigued by Osterweis' understanding of the role of great oratory in history. David remembered, "He was a courtly man with Southern manners who grew up in New England. Some of his relatives had lived in the South. He had written a biography of his ancestor, Judah P. Benjamin, who served in the cabinet of the Confederate government."

In his final years, Osterweis worked on many historical projects, including a Public Broadcasting System (PBS) series about the importance of the right of free speech and the great important American speeches from Colonial times to the present. David gathered with other former debaters to view the series, but death already had taken their beloved coach.

Because of the Yale experience and having been exposed to so many great speakers while in college, David, as president of OU, has supported efforts to expose OU students to as many great speakers as possible.

Other professors who made a lasting impression on the young American History major were Edmund Morgan, a respected Colonial historian, and C. Vann Woodward, "an incredible teacher" and perhaps the greatest scholar of the history of the American South living at that time.[10]

David played in the Yale band, but it was unlike any experience he previously had encountered. "It was not a precision marching band," David said, "we never concentrated on perfection." Football in the Ivy League was a social event without a serious emphasis put on winning. The band was not expected to perform in a manner to which David was accustomed. Rather than uniforms, band members wore blue blazers, grey slacks, and black shoes. Often the clothing did not match and sometimes members of the band "got lost" during the half-time performance. But it was fun and kept David involved in campus activities.[11]

At Yale, David was surrounded by great music and theater and heard the leading politicians and thinkers of the day in lectures and debates. He also was involved in campus politics. The Yale Political Union was a mock parliamentary debating society made up of several parties that ranged from the far right to the far left. There were two centrist parties, the moderate liberal party and the moderate conservative party, the latter of which David was a member. David was elected as speaker of the Yale Political Union, one of the group's top two posts.[12]

In the summers, David returned to Washington, D.C., and interned at a federal agency called the Office of the National Civil and Defense Mobilization. It was part of the executive office of the President and was housed in the Old Executive Office Building adjacent to the White House. He worked directly for Leo A. Hoegh, the former governor of Iowa.

Hoegh was an appointee of President Dwight D. Eisenhower and was energetic about his responsibilities in the federal government. Hoegh invited David to sit in on high level planning sessions to develop responses to possible missile attacks, nuclear war, as well as natural disasters.

Not only was the internship a great learning experience, David enjoyed looking out his window to see President Eisenhower, an avid golfer, practicing his putting on a small green outside the Oval Office. David also had the chance to attend formal welcoming ceremonies on the South Lawn of the White House.

During his Washington summers, David dated among other girls, Cokie Boggs, the daughter of Louisiana Congressman Hale Boggs. Cokie later married and, as Cokie Roberts, became a respected national journalist and Washington correspondent for ABC News and National Public Radio.

David also had the chance one summer to work at the United States Information Agency (USIA) where legendary newscaster Edward R. Murrow was director. Murrow was one of the most respected American journalists, known for his work investigating controversial national stories. David was able to attend strategy sessions led by Murrow. David remembered, "Mr. Murrow impressed me by constantly trying to teach people how free discussion contributed to the greatness of America."

In 1960 David was involved in the national presidential campaign. An old family friend was Lyndon B. Johnson, United States Senator from Texas, who was campaigning for the Democratic presidential nomination against Senator John F. Kennedy and others. Oklahoma United States Senator Robert S. Kerr, also a longtime Boren family friend, asked David to generate publicity for Johnson. Senator Kerr called David and said, "It would be great for the campaign if we could get some publicity saying that a students-for-Johnson movement has begun at Yale, at the other end of the geographical spectrum from Texas."[13]

David formed a Johnson-for-President Club on the Yale campus, put out a press release, and "made a lot of noise." He lined up support from several students from Oklahoma and Texas who supported Johnson. Even though the club had only about 20 members, David was able to get national publicity about the fact that a Johnson-for-President Club had been organized at an Ivy League School. That made Senator Kerr very happy.

After Kennedy received the nomination and selected Johnson as his running mate, David worked for the ticket. After they were elected, David attempted to return the next summer to his internship. However, he was told that the agency was hiring only Kennedy supporters, not students who campaigned initially for Johnson. David called Senator Kerr with the news. The senator was startled and said, "Stay by the phone. I will call you back." Within a few minutes, someone from the federal agency called to offer David his old internship, obviously because of the direct intervention of Kerr who had huge influence in the nation's capital and was called the uncrowned king of the United States Senate.[14]

Kerr's involvement in David's life had begun in 1952 when Kerr was seeking the Democratic nomination for president. David was one of several young men and women who served as Kerr's pages and ran errands for him on the floor of the Democratic National Convention. It was the beginning of regular attendance at Democratic National Conventions for David. His father, Lyle, was also in attendance and the conventions allowed them to spend quality time together, studying and observing the political process. David was first elected as a convention delegate in 1968 and went as a delegate every four years until he became president of OU in 1994 and assumed a non-partisan role.

Both Kerr and Oklahoma Congressman Carl Albert were kind to David and shared their political wisdom with him. During David's time at Yale, Albert was House Majority Leader. He did not become Speaker of the House until 1971. When David rode the train home on weekends to visit his parents, he often spent Saturdays at the Capitol. He knew Albert worked on weekends and would be generous with his time.

One weekend, David had a lengthy visit with Speaker Albert and his chief of staff, Charles "Charlie" Ward, from Poteau, Oklahoma. Both said they hoped someday David would run for Congress from Oklahoma. David said the only way he would ever run for Congress was if Ward would be his chief of staff. Many years later, after David was elected to the United States Senate and Albert had retired, Ward indeed became David's chief of staff.[15]

Even though he would be a leading Democratic officeholder in later years, David was quite conservative in his political views at Yale and did not hesitate to become embroiled in many controversies. At the time, he had not developed a full understanding of how he truly felt about the use of civil disobedience to bring about changes in the civil rights arena. He sincerely believed in civil rights for all citizens, but questioned whether civil disobedience was an appropriate method because it involved breaking the law.

In the school newspaper, David criticized Yale Chaplain William Sloane Coffin, Jr., a liberal Christian clergyman who was a peace activist of international stature. Coffin used his pulpit at the Yale chapel to advocate civil disobedience. David thought Coffin was wrong to use his position as chaplain to preach politics. Coffin was so upset that he called David's name in one of his sermons and criticized his stand against civil disobedience.

While he disagreed, Coffin continued to welcome discussion times with David. Coffin even taught David how to ice skate. Over time they developed a mutual respect for each other. When David ran for the state legislature, Coffin was one of his first contributors.[16]

During his dispute with Coffin, the chaplain deliberately placed David next to the most outspoken proponent of civil disobedience, Dr. Martin Luther King, Jr., at a luncheon before Dr. King spoke to Yale students. David kindly but firmly told Dr. King that he disagreed with his position on civil disobedience. Dr. King did not convince David to change his position, although the civil rights leader was "extremely courteous and warm" toward David. He also was very patient with the 19-year-old student who never passed up a moment to tell someone his opinion about the subject at hand. David remembered, "It is a memory I will always cherish because this patient man truly tried to be a teacher to a young man who thought he knew more than he really did know at the time." Later, David came to understand why Dr. King had been right to use civil disobedience to bring about long-needed changes in civil rights in America.[17]

Later, thinking back on the patience of Dr. King and many leaders such as Yale President Griswold whom David had criticized in his student activist days, David realized how important that patience had been in his personal and intellectual growth. One day after he spent several hours in a long conversation with a student at OU and backed up the remainder of his appointments, his assistant, Sherry Evans, asked why he had taken such a long time with the student. David replied, "I am paying back those at Yale who spent so much time with me and had such great influence on my life."

Much to David's surprise, he was invited at the end of his junior year to become a member of The Order of Skull and Bones, a secret society at Yale. Skull and Bones was the most prominent of Yale societies and had produced great national leaders including members of the Taft and Bush families, writer Archibald McLeish, Yale Chaplain Coffin, environmentalist Gifford Pinchot, and many more.

In fact, three generations of the Bush family were members of Skull and Bones—Senator Prescott Bush, President George H.W. Bush, and President George W. Bush. When the latter ran for president, his Democratic opponent was another Skull and Bones member, John Kerry.

"Bonesmen," as members were called, met on Thursday and Sunday evenings during their senior year at the Skull and Bones "tomb," an architecturally interesting building on the Yale campus. There is no doubt that contacts made during his senior year at Yale helped David reach his career goals. After Skull and Bones began admitting women in 1990, David and his daughter, Carrie, Yale Class of 1993, became the first father-daughter members of the prestigious organization.[18]

David's membership in Skull and Bones expanded his horizons. It was a diverse group made up of athletes, artists, musicians, and David, a scholar and student journalist. All sides of campus life were represented in the small group of 15 students. David learned that although people may look different on the outside, we are all very much alike beneath the skin. He said, "We worry about the same things, we have the same insecurities, and we have the same hopes for our lives." Those valuable lessons have served David well in his career in public service.[19]

David's experiences in Skull and Bones also gave him the foundation for feeling strongly about building diverse friendships. That concept that was developed while in college later guided David, as president of OU, to diversity housing, to make certain that students would grow and learn by being with people unlike themselves, to form fast friendships with people from different parts of the country and different nations and races, religions, and cultural backgrounds.[20]

At the same time, several Skull and Bones alumni became important in David's life. Prescott Bush, United States Senator from Connecticut and Yale alumnus, was the father of the first President Bush and grandfather of the second President Bush. Senator Bush was kind to David and often invited him and other Skull and Bones members who were interested in politics to have dinner with him.

Bush was very interested in David's political ambitions. Bush was a moderate pro-business Republican. He had been treasurer of the first national capital campaign of Planned Parenthood and an early supporter of the United Negro College Fund, both positions contrary to most New England Republicans.[21]

Senator Bush's diverse political stances made him an interesting conversationalist. David enjoyed time spent with Bush who introduced him to his son, George H.W. Bush, with whom David developed a friendship during his service in Congress, as United States Ambassador to China, Republican National Chairman, director of the Central Intelligence Agency (CIA), vice president, and later as the nation's 41st president.[22]

Skull and Bones also allowed David to get to know William F. Buckley, a former society member and leading conservative thinker of the time. Buckley often invited him to spend Sunday lunches with his family.

Another controversy that involved David grew from his sincere belief that the conservative point of view was not being adequately presented at Yale. He became a leading activist for more conservative students and faculty members. David's agitation for more balance on the faculty put him at odds with Yale President Griswold who believed David wanted faculty members hired based solely on their political beliefs. David saw it differently. He believed that he was seeking to make Yale an even greater marketplace of ideas.[23]

Griswold was an advocate of broad liberal arts education. He often spoke passionately about the need for a university to be a place where ideas could freely be exchanged. He argued that if we are to learn and grow, we must have debate and must broadly educate ourselves. Griswold placed great emphasis upon knowing literature and history to be able to understand the times in which we live and understand each other.

President Griswold allowed David to come to his office many times to hear him out. "He respected my opinion as a student leader and he certainly had an impact upon my thinking both then and later in life. I truly felt I was trying to get him to more fully implement his own ideas."[24]

Later when David was a member of the Oklahoma House of Representatives, defending the actions of OU President George L. Cross for bringing controversial speakers to campus, he found himself using some of President Griswold's language. He argued to fellow state legislators, "Even if we disagree with someone strongly, they should be allowed to speak. Because in debating them, we will strengthen the truth and strengthen the right side of the argument."[25]

It was from President Griswold that David first heard a reference from John Stuart Mill's essay, *On Liberty*. Mill, a nineteenth century philosopher, political economist, and Member of Parliament, gave an impassioned defense of free speech in *On Liberty*. The essay, which David has read and re-read hundreds of times since his college days at Yale, has become one of the great influences on his own political thought.

Mill argued that free discourse is a necessary condition for intellectual and social progress. He contended that we can never be sure that a silenced opinion does not contain some element of the truth. Mill also argued that allowing people to air false opinions is productive for two reasons. First, individuals are more likely to abandon incorrect beliefs if they are engaged in an open exchange of ideas. Second, by forcing other individuals to re-examine and reaffirm their beliefs in the process of debate, their views are strengthened and enlivened.[26]

From his discussions with President Griswold and reading Mill's essay, David developed strong feelings about the place of a university. He said, "It must be a place where ideas are vigorously debated and where there is diversity of thought. At Yale, hearing some of the people who disagreed with me did not change my mind, but it helped me understand where I stood and what I believed in. Truth is strengthened when it is tested."[27]

Even today, as president of OU, David returns in his mind to the truths he learned at Yale. "Debate is healthy for our society and essential for our intellectual growth," he said. While listening to students who are not in agreement with his decisions as the leader of OU, David thinks back to President Griswold who heard him out.

In addition to writing pieces for the school newspaper, David chose former Oklahoma Governor William H. "Alfalfa Bill" Murray as the topic for his senior thesis. The populist governor, certainly the most colorful politician in Oklahoma history, was a frequent visitor to the Boren home when David was in elementary school. Murray was a staunch supporter of Lyle Boren's candidacy for Congress.

In research for the thesis, Johnston Murray, Alfalfa Bill's son and also a former governor of Oklahoma, gave David full access to Alfalfa Bill's papers, letters, and tax returns. David was able to write his thesis based upon fresh material that was not available to previous biographers of Murray. He discovered from the former governor's tax returns that Murray, who was chairman of the Oklahoma Constitutional Convention and the first Speaker of the Oklahoma House of Representatives, made almost no money in his entire life. Even though Murray was controversial, he obviously never profited personally from his public service and was scrupulously honest about the use of public money.[28]

David was a member of the Army Reserve Officer Training Corps (ROTC) at Yale and was chosen cadet of the year his first three years. He was promoted through the ranks to third in command of a cadet company. At graduation, he was selected as a distinguished military graduate of the program. One summer he went through basic training at Fort Devens, Massachusetts. General William Westmoreland was in charge of the training that summer and was determined to make certain his trainees were the toughest. David learned to run long distances with a backpack and use a bayonet in hand-to-hand combat.[29]

David was the only Oklahoman in his basic training squad. Most of the young men were Irish from the Boston, Massachusetts, area. They could hold their own in tough neighborhoods and had the scars to prove it. They did not particularly like people from beyond the Boston area. When David revealed his roots extended to Ennis, Ireland, he was immediately accepted. The Boston Irishmen helped David successfully complete basic training and watched out for him. At graduation, David earned a commission as a second lieutenant.[30]

While David had been elected Speaker of the Yale Political Union, Yale's model parliamentary debating association, he had never run for a class office until he ran for the position of senior class secretary, equivalent to president of the Yale student body. Because David was not in a fraternity, it was rather shocking that he ran at all because the job had been held only by fraternity men in the past. David wanted to break the monopoly.

Most Yale students were not members of a fraternity, but the organizations wielded much power in student elections. David lost the race because of a weighted system in which voters were allowed to vote for more than one candidate. David actually received more first-place votes than his opponent, but lost in the total tally because the fraternity block all ranked him fifth. It was after he lost the class election near the end of his junior year that he was selected for membership in Skull and Bones, arguably Yale's most prominent honor. Perhaps the Bonesmen who elected him were impressed by his political courage.

As David's career at Yale was coming to a close, he began thinking of his future. He knew he would end up in law school and in public service, but several professors wanted him to delay enrollment in law school and continue his education in England.

I told the Rhodes Scholarship interview committee
that I hoped to be a public servant in Oklahoma,
that I believed in the Oklahoma values, and wanted to give back
to the state which had given me so much by
playing a leadership role in the future of Oklahoma.

DAVID L. BOREN

SEVEN

Rhodes Scholar

AVID HAD NOT SPENT MUCH TIME thinking about applying for a Rhodes Scholarship, the world's oldest and perhaps most prestigious international fellowship. Instead, he was anxious to return to Oklahoma and attend law school at the University of Oklahoma. His primary goal in life was to enter Oklahoma politics. Getting back to the Sooner State was the first step in that process.

However, Professors Howard Lamar and Rollin Osterweis convinced David to at least apply for the Rhodes Scholarship, to broaden his educational experience by studying two years at Oxford University in England.[1]

Cecil John Rhodes, the British-born South African mining magnate who founded the De Beers diamond company, left his large fortune upon his death in 1902 to establish the Rhodes Trust in Oxford to provide scholarships for students around the world who exhibited worthy qualities of intellect, character, and physical ability. Rhodes hoped to maintain British influence in the world by having future leaders from former colonies educated at Oxford.

The list of former Rhodes Scholars read like a "Who's Who" in world leadership. In the five decades before David became a

Rhodes Scholar, many world leaders and influential citizens had studied in the program at Oxford. They included Arkansas United States Senator J. William Fulbright, the originator of the Fulbright Fellowship; Dominic Mintoff, prime minister of Malta; Sir Zelman Cowen, Governor General of Australia; R.W. Burchfield, editor of the *Oxford English Dictionary;* American poet Robert Penn Warren; Oklahoma Congressman and Speaker of the House Carl Albert; Secretary of State Dean Rusk; Oklahoma native and Librarian of Congress Daniel J. Boorstin; Oklahoman George C. McGhee, who served as American Ambassador to Turkey and Germany; United States Supreme Court Justice Byron White; Navy Admiral and Central Intelligence Agency (CIA) Director Stansfield Turner; United States Senators Richard Lugar and Paul Sarbanes; musician Kris Kristofferson; and United States Supreme Court Justice David H. Souter.[2]

David and his father spent the night before the Rhodes Scholarship interviews in Oklahoma City at the Skirvin Hotel. The following day, David appeared before the committee that would choose Oklahoma's applicants for the prestigious scholarship. OU President Dr. George L. Cross was chairman of the panel that included Savoie Lottinville, director of the University of Oklahoma Press, and Norman attorney John Luttrell.

The committee members asked questions primarily about what David wanted to do with his life. He told them that he truly believed in Oklahoma values and that he wanted to spend his life in a leadership role in his home state. Dr. Cross asked questions about Oklahoma history and quizzed David about his senior thesis about Alfalfa Bill Murray.[3]

David was somewhat surprised when he was chosen as one of two Oklahomans to advance to the regional finals of the Rhodes Scholarship competition in New Orleans, Louisiana. The other

Oklahoman was a young man from Tulsa, James Woolsey, Jr., who was graduating Phi Beta Kappa from Stanford University. Later Woolsey served as a strategic arms limitation treaty negotiator, as undersecretary of the United States Navy, director of the CIA in the administration of President Bill Clinton, and one of the nation's most respected foreign policy specialists. David would later introduce Woolsey to the United States Senate committees considering his confirmation to each of the federal posts.

David and Woolsey first met in December, 1962, when they arrived in New Orleans and attended dinners and social events leading up to the all-important final interviews. With them were two students from each of six other states in the region. From the 14 applicants, only two would be selected as Rhodes Scholars, and seldom were both winners from the same state. David and Woolsey talked about that fact and wished each other luck.[4]

Much to their surprise, both of them were selected. It was only the second time in history that two Rhodes Scholarship winners had come from Oklahoma. David believes he was selected because he was so relaxed. He remembered, "Some people had for many years lived their lives to be Rhodes Scholars. I had not even thought about it until a few weeks before."[5] David had applied only to humor his professors.

Oklahoma newspapers trumpeted the accomplishments of David and Woolsey. When they arrived at the airport in Tulsa, it was like a rally for a returning football team. The mayors of Tulsa and Seminole were there, along with the Seminole High School Band.

David graduated from Yale summa cum laude and Phi Beta Kappa with a bachelor's degree in history in May, 1963. In September, he, Woolsey and 30 other American Rhodes Scholars, all males, headed for England. Among the other scholars were Walter Slocombe, later Undersecretary of Defense.

The group of scholars sailed from New York City to London aboard the SS *France*. After five days at sea, David had developed a close friendship with Bill Lewis, a Rhodes Scholar who had a similar small town upbringing. Lewis had been raised in Blacksburg, Virginia. He later became Assistant Secretary of Energy and for several years was chairman of the McKinsey Global Institute, an educational arm of the well-known McKinsey & Company, counselor to the world's largest companies.

David also struck a lasting friendship with Bob McNeil, a Notre Dame graduate whose father, Don McNeil, was host of the Nation's most popular morning radio show, *The Breakfast Club*. David had come to know Russ Carpenter, a Princeton graduate who had served with David on a committee to choose which ship the American Rhodes Scholars would travel to England. David already knew his Yale classmate, Joe Wood, from Indiana, later a vice president of the World Bank.[6]

On his way to Europe, David thought about how homesick he would surely be in England, so far from his family. There were no cell phones and transatlantic phone calls were expensive. David knew that he probably would not be able to come home during the two years of the scholarship.

On the day he arrived at Oxford University, it was cold and damp. He was met at the gate of Balliol College, where he would live and study, by a porter with a thick, English accent. The porter opened the gate and asked David where he was from. He said, "I am sure you have never heard of my hometown of Seminole, Oklahoma." The porter surprised David when he replied, "Oh yes, I know about Seminole." It turned out that a few years before, Oliver Johns, the son of the Seminole school superintendent, had studied at Oxford and also lived in Balliol College. David thought, "It is a small world!"[7]

David was assigned to live in a two-room suite that had been occupied two centuries before by the famous English economist, Adam Smith. The rooms had stone walls two feet thick. One room was a sitting room with a desk. The other room was the bedroom with a large wardrobe for his clothing and personal items. David often said that the room surely had not been renovated since Smith's days and were often very cold in winter. The electrical wiring allowed for only one small, single-bar electric stove.

As he drifted off to sleep on his first night at his new post of learning, David reflected on the mountain of information he had read about Oxford and its place in the history of education.

Oxford University is the oldest university in the English-speaking world, laying claim to eight centuries of continuous existence.[8] European travel author and expert Jan Morris described Oxford:

> Oxford sits in the middle of a fairly ordinary mercantile and industrial city...its buildings are a baffling jumble of structures ancient and modern, with no obvious center to them, no dominating campus or architectural pattern. And most crucially, Universitas Oxoniensis is unique in its attitudes: eager, modernity beside medieval loyalties, skepticism tempered by tradition, and the whole venerable entity spiced with anomalous quirk and absurdity.[9]

David was well aware of Oxford graduates who had made their mark on history. Oxford played a role in educating four British and eight foreign kings, 47 Nobel prize-winners, 25 British prime ministers, 28 foreign presidents and prime ministers, seven saints, 86 archbishops, 18 cardinals, and one pope of the Catholic church. John Wesley, the founder of Methodism, studied at Oxford. Seven of the previous ten prime ministers of Great Britain were Oxford graduates. The world of literature was filled with Oxford alumni including Lewis Carroll, Aldous Huxley, C. S. Lewis, J. R. R. Tolkien, Percy Bysshe Shelley, and Thomas Warton.[10]

Oxford had begun with students fending for themselves in small groups based in inns and lodging houses. From those small groups evolved the modern Oxford consisting of an association of autonomous colleges. About 1260, John Balliol, one of King Henry III's most loyal lords, rented a house in the suburbs of Oxford and maintained it for poor students. Balliol College, which resulted from that act of charity, points to 1263 as its founding year, making it the oldest of all the colleges in Oxford University.[11]

David entered Balliol College with approximately 300 other students from more than 30 countries. The college had a particular reputation for academic excellence, students who thought for themselves, internationalism, and a strong sense of student involvement.

Student life at Balliol College was unlike any other place on earth. David was assigned the services of Jack Walton, a "scout" who kept his rooms clean and brought him hot tea in the afternoons. It was like being transported back in time of the English gentlemen of Oxford. Walton was paid by the college but David was expected to give him a gratuity at the end of each of the three terms in the academic year.[12]

Walton was quite a character. He was dressed in a white jacket and necktie and was responsible for keeping David on the straight and narrow. As a disciplinarian scouts enforced rules of having no ladies in rooms past a certain hour in the evening. If David entertained friends for sherry or tea, he was expected to send a written invitation that would be delivered by the scout.

David learned English etiquette quickly from Walton, who also liked to talk politics. Officially, Walton was a Socialist but seemed to vote for every conservative aristocrat in British elections. David had been brought up in a home that did not believe in classes of citizens—everyone was equal. He discovered the opposite in England. His scout was living in the midst of a society that was based upon classes. David soon learned that although England had changed somewhat after World War II, there were still class divisions. He could determine a person's social class or economic grouping from his or her accent and how they conducted themselves.[13]

David's neighbors in his building were unique. Allan Taylor, who lived one floor above him, was like a roommate. He was from Tasmania, Australia. David and Taylor became close friends. After Oxford, Taylor became a member of the Australian foreign service and served as ambassador to a number of countries, including Indonesia, and later as director of the Australian intelligence agency, the Australian equivalent of the CIA . On the top floor lived the grandson of Harold Macmillan who had recently concluded service as British prime minister.

Also at Balliol College was Richard Fletcher, an Englishman who later became the number-two person in British intelligence, the Secret Intelligence Service, commonly known as MI6. Many years later, there was a meeting of the world's top four intelligence officials including George Tenet, who called David his mentor in a 2007 autobiography, Allan Taylor, and Fletcher, who was acting as chief of British Intelligence. It was ironic that three of the world's four leading intelligence directors were David's personal friends and associates. During the high-level meeting, Tenet, Taylor, and Fletcher sent David a message letting him know they were all together.[14]

One of the quick lessons in the English way of life David learned was proper etiquette in introducing one's self to others. It was not acceptable to the British to walk up to someone, stick out your hand, and introduce yourself. Instead, David learned to wait quietly in the dining hall until another student came to him and "broke the ice." At first, it was difficult to make friends at Oxford. However, David learned that once British fellow students did decide to count you as a friend, they were loyal and devoted friends for life.[15]

Richard Bevan and George Hallahan were Brits who became David's close friends. They rowed on the crew with him representing Baillol College in the hotly-contested boat races between colleges. They traveled together to the Scandinavian countries of Norway, Sweden, and Denmark, all the way to Lapland and to the border with the Soviet Union.

In addition to rowing, David also had a full social life, attending balls at Blenheim Castle with a special English friend, Allison Ellicott, on his arm, or learning how to punt down the rivers at Oxford. Punting involved using a pole to steer and move a flat-bottomed barge. Often, David punted the barge up river to a beautiful picnic location in the company of one of the two young American women, Gail Clements and Eileen Baker, who David dated in his time at Oxford.

The Oxford method of teaching was unique. Students did not attend classes, but instead met individually or in very small groups with a professor in what was called a tutorial. Once a week, David spent an hour with each of his tutors. He took courses in politics, philosophy, and economics, working toward an interdisciplinary degree in those areas. The tutor assigned a topic each week and David was required to prepare an essay on the subject.[16]

At the next weekly meeting, David read his essay aloud and the tutor gave his criticism and asked deep questions. If another student was present at the tutorial, the student was also expected to cross examine.

David found much more time for personal reflection at Oxford than had been possible at Yale. There were fewer hours spent in class. There was no identifiable set of extracurricular activities in which to participate which defined success as a student leader. It gave him time to think about what he wanted to do with his own life and how he wanted to make a positive contribution. He kept a diary during the period and also composed works of poetry.

Jim Woolsey, David's fellow Rhodes Scholar from Oklahoma, ended up being assigned to St. John's College which was next door to Baillol College. Woolsey remembered, "David and I looked at most political issues from the same perspective. We were both conservative Democrats. David was obviously brilliant and enjoyed the tutorial system in which a bright individual would sit with him and argue the content of his essays." Woolsey said, "One of Oxford's substantial strengths is having someone of great intellect pay a lot of attention to how you wrote about the topics of the day."[17]

Between the eight-week terms was a six-week reading period in which students could complete additional research or travel. With different groups of friends, David took advantage of being in Europe where travel was relatively inexpensive and many countries were only a short train ride away. During his years at Oxford, he visited 50 countries. David not only visited the countries of western Europe that were accessible to Americans, he and several friends were able to obtain travel visas to go behind what was then called the Iron Curtain to East Germany, Poland, Czechoslovakia, and Hungary.[18]

On one trip to Hungary, David and his friends met with a group of young people in a cellar beneath a vineyard. The young men were anti-communist and were hoping to end the Communist regime and return control of the Hungarian government to the people. In Budapest, David heard the steps of Cardinal Jozsef Mindszenty walking about in his room one floor above the reception area of the American Embassy. The Catholic leader had sought exile from the Communists and was a prisoner in his own country.

On a trip to Poland, David and his travel companions could not find a hotel and had to spend the night with a group of Polish miners in a barracks. The miners had been taken from their families and placed in a new area to develop a mining complex. One of the miners played the accordion during a discussion of politics so the Communist overseers could not hear their conversation. Some of the miners took David and his friends to church during Holy Week, despite the fact that those known for attending religious services were denied good housing and good jobs. David said, "The trips gave me a real insight of what it is like for people to be held in their own country under the occupation of an outside government in which they did not believe."[19]

During one Christmas season, David and a group of fellow students visited the Holy Land. They rode the Orient Express, then traveled by boat from Italy to Greece, and took passage on a very old train from British Imperial days from Istanbul, Turkey, to Beirut, Lebanon, across Syria. David thought Beirut was a beautiful city, the Paris of the Middle East. Before years of war and destruction, Beirut was filled with sidewalk cafes and many young people who spoke English and who were friendly to Americans. Being in Beirut also gave David the chance to try to speak his "very primitive" French.[20]

One of his most unforgettable trips was made in a Land Rover from Jerusalem into the desert to the settlement where Lawrence of Arabia had made his headquarters. A Bedouin they met at the last Jordanian Army outpost joined the students as they crossed trackless spans of blowing sand to a distant village where the guide had family. The Bedouin spoke only a few words of English and David's only key to the Arabic world was a guide book that had been written in the early part of the century.

The first two nights of the trip were spent in a Bedouin tent village, sitting around a campfire with the men of the camp drinking coffee from a single huge cup that was passed from man to man. They sat and slept on sacks of surplus American grain sent as foreign aid. When the group arrived at their destination, the entire town turned out to greet them. They were the first non-Arabs to visit the town in a long time. Because there was no hotel, two young school teachers asked David and his group to spend the night in a large, one-room house.[21]

More than 60 neighbors attended an impromptu dinner held in the students' honor. Each local brought a particular dish that ranged from raw meat to yogurt. Even though David was afraid to eat some of the offerings, he did not want to offend the visitors who closely watched him. He put his taste buds on hold and ate what was placed in front of him.

David was intrigued with village families and their children who were learning English in the local school. The young students recited what they had learned in English. When David returned to Oxford, he and his companions combined their funds, bought books on American history that had been translated into Arabic, and sent them to the school library in the Jordanian town they had visited.[22]

David and his troupe took a trip by camel between groups of pyramids in Egypt. At the time, they could not visit Israel because, if they had an Israeli stamp in their passport, many of the surrounding Arabic countries would not allow them to cross into their territory. Jerusalem was under Jordanian control and they were able to visit the historic city. David also visited several Palestinian refugee camps and argued with several refugees his age about Israel's right to exist. While he strongly favored the independence of Israel, he left feeling that the Palestinians also deserved a homeland as well and that there would never be peace until such a homeland was created.[23]

On other trips, David went to Morocco, Spain, France, and bicycled across Holland with fellow Rhodes Scholar Bob Munford from Mississippi. On a trip to Vienna, Austria, David and his friends pooled their money and stayed in hostels to save money so they could attend a performance of the music of Richard Wagner at the Vienna Opera House conducted by Herbert von Karajan.

Once, while studying for final exams, David and Australian friend, Allan Taylor, traveled to Scotland to isolate themselves for the very long and difficult exams which covered the entire two years of study. They lived in an inn in Durness, an isolated village on the north tip of Scotland. Between study breaks, David walked on the heather and into the highlands along the edge of the sea. He will never forget the sounds of the waves crashing into the Scottish coast or the serene sight of long-haired cattle grazing.[24]

When he was between terms, David worked as a member of the Speakers Bureau at the American Embassy in London. He spoke at garden clubs, civic clubs, sporting clubs, and other groups all around England about life in the United States. It was during the time of the presidential race between Barry Goldwater and Lyndon Johnson, a subject in which the British people were very interested. The British were mesmerized by the Kennedy family and listened intently to David's stories of meeting Kennedy and the Boren family's friendship with Johnson.

David was in London in January, 1965, when former British Prime Minister Sir Winston Churchill died. He stood outside St. Paul's Cathedral, along with hundreds of thousands of others, to observe one of the largest gatherings of world leaders ever. It was a remarkable moment in history. David was only a few steps from French President Charles De Gaulle and other leaders who led the funeral procession to St. Paul's. Thousands of former British soldiers wore their World War II uniforms to honor the man who brought England through the war.[25]

David was touched by the outpouring of feeling for Churchill. He said later, "To me, it was a tribute to Churchill's moral courage." David always has revered Churchill and considers him among his greatest personal heroes that include George Washington, Abraham Lincoln, Thomas Jefferson, Harry Truman, Franklin D. Roosevelt, and Nelson Mandela. Churchill has been a role model for David because Churchill was never afraid to stand alone. "He had the courage to do what he thought was right to protect his country even though at the time he had every reason to believe that he was sacrificing any chance to have a political career," David said. Even though David recognizes that other politicians perhaps may have achieved as much for their nations, he does not believe that any political leader ever exceeded Churchill in integrity and courage.

Back at Oxford, a memorable time for David was the visit of former Prime Minister Harold Macmillan to the college. One evening, David and other students had dinner with Macmillan in what was called the Hall, a beautiful gothic room with long tables and low benches where students sat below the High Table, at which Macmillan and other dignitaries sat. Macmillan was serving in an honorary position as the chancellor at Oxford following his time as prime minister.

On that occasion, in the candlelit room, Macmillan was asked to speak. A graduate of Balliol College himself, he began to talk about the former students who were memorialized in portraits that graced the walls of the Hall. Many of the young men were in military dress, heroes of particularly World War I. Macmillan described the men so clearly that David thought he almost knew them. Macmillan spoke extemporaneously without a microphone. David remembered, "He painted such a complete picture of each one of the heroes that I felt like I knew them. He described their contributions and how they were killed in battle and what it meant for the British to lose an entire generation of potential leaders." David never forgot the beauty of Macmillan's language—he described it as "almost pure poetry." It was an emotional moment for David and helped him understand the toll that World War I and World War II had taken on Great Britain.[26]

David had heard many of the great speeches of the century, both in person and by recording. But for him, Macmillan's speech in the Hall that evening ranked near the top. David became a fan of Macmillan who had a difficult role in transitioning Great Britain from its role as the leader of an empire, of literally ruling much of the world during the Victorian Period, to the role of a single country that needed Allies to exert influence in the modern world. David often read Macmillan's speech, "The Wind of Change," in which the prime minister prepared Britain for exercising a new kind of influence based on values, diplomatic skills, and friendships with other nations which allowed it to play a major role in world affairs even after the end of the British Empire. Macmillan's thinking was to continue for many years to influence David's views on foreign policy.[27]

After two years at Oxford, David had to make decisions about his future. He had earned a master's degree in political science, but could have stayed one or two years longer for a doctorate degree. He also met with Headley Donovan, editor of *Time* Magazine, who tried to recruit David to write for *Time*. David still toyed with the idea of pursuing a career in journalism. He also had enjoyed visiting foreign countries and talking about the American way of life, so a career in the foreign service also appealed to him.

But David was anxious to get home—he felt time was passing him by. He listened to the advice of Earl Sneed, dean of the OU College of Law, that if he ever wanted to be successful in Oklahoma politics, he should attend law school in the Sooner State. Sneed had given David a personal tour of the law school before he left for Oxford and had convinced him of its high standards and excellence as a college of law. In addition, Sneed reasoned that friendships formed in law school would benefit any run for public office and attendance at alumni functions would introduce David to the leading lawyers and judges in the state.[28]

The firm decision was made. David would not stay at Oxford to complete a doctorate, nor would he join *Time* Magazine. Instead, he would return to Oklahoma, enroll at the OU College of Law, and pursue his dream of public service.

*I was already busy, going to law school and serving
as a counselor in Worcester House, an OU residence hall.
Then came a telephone call which changed my life.*

DAVID L. BOREN

EIGHT

Law School and Race for the House

HE UNIVERSITY OF OKLAHOMA College of Law began classes in 1909 with Professor Julien C. Monnet of the George Washington University Law School as dean. The law school's first class was made up primarily of six aspiring law students from Epworth University School of Law, now Oklahoma City University. Epworth's law school had begun five years earlier, but because of lack of support from feuding camps of Oklahoma Methodists, and the desire to have a law school at a state-run university, the OU Board of Regents established the OU College of Law. Classes were held in the Science Building at first, then were moved to the basement of the Carnegie Building.[1]

The OU College of Law grew in stature from 1909 to the 1940s when most county and district judges and justices of the Oklahoma Supreme Court were OU Law graduates. In the mid-1940s, an African American young lady from Chickasha, Ada Lois Sipuel Fisher, applied for admission to the law school, but was denied solely on the base of race. Fisher, represented by later United States Supreme Court Justice Thurgood Marshall, was the plaintiff in a landmark civil rights case. In 1948, the high court ordered her admitted, breaking barriers for African American students at law schools across the nation. That event is memorialized in a garden on the present law school campus.

David said goodbye to many friends he had made at Oxford and sailed for America. After visiting a few days with his parents, he reported to the law school in Norman. To assist in the payment of tuition and fees, he became a resident advisor (RA), or counselor, at Worcester House, one of the aging World War II-era dormitories on the OU campus. Worcester House was filled with 120 freshmen men for whom David and his fellow RA, Lewis Parkhill, later a professor at Murray State College at Tishomingo, Oklahoma, were responsible. Students came to David for advice, and he patrolled the halls to enforce a mandatory study hall each evening.[2]

David truly was interested in the academic advancement of the freshmen under his tutelage. He arranged for faculty members to speak informally with students over dinner in the Wilson Center cafeteria. David was the victim of many good-natured student pranks. One of the more memorable occasions was when his dormitory-room door was nailed shut. David remembered, "It happened so fast. I was studying when I heard the first sounds of hammers." However, by the time David jumped from his chair and approached the door, the students had hammered at least a dozen nails through the door into the door jam. After an hour of freshmen enjoying their accomplishment, they freed David from his room. David said, "Those kind of pranks certainly built my ties to OU immediately."[3]

In 1965, the OU College of Law was headquartered in Monnet Hall, a stately building on OU's North Oval adjacent to Evans Hall, the university administration building. David instantly was surrounded by a group of law school friends who became his friends for life. One good friend was Dan Little, the son of Reuel Little, a successful oil man and entrepreneur in

Madill, Oklahoma. Dan had attended Harvard College for his undergraduate studies, so he identified with David's time at Yale. There were other ties with Dan—David defeated him by the slim margin of one vote in the election for freshman class president, and Dan later introduced David to his sister, Janna, who would become David's wife.[4]

David made friends with both law students and freshmen men in Worcester House. Many of those friends would later become involved in David's campaigns for public office, including Von Creel, Mike Weaver, Lynn Windel, Tom Cornish, Charles Cashion, Glenn Floyd, Prudence Little, John Ray Green, Phil Redwine, Danny Binns, Jack McCarty, James Kirk, Farrell Hatch, Elaine Schuster, Pauline Fahle, Phil Horning, Randall Mock, Coy Morrow, Harvey Chaffin, Carlisle Mabrey, and many others.

From his first days on the Norman campus, David sought time with OU President George Lynn Cross. Dr. Cross had been at the helm of the university since 1943 and was one of America's most respected university presidents. Just as with his encounters with Robert Frost, David calculated when Dr. Cross would leave the front door of Boyd House, the presidential residence, for a stroll across the street to the Oklahoma Memorial Union for a morning cup of coffee. Dr. Cross remembered David from his Rhodes Scholarship interview, so he was delighted that David wanted to accompany him on his morning walk to coffee.[5]

Dr. Cross was an educational hero and mentor to David. Strolling along with a pipe in his hand or mouth, Cross was the epitome of a revered president of an institution of higher learning. He offered deep insight into the events of the day, both nationally and in Oklahoma, and was genuinely interested in David's future. Their friendship became solid within a matter of a few weeks over morning coffee.[6]

Conversations with Dr. Cross gave David his first real insight into what it was like to be a university president, the huge responsibilities that the president bore in making a difference in the lives of OU students. Cross was accessible to all students, but David took advantage of the president's willingness to share his knowledge. No doubt, the time spent with Dr. Cross influenced David's decision to ultimately leave a powerful post as Oklahoma's senior United States Senator and return to OU as president, a decision that David was able to talk over with Dr. Cross before he made it. In fact, a telephone call from Dr. Cross urging David to come back to OU probably tipped the balance in his decision.[7]

In addition to becoming close friends with his mentor, David also was blessed with a wonderful relationship with Cleo Cross, the wife of the president. David said, "She was so kind and understanding. Her advice on studies, relationships, and good manners were very important to me." David's close friendship with Dr. and Mrs. Cross continued until their deaths.[8]

Even after beginning law school, David was not completely certain where his future in public service was headed. He took examinations that would allow him to work in the diplomatic service of the American government. He had passed the written foreign service examination and was waiting to take his oral interview when he changed course and entered politics. At Oxford, he had been offered a job to write for *Time* Magazine and also considered journalism as a possible career. To consider his options, he visited with Raymond Reed, the state representative from David's home district in Seminole County. District 28 included most of the county.

David told Reed that he might want to run for the Oklahoma House of Representatives, but would never oppose Reed while he remained in office. David also talked to newspaper publisher Milt

Phillips, oil man Melvin Moran, Seminole Mayor Fred Adwan, A.C. Kidd of Wewoka, and other Seminole County residents about the possibility that he might want to be the representative from Seminole County. David had kept in contact with Phillips because he often wrote columns for the newspaper when he was at Oxford. Everyone with whom David talked was positive about his future role as a leader in the county.[9]

To be eligible for election to the legislature from Seminole County, David always had kept his permanent residence in Seminole. He rented a room from Mrs. Noel Summers who lived next to the house where David grew up. In fact, David had voted since age 21 in Seminole, including by absentee ballot when he was in England.

David genuinely liked law school. He was challenged by professors and intrigued by discussions of case law and world events with fellow students. He had his plate full with entering law school, being elected freshman class president, and avoiding pranks of his students as an RA in Worcester House. However, an opportunity of a lifetime occurred in the form of a telephone call from Representative Reed in December, 1965.

Reed told David that he had an opportunity to run for a vacant county judge position and would not run for reelection to the House of Representatives. David thanked Reed for the early news and quickly conferred with his father, law school friends, and old family friends in Seminole. Within days, David was telling people he wanted to be the next state representative from Seminole County.

He immediately made an appointment with the publishers of the two newspapers in the district, Milt Phillips of the *Seminole Producer* and Gary Reed of the *Wewoka Times*. There would not be much time to canvass the district because the Democratic primary was in early spring. An important early endorsement was from legendary attorney Dick Bell in Seminole. Bell had been a Boren family friend since David's birth.[10]

David had ties in the three major towns in District 28. He was well known in his hometown of Seminole, the largest city in the district. He had family and friends in the smaller town of Wewoka, the county seat. His uncle, Dale Boren, owned the Boren-Malone school supply store in Wewoka, where poor children were often given textbooks they could not afford. David's aunt, Juno Boren, was the Wewoka town librarian. His grandparents, Mark and Nannie Boren, were beloved in Wewoka and were known for giving credit to the poor at their grocery store during the Great Depression.

All of David's family members in the area were stalwart members of their respective churches and knew many of the voters. David's maternal grandparents were leading citizens of Maud where his grandfather served as postmaster. In fact, during law school, David drove each Sunday afternoon for dinner with his grandparents.

David had two formidable opponents for the House seat. William C. "Bill" Wantland was a 32-year-old Seminole attorney who served part time as priest for the local Episcopal congregation. David was single and only 24—Wantland had a family and was well established in Seminole. The third candidate was a last-minute entry into the race, Bill Nicholson, in his late sixties and a recently-retired and very popular longtime county sheriff. David knew it would take "a lot of elbow grease and shoe leather" to win the race.[11]

Law school classmates and Worcester House freshmen made up much of the first Boren campaign team. They traveled after classes to Seminole County to knock on doors, deliver handbills, and assist David in any way he requested. Students were organized by Carrie Abernathy Bell, the wife of one of David's law school classmates. Carrie and David developed maps of the communities in the district. It was his goal to deliver literature to every single house in the county, including residents of the smaller towns of New Lima and Cromwell.[12]

David's youth was a campaign issue. His opponents charged he was inexperienced. He was accused of being a "carpetbagger" and that he had really lived the past decade either in Maryland, at Yale, or in England. David's theme was "Give a young man a chance."

It was old-fashioned campaigning. David appeared at pie suppers in rural areas where pies were auctioned to the highest bidder and at "speakings" at civic clubs and before a large crowd at the Seminole Municipal Auditorium. At one such event, Wantland, who after the election became good friends with David for life, openly criticized David for not having roots in the area as a "carpetbagger." David countered with a long list of his relatives in the area and the fact that he attended public schools in Seminole for ten of the 12 years.[13]

During the debate, David pointed out that his family was deeply embedded in the fabric of the county. The debate was dramatic at best. Wantland's speech was disrupted by Nellie Janes, an elderly Seminole woman and beloved pillar of the Methodist Church who could not hear well. She stood up from her seat on the front row and said, "What's that he's saying about David Boren? I can't believe it. That's a terrible, terrible lie. Shame on him! He shouldn't say things like that about David. He's a fine young man."[14] People thought Mrs. Janes was just talking too loudly because of her hearing problem. However, as she left the auditorium that night, she winked at David and said, "How'd I do?"

At the same candidate forum, attorney Dick Bell defended charges against David that he had never been registered in the county and had never voted. Bell stood from his seat in the middle of the auditorium and dramatically announced that he, as county election board chairman, had personal knowledge that David was always registered in Seminole County and that he had voted in every election. Bell insisted that Wantland apologize. David took the high road, stayed positive, and came out of the debate with momentum.[15]

The large group of African American voters in the district also played a major role in the campaign. Seminole and Wewoka still were segregated—African Americans were concentrated in one area of each city. One of David's opponents handed out $5 and $10 checks to potential voters and hired drivers to pick up voters and take them to the polls.

On the other hand, David, as a white candidate, went campaigning door to door in African American neighborhoods, an unusual action in rural Oklahoma in the 1960s. He had dinner as a guest in the homes of prominent black leaders which was unheard of in Seminole County. David's stance on equality for all won him endorsements from several African American leaders, including Dr. C. R. Johns who had been school superintendent of all-black schools during segregation days and later served as a city council member in Seminole.

The long battle between citizens of Seminole and Wewoka peaked during the House campaign. Wewoka had been the county seat since statehood, but Seminole had an oil boom and passed Wewoka in population in the 1920s. There were rumors during David's campaign that Seminole was again interested in becoming the county seat. Wewokans were defensive about such rumors and the rivalry was on. The deep roots of David's family in Wewoka was very reassuring to the citizens of that community.

David picked up support from Bessie Harris, a former chairman of the Seminole County Democratic Party. Mrs. Harris was a good friend of David's grandmother, Alice McKown, and used her influence to sway many rural voters to David's corner.

David's newspaper advertisements were to the point. He promised, "Each issue will be weighed with independent thought and decided on its merits." Another ad mentioned that David was a Rhodes scholar, but also had common sense. A theme of the advertising was that David had time for the job and was best qualified because he had a concrete, eight-point platform and was a veteran of government service, having spoken "for Oklahoma and the U.S." in 30 countries around the world. He also stressed that he would run a positive campaign because he did not believe in trying to build up one's self by tearing down someone else.[16]

A few days before the primary, Sheriff Nicholson approached David and said he regretted getting into the race. He publicly withdrew and endorsed David. However, it was too late for the county election board to remove his name from the ballot.

On election day, balloting was close. Wantland led the field with 3,137 votes to David's 2,934. Because Nicholson was still on the ballot, he received 327 votes, enough votes to throw David and Wantland into a May 24th runoff. It was clear where David was strong in the district. He carried Maud and Wewoka and African American boxes in Seminole and Wewoka, but lost Seminole to Wantland.[17]

The runoff was fiercely contested. The *Seminole Producer* called it "one of the most heated political races in recent years."[18] David and his army of OU students again delivered literature to every house in the district. David took advantage of every opportunity to espouse his beliefs and qualifications to civic and church groups.

There was much interest in the runoff election in 1966. Former Governor Raymond Gary and Preston Moore were in a hard-fought contest for the Democratic nomination for governor.

And, for the first time in state history, Republicans had a runoff for the gubernatorial nomination. State Senator Dewey Bartlett, the eventual winner in the general election, was pitted against John N. "Happy" Camp.

On May 24, David squeaked out a 92-vote victory over Wantland, 2,961 to 2,869. David carried all four boxes in Wewoka and the Maud precinct. Wantland won the most votes in the Seminole precincts. Wantland immediately asked the State Board for an official recount. The ballot boxes were kept under lock and key at the county courthouse. David and his advisors were concerned about someone tampering with the ballots, so several friends took turns sleeping with the ballot boxes until a judge could oversee the recount. District Judge Lee R. West of Ada was assigned the task of presiding over the recount in which David picked up eight votes and was declared the winner by 100 votes.[19]

Because Seminole County had an overwhelming number of voters registered as Democrats, winning the Democratic nomination for House District 28 was tantamount to election. However, David drew a general election opponent, Republican Clifford Conn, also a student at OU. It really was not a contest and David won the race 4,528 to 1,687 with the endorsement of Bill Wantland whom David had defeated in the Democratic runoff. David carried every precinct in the district. Wantland later became the Episcopal Bishop of Eau Clare, Wisconsin. After his retirement as bishop, he moved back to Seminole.[20]

The general election was not only an important day for the Boren family, the vote counting produced two monumental decisions. Voters elected Bartlett as the second consecutive Republican governor after nearly a half century of Democrat-rule in the governor's mansion. Even a more significant election was the defeat of longtime Speaker of the House J. D. McCarty in Oklahoma City.

Funeral home operator Vondell Smith beat McCarty, a symbol of the power of what David would later label the "old guard."

One person who David impressed with his campaign was Rob Pyron, a 16-year-old Wewoka High School student. Pyron, who later would become David's first staff member in his 1974 run for governor, said of David's first campaign, "The campaign was hotly contested, but David established a tradition of positive campaigning and not debunking an opponent for political gain."[21]

Pyron was working at a gas station when he first met Boren and they had conversations while he washed the windshield and checked the oil. Later, when Pyron was the governor's press secretary, he was asked what he was doing when he first met David. Pyron jokingly replied, "I was in the oil business."[22]

---

*I would have nothing to do with dirty political tricks,
so I walked out of the room.*

DAVID L. BOREN

NINE

Maverick Legislator

WITH HIS FIRST SUCCESSFUL POLITICAL CAMPAIGN behind him, Boren returned to law school. In fact, OU College of Law Dean Earl Sneed wrote a tongue-in-cheek letter to Boren's father, Lyle, commenting about the large number of law students who had spent much of their spring helping in the Boren campaign. Sneed said, "We will be glad when this election is over so we can get back to having law school!"[1]

With the new responsibility of serving in the Oklahoma legislature, Boren gave up his position as residential assistant at Worcester House. He moved into an apartment in the Westwind Apartments near the Duck Pond east of the OU campus. He continued to spend Sundays with relatives in Seminole County. It was a special time for family. David remembered, "We all sat around the same table every Sunday in the same chairs. I was generally asked to give the invocation before lunch." Needless to say, his grandparents were extremely proud of their young grandson being elected to political office, following in the footsteps of his father.

Boren was seated in the Oklahoma House of Representatives on the back row with Representative Charlie Morgan of Prague, a Boren family friend. Ironically, years later, when Dan Boren was elected to his father's former seat in the House of Representatives, he was seated beside Representative Danny Morgan, the son of Charlie Morgan.[2]

It was not long before Boren began to show his independent streak as a legislator. Governor Bartlett asked Boren to be a Democratic sponsor of a bill that affected the state treasurer's ability to decide which banks held state deposits. At the time, Democratic State Treasurer Leo Winters was in complete control of the deposit of state funds in Oklahoma banks. It was a lucrative venture for a bank to hold huge deposits of state money until the treasurer needed the funds to pay state bills. A bank was allowed to pay the state a small rate of interest on the deposit and then loan money to its customers at a much higher rate. Because the "idle deposits" sat in banks for extended periods of time, bankers prospered.

It was not just coincidental that the banks receiving large state deposits were avid supporters of Treasurer Winters. Boren reflected, "The bankers incurred favor with legislators who were awarded with state deposits in banks in their home counties. It was quite a network with the state treasurer, large banks, and state legislators keeping the status quo."[3] Democrats enjoyed a large majority in both the Oklahoma State Senate and House of Representatives, so Republican Governor Bartlett had an uphill battle to pass reform legislation.

Bartlett announced to the world in his state of the state message early in the 1967 legislative session that Boren would be the Democratic sponsor of the bill. Democratic leaders were furious. Later that day they held a closed-door caucus and demanded Boren withdraw his sponsorship of the bill. Boren refused and a motion was made to censure Boren for his "maverick" action. The motion passed with only three dissenting votes—Boren, Representative Don Coffin of Guthrie, and Representative David Stratton of Clinton. Boren said, "What a first week for my legislative career."[4]

Boren looked at the issue with non-partisan eyes. If banks had to bid competitively for the deposit of state funds, state government would benefit by receiving larger interest payments. It sounded like good government to Boren. However, Democratic leaders killed the bill in committee. Boren later advocated the idea in his race for governor in 1974 and a bill to implement it passed the legislature in 1975.[5]

Boren made friends on both sides of the aisle in the legislature. It was indicative of his bi-partisan stance throughout his career in public service. On pieces of legislation, he often teamed with Republican Representatives Ralph Thompson and James Inhofe. Thompson later served as a longtime federal judge and Boren defeated Inhofe for governor in 1974. Later Inhofe replaced Boren in the United States Senate.

Boren's new role as a member of the House of Representatives also allowed him to make influential friends outside the legislature. Oil man Jack Abernathy set up a luncheon between Boren and Edward L. Gaylord at the Skirvin Hotel. Abernathy thought Boren and Gaylord needed to know each other because he recognized that both men deeply cared for Oklahoma. Gaylord's father, E.K. Gaylord, was still publisher of *The Daily Oklahoman*, but the younger Gaylord was active in civic affairs.

Boren and Gaylord found much common ground between them. A close, personal friendship began and lasted more than 35 years until Gaylord's death in 2003. They had lunch every four to six weeks. Even when they disagreed on politics, their friendship was not affected.[6]

Fortunately for Boren, the legislature met only four days per week for the first few months of each year. After all, he was a full-time law student who was devoted to earning good grades and getting the most out of the law school experience. He was selected for the OU *Law Review* and published an article on unclaimed property. Boren also was named to the Dean's Honor Roll for each of his semesters at law school.

Being a member of the state legislature did not give Boren an upper hand in law school, but the prestige certainly did not hurt his relationship with professors. Professor Frank Elkouri, who had been associated with the OU College of Law since he enrolled as a student in 1939, was impressed with how Boren could earn superior grades while spending so much time with his constituents and with the legislative process. Elkouri said, "I was in awe of his academic performance. Several of our students had outside jobs, but David was superior and a real leader even though he had his hands full as a state legislator."[7]

Although he often had to be at the State Capitol during the legislative session for an important vote, Boren's attendance in law school was "quite good," according to Professor Daniel G. Gibbens. Gibbens remembered a constitutional law class of which Boren was a member. Gibbens said, "I remember exactly where he sat, second row, right of center. I tried not to pick on him and call on him to recite more than other students. But when I did call on him, he was always prepared."[8]

Boren's occasional absences caused by legislative duties did affect his grade in another class. Professor Elbridge Phelps penalized Boren because of the few classes he missed due to legislative work, even though Boren's work frequently benefited OU. Professor Gibbens said, "Professor Phelps routinely had a tighter attendance requirement than the rest of the faculty and clearly made no exceptions."[9]

Boren's friends in law school saw his devotion to family, law school, and his new-found purpose—public service. Tom Cornish, who began and completed law school with Boren, said, "His love and compassion for family, friends, and his public constituency is his legacy in Oklahoma." Cornish saw Boren "pecking away on a manual typewriter" answering letters from Seminole County people who were seeking his help on some matter. Cornish said, "Throughout his entire career in public service, he never forgot his

Seminole County roots. He has always made time to respond to requests for help to deal with the problems of the people from the forks of the creek in Oklahoma."[10]

Fellow student Jack Mattingly, who later would become Boren's law partner in Seminole, said, "David was bright, a true gentleman, and had the qualities that allowed him to become both a successful student and budding politician." Mattingly believed Boren was the perfect politician because of his intelligence and aspiration for public service.[11]

Boren settled down in his law school work and his position as state legislator from District 28. He was able to overcome the first month of ruffled feathers over the state deposit legislation and was named to the House Elections Committee. He authored a bill that allowed county election boards to not print the name of unopposed candidates because they were automatically elected or reelected. The law saved election boards money in the cost of printing ballots. In some counties, the general election ballot was greatly shortened because many local officials, with no opponents, were officially elected in primary elections.[12]

Boren also was a member of the House committee that oversaw the operation of state parks and economic development. He learned much about state parks and lodges and helped appropriate funds for major renovations. To add to his duties, Boren became the nation's youngest member of the Rhodes Scholarship selection committee.

Over time, Boren became less controversial and was often defended by House Speaker Rex Privett. Slowly, but surely, fellow Democrats forgave Boren for authoring the state deposits bill and backed Privett in naming Boren to the powerful Rules Committee where the Speaker often sent bills that he intended to die without being voted on by the full membership of the House. The Rules Committee process allowed the Speaker to kill a bill behind closed doors without individual members' votes on the measure ever being recorded.[13]

Boren saw first-hand that often citizens never knew how their elected representative voted because the fate of many bills was "taken care of" in clandestine fashion. There was not only the Rules Committee in which bills died, but other measures were killed by a vote of the entire House voting as a Committee of the Whole. There was no recorded vote, only a voice vote. Boren said, "I felt both of these procedures really kept the people from knowing what was going on." Later, Boren introduced legislation to make House members more accountable. His proposals required that all committees meet in open session and that votes be taken on all matters in committees and when the House met as the Committee of the Whole. He also wrote a bill, later known as the Open Meetings Act, which applied to all state and local public bodies. [14]

Boren kept in touch with the people in Seminole County whom he served in the legislature. He held frequent town meetings, placing notices in local newspapers of the time and place of such meetings. He was diligent to make certain every request for help was answered. He attended every public gathering he could. Along the way, he built strong local support for his continued service. In the next three House elections, 1968, 1970, and 1972, Boren drew no opposition.

Boren graduated with honors from the OU College of Law in May, 1968. He received the Bledsoe Prize as the outstanding law graduate. During his senior year, classmate Dan Little had introduced his sister, Janna, to David. Janna had studied communications at Boston University and was working at a television station in Oklahoma City. David and Janna began dating and were married in 1968. They purchased a small home on Wilson Street in Seminole. Liz Robertson was their neighbor across the street. She said, "We felt honored to have our state representative as our neighbor." Liz helped Janna develop a list of community leaders to invite to dinner so she could become better acquainted in Seminole. [15]

Boren passed the Oklahoma bar examination and opened law offices in both Seminole and Wewoka. In Seminole, he shared office space with an elderly lawyer, Elmer Sutherland, down the hall from Dick Bell, who offered Boren additional advice on his new law practice. In Wewoka, Boren officed with attorney A. C. Kidd who became a mentor to the brand new lawyer. When Boren had an unusual case which required a court appearance, Kidd accompanied him to the courtroom and "walked him through it so he didn't make any mistakes."[16]

By 1970, Boren had become an influential state legislator and was asked to participate in Democratic efforts to unseat Republican Governor Bartlett. Boren admired Bartlett but agreed with Democrat David Hall's platform of increasing state funding for education. Hall was county attorney in Tulsa County and was running as a reformer. Boren was one of three or four people who helped write Hall's speech in which he announced he was running for governor.[17]

As part of Hall's "inner circle," Boren was invited to meetings in which campaign strategy was discussed. At one such meeting, campaign operatives were preparing to call Bartlett a polluter by staging an oil spill at one of his Keener Oil Company wells in Seminole County. Boren heard Hall supporters planning to open a valve on Bartlett's well so the oil would flow into a nearby creek. Photographs would be taken and the media would be alerted. Boren said he did not approve of such underhanded tactics and he would not be a part of it. He left the meeting—and never returned.[18]

Boren told Governor Bartlett about the plan hatched against him. Bartlett was able to prove that someone had deliberately sabotaged his well in an attempt to label him a polluter. The Hall plan backfired. Boren never had a confrontation with Hall over the event—he simply pulled back and ceased any activity on behalf of Hall's campaign.[19] Hall defeated Bartlett in the 1970 general election, returning the governor's mansion to Democrats after two successive Republican governors, Henry Bellmon and Bartlett.[20]

*When a banker takes the depositor's money,
we call it embezzlement. When a politician goes
on a personal trip at public expense, we call it politics.*

DAVID L. BOREN

TEN

Professor Boren

N **1969, SHORTLY AFTER BOREN WAS MARRIED,** he began teaching as an assistant professor of political science at Oklahoma Baptist University (OBU) in Shawnee. He still was practicing law in Seminole and Wewoka and taught the young couples' Sunday School class at First United Methodist Church in Seminole. He also was a member of the Seminole Rotary Club, a board member of the Wewoka Chamber of Commerce, a member of the Seminole Chamber of Commerce, vice chairman of the Law Schools Committee of the Oklahoma Bar Association, and a member of the Governor's Task Force on Vocational Technical Education.

OBU was founded in 1906 when the State Baptist Convention of Oklahoma voted to make plans to open a Baptist university in the state. In 1906, a board of trustees was named. Classes began in the basement of the First Baptist Church of Shawnee and in Convention Hall in September, 1911. The City of Shawnee contributed the original 60-acre campus north of the city. The first building, Shawnee Hall, opened in 1915.[1]

Boren was familiar with OBU. His parents were close friends of the former long-time OBU president, John Wesley Raley, and his wife, Helen. Raley retired in 1961 after serving longer than any other president of the university. He died in 1966. At the time Boren began his teaching career, Grady C. Cothen was president. Shortly after Boren arrived at OBU, Cothen left the university to become president of New Orleans Baptist Theological Seminary.[2]

When Boren arrived on the OBU campus, it was far different than today. Dr. Jim Farthing became a professor of history at about the same time Boren joined the faculty. Farthing and other OBU academicians were proud of Boren's credentials as a graduate of Yale and Oxford and his fame as a Rhodes Scholar. Farthing said, "The assets that made David an effective politician made him an effective instructor with unique insight into the American political process."[3]

Boren was a popular professor and was named chairman of the OBU Division of Social Sciences in 1971. Two years later, he was promoted to associate professor and was tenured in 1974. Even though students "lined up" to enroll in Boren's classes, OBU archivist J. Thomas Terry recalled the time when an obstinate student who wanted Boren to hold class outside on a beautiful day laid on the floor of the classroom door as a protest. Boren quietly told the other students to "step over her" and join him in the classroom.[4]

While Boren had turned much of his attention to teaching, he still practiced law. He prepared a Last Will and Testament for John W. Parrish and his wife in 1970 for a $10 attorney's fee. Parrish served OBU in many capacities throughout the years, including being named interim president in 2008. He said, "Students liked David's classes so much that they began quoting him and his views on world and national politics." Parrish called Boren "a very effective communicator."[5]

Rudolph Hargrave, later a justice of the Oklahoma Supreme Court, practiced law in Seminole County. When Boren agreed to handle a divorce case for a client, he admitted to Hargrave, "I have no idea what I am doing." Hargrave guided the young lawyer through the process.[6]

Boren was OBU's primary instructor of political science. Even though he was versed in American and world history, he did not teach history classes. Because his class offerings were popular, larger classes were taught in the basement of Raley Chapel. During the legislative session, Boren's classes were scheduled early in the morning, so he could jump into his car and drive to Oklahoma City for committee meetings and House sessions.[7]

Boren created a special internship program at OBU funded by the Kerr Foundation through which political science majors and minors could intern for state legislators. David Smith, now a successful attorney in Ada, and other students drove from Shawnee to Oklahoma City to spend the day with their assigned legislator, attending committee meetings, watching debate on the House floor, or completing research. Each day ended with a session with Boren discussing what each intern had learned that day.[8]

Boren invited students to his home in Seminole for dinners of chicken or steak. He also hosted election night gatherings for students. Smith remembered, "At those famous dinners we talked about politics and law. He was our mentor." Smith called Boren the best professor he had in his college and law school experience.[9]

Even though Boren wore glasses and "looked like a professor," Smith said it was Boren's personality that made him a favorite with students. Smith said, "He was kind, sincere, honest, and genuine. His teaching style was very thought-provoking. Each day, there was a spirited discussion about how the social, political, and legal events in the morning newspaper related to the Constitution and text book lessons. It was current events at its best."[10]

Boren's students admired him. Jim Hopper said, "He made a difference in my life. He is absolutely my mentor professionally. If I was ever in trouble, he is the first person I would call." "He was a great teacher," Sam Hammons remembers, "It was clear he loved the classroom and the students loved him."[11] David Cox believes that Boren is a "teacher at heart." Cox said, "The quality I admire most in him is his gift in motivating and inspiring people to be better than we are."[12] David Berrong tried to never miss one of Boren's classes. He said, "He made what some people considered boring political and government topics come alive. We knew he was a special person headed for greatness."[13]

Boren loved to debate his students in the classroom. He would allow students to present their opinions, then he would take the opposing position. In the process, he enlightened students as to the strengths and weaknesses of both positions. His excitement about the political process was contagious. Boren was a confidant of OBU President William Tanner as well as Academic Dean Dr. William Neptune and Dean of Students Don Osborne.[14]

Boren addressed a student and faculty assembly at OBU in May, 1970. College campuses had been torn with frustration with the war in Vietnam and what many college students believed to be an uncaring federal government. Demonstrations on college campuses made the nightly news. Boren said, "Our world is confused and polarized. Irrationality breeds irrationality. Force breeds force. Demonstrations are counterproductive. Confrontations breed suffering and death."[15]

Boren summarized his belief that confrontation was dangerous to intellectual freedom:

Never before have we so needed to say "stop"—stop the confrontations, stop the mobs which shout down speakers, stop our frenetic action which further confuses us, stop the burning of books which contain ideas we do not like. Stop trying to "feel" our way out of our dilemmas and start trying to THINK our way to solutions. We live in an age of anti-intellectualism, even on the campus itself. We have let our frustrations get the best of us. We have copped out and dropped out.[16]

Reporting on Boren's speech that day was Shawnee High School student Robert Henry, later a state legislator, attorney general of Oklahoma, dean of the Oklahoma City University School of Law, and chief judge of the United States Court of Appeals for the Tenth Circuit. Henry said, "When we got back and I did a report, my colleagues said, 'You didn't do a report. You virtually repeated Boren's speech verbatim.'" Henry's excuse was that Boren's speech was so good and "spoke" to him, he remembered the speech word by word and phrase by phrase.[17]

Boren believed that his role as a teacher was a form of ministry. He described teaching as the "most satisfying experience of my life" to that point in his life's journey. "While, of course, there is the excitement of the exchange of ideas in the classroom," Boren wrote, "of even greater importance is the development of close personal relationships with students. A college student, whose character is forming, so open and honest and yet still so uncertain in his direction, is in need of compassion, help, and reassurance."[18]

Boren compared teaching to being a pastor of a church. He said, "A teacher must share himself and his own shortcomings in an honest relationship with a student while drawing from the student the tremendous potential which is there, not only in scholarship, but also in personhood. What situation could present a greater opportunity for ministry to others?"[19]

Boren spoke publicly about the issues of the day. When a student asked him, "Where is our country headed?" Boren struggled for an answer, reflecting on scandals, abuses of power, and petty corruption in government. He wrote in a column in the *Baptist Messenger*, "We are not undergoing a political crisis in this country. We are undergoing a moral crisis. For too long we have tolerated immorality in politics...When a husband violates the trust of a marriage relationship, we brand his act adultery. When a public official violates his public trust, we call it politics."[20]

Boren continued, "As Christian men and women, we are called to serve our fellowmen and our God in the political life of our society as surely as in any other field. Why do we tolerate wrong-doing and evil here more readily than elsewhere? Every week we wink approvingly at moral compromise in the political arena, we sow a seed which will produce a bitter harvest...Integrity is not out of place in politics."[21]

Boren also shared his wisdom with students at the OU College of Law. Steven Taylor, long-time district judge in McAlester and now a justice of the Oklahoma Supreme Court, was an OU law student who took advantage of Boren's presence at the law school to meet with students who had an interest in entering public service. Even though only three other students showed up at the appointed hour with Taylor, Boren spent more than two hours telling the students about his experience as a legislator. Taylor said, "Those two hours provided a major inspiration for my interest in public service. He told us that he intended to devote his entire life to serving his state and country, and he encouraged us to do the same."[22]

As Boren's prowess as a college professor was being developed, his distrust of the administration of Governor David Hall grew. Boren was disturbed about rumors from honest highway contractors who alleged that they were "being shaken down" by being forced to buy bonds from certain supporters of Hall. Boren was crushed at such allegations because he genuinely liked Hall's charisma and identification with the electorate.[23]

Boren took news of allegations of abuse of power directly to Governor Hall. Boren urged the governor to take a close look at certain people around him. The first time Boren visited with Hall about his concerns, Hall thanked him and said he was shocked to hear such rumors. Hall assured Boren he would check into the matter.[24]

Boren continued to hear from his own respected supporters that Hall's personal debts were being paid by cronies who were benefiting from state business. Still loyal to the governor, Boren reported such rumors to Hall. Finally, after several visits, Hall's tone changed. He became hostile and told Boren he did not want to hear any more about it, it was none of Boren's business, and he hoped Boren would quit spreading the false rumors. Boren left the governor's office disappointed and disillusioned, vowing to never return to tell Hall about the things he was hearing or urge the governor to stop any corruption in his administration.[25]

Boren's relationship with Governor Hall further deteriorated because Boren opposed Hall's plan for a large income tax increase. By the middle of Hall's term, Boren had become an outspoken critic of Hall's policies. Some Capitol observers suggested that Boren might run against Hall in the 1974 Democratic primary, although most people laughed at that idea because they thought Boren had no chance whatsoever to defeat a sitting governor.[26]

Boren introduced a series of reform measures, but most were killed in the House Rules Committee. Boren was unsuccessful in passing legislation to require competitive bids on state deposits, to require the House Rules Committee to meet in open session, and to take roll call votes on issues brought before the committee. Boren also introduced a bill that would do away with the Committee of the Whole and provide for the installation of a voting machine in the house so a permanent record could be made of how House members voted on amendments. Even though Boren's ideas were repudiated by House leaders at the time, eventually, after he was governor, voting machines were installed in the chambers of both the State Senate and House of Representatives.[27]

Boren's vocal criticism of Governor Hall made Democratic legislative leaders nervous—after all, the governor was the titular head of the state party. The more Boren criticized Hall and introduced reform bills, the greater the pressure being applied by his foes. When Boren pushed his bill to competitively bid interest rates on state deposits, all state funds in banks in Seminole County were withdrawn. Boren was undaunted in his support of the idea.[28]

There was other punishment for Boren's campaign to rid state government of corruption. A tunnel was being excavated to reroute Northwest 23rd Street under state property that connected the State Capitol to new state office buildings being built north of the Capitol. State officials decided to give the excavated dirt to the contractor in consideration of him hauling it away. Boren was upset when he learned that the state then purchased the dirt it had given away for several hundred thousand dollars to construct parking lots on Capitol grounds.

Boren called it a "dirty deal" and publicly called for an investigation. His punishment for blowing the whistle on the deal was swift. Before his latest revelation, the sign on Boren's door on the fourth floor of the State Capitol read, "Vice Chairman of the Elections Committee, Chairman of the Economic Development Committee, and Member of the Rules Committee." The next day, all references to committee membership had been removed. The House Speaker had stripped him of membership in all committees. He was the only member of the legislature not assigned to at least one committee. Boren also found that his office had been moved to the fifth floor with Republican members.[29]

Relegated to the back row of the House was not all bad for Boren. Frankly, it gave him a splendid vantage point from which he could see all action during debates and times of voting on bills. Boren recognized he was an outcast for standing up for the issues in which he believed. Over a period of days and weeks, Boren began thinking that the only way he might bring reform to Oklahoma was to run for governor himself.[30]

State government in Oklahoma was being run like a country club—in privacy and with privilege for a chosen few.

DAVID L. BOREN

ELEVEN

Loss of Trust

O KLAHOMANS HAD LOST CONFIDENCE in their government by 1973. Their leaders, for generations held in high esteem because of their lofty positions, were now considered to be as bad as the scoundrels who made headlines for bilking innocent senior citizens and compromising principles of decency and honesty.

The federal government was floundering in the midst of the Watergate Scandal. Americans were growing tired of turning on the evening news to hear more rumors and reports of corruption that ascended literally to the highest levels of government, to the leader of the free world, President Richard Nixon.

In Oklahoma, Governor David Hall was plagued with grand jury investigations and frequent critical newspaper stories. His political fortunes had gone from meteoric to low in a few short months. For Boren, the public announcement of Hall's troubles was sad, but not unexpected. For years, Boren had suspected foul play in the Hall administration.

From the moment Hall had left his secure job as a young attorney for an oil company to become an assistant county attorney in Tulsa County, Oklahoma, his persistence in politics was carved in stone. After twice being elected county attorney in Tulsa County, he ran third in the Democratic primary for governor in 1966. Four years later, he upset incumbent Republican Governor Dewey F. Bartlett and took over the leadership of Oklahoma state government.

Within weeks of assuming power, Hall irked many Oklahoma politicians and business leaders by asking for a huge tax increase. Before bitterness and hurt feelings from the tax battles could be healed, Hall unveiled a controversial bond issue to provide road money for each of the state's 77 counties. Freeway 77—some opponents called it "Hall's Highway Hoax"—was soundly defeated three-to-one by Oklahoma voters. In only six counties did voters approve the proposal.[1]

Even with two long and costly battles under his belt, Hall was still a good bet to become the state's first two-term governor. But in May, 1973, Hall's career as a silver-haired charismatic political leader began a painful road to disaster. Newspapers revealed that the Internal Revenue Service had been conducting an investigation of Hall since 1971. State grand juries in Tulsa and Oklahoma City probed alleged kickbacks in state building projects. Hall was not indicted in the kickback scheme, but several of his key supporters and aides were.

The cloud of alleged corruption caught the attention of federal prosecutors in early 1974. United States Attorney William Burkett announced on January 2 that his office and the Federal Bureau of Investigation (FBI) were investigating political contributions from state contractors with an eye toward a possible extortion indictment against Hall.[2]

As if the federal investigation and the state grand jury probes did not provide enough of a hindrance to Hall's future, legislative leaders were pushed by Republicans to investigate the governor. The leaders of the House of Representatives and State Senate, both fellow Democrats, told reporters they would take a "cautious and deliberate approach" to any proposals for an investigation.[3] Despite the swirling rumors, Hall announced he would run for reelection.

The scandals, whether real or imagined, and the resulting loss of faith in state government formed the backdrop of the 1974 gubernatorial campaign. The stage was set for an unknown state representative to mount Oklahoma's most phenomenal grassroots campaign—the Boren Clean Sweep.

Boren had been contemplating a run for Oklahoma's highest elective position since he had been stripped of committee assignments and realized he could probably never make a difference in state government as a member of the legislature. He wanted to be governor and have a bully pulpit to advance a series of changes to make government more efficient, streamlined, and honest.

Behind the scenes, Boren began raising money and talking to potential supporters. His father, Lyle, still had many contacts in the Fourth Congressional District he had represented in Congress a quarter century before. The younger Boren had established relationships with students in law school, the dormitory where he was a resident advisor, at OBU, and in the United States Junior Chamber of Commerce (Jaycees), an organization that had named him one of the ten outstanding young Jaycees in the nation in 1967.

Boren's first volunteer staff member was Rob Pyron, who worked at the newspaper in Wewoka. Pyron had been a Boren supporter since his teenage years and Boren's first race for the Oklahoma House of Representatives. When sufficient campaign funds were available, Pyron was hired as the campaign press secretary and began scouring the state for support in a tiny Ford Pinto. Another early campaign staff member was Sven Holmes, whose father worked for Phillips Petroleum Company in Bartlesville. Holmes was a student at Harvard College and had met Boren when Holmes was a candidate for a Rhodes Scholarship. Other early staff members were Sam Hammons and Gary Morris.[4]

On July 12, 1973, a year before the Democratic primary, Boren announced his intention to run for the Democratic nomination for governor. It was decided that the campaign must be people-to-people and issue-oriented.[5]

Even the announcement by the unknown state legislator went without major fanfare in state newspapers. David chose three venues for the formal announcement—Oklahoma City, Tulsa, and in the community center at St. Gregory's College in Shawnee where many of his hometown supporters from Seminole County cheered his vision.

In Tulsa, Pyron had made reservations for a meeting room at the Skyline East Hotel for Boren to hold a news conference to announce he was running for governor. He also arranged for the marquee to welcome David Boren, "Oklahoma's Next Governor." However, there was concrete proof that Boren was unknown. When Boren and Pyron arrived for the news conference, the marquee at the front of the hotel declared, "Welcome Rob Pyron, Oklahoma's Next Governor."[6]

Only 20 to 30 people showed up for the announcement in Tulsa, including former Tulsa Mayor George Norvell and his wife Opal. Both were tireless workers from the first day. Mayor Norvell, who always was optimistic, told Boren, "There may not have been many people here, but all were high quality."[7]

The first order of business for the campaign was to build an organization. Boren crisscrossed the state, clearly impressing people with his delivery and his vision before an estimated 400 civic clubs in all 77 counties.

From the beginning of the 16-month formal race, Boren's theme was the need to sweep out the "old guard," the contingent of entrenched politicians that had maintained control of the legislature and state government for many years. Boren talked about reform and open government. He said the operation of state government was like that of a private club run in secrecy and with privilege available only to a chosen few.[8]

Advisors told Boren he needed a poll to assess his popularity in the state. He spent $2,000, nearly half of the total campaign war chest, to find that only two percent of the people recognized his name—and surely some of that number counted old-timers who remembered his father serving in Congress decades before. Boren was discouraged. When asked about the poll, he often would not show the results and simply say that it showed great potential to increase his support.[9]

Sven Holmes' job in the campaign in the fall of 1973 was to prepare a combination campaign-platform legislative program called the Boren Plan. Boren advocated many of the reforms he had tried to pass in the legislature. He believed that legislative votes should be public, that even the smallest campaign contribution should be disclosed, that architectural and engineering contracts for state projects should be competitively bid, and that the merit system for state employees should be expanded to curtail political patronage.[10]

The Boren Plan also called for the elimination of the state inheritance tax between husband and wife. Along the campaign trail, Boren heard stories of widows who had to sell their family farms in order to pay inheritance taxes. That issue began as a small part of the platform, but in the end was a significant reason many Oklahomans chose to support Boren for governor.

Boren also called for an end to double taxation, the assessment of state income tax on federal income tax paid by taxpayers. The double taxation had been allowed by Governor Hall's tax increase bill. Boren did not believe that citizens should pay the state a tax on money they already had paid the federal government. That issue also resonated with the people.

Boren's long membership in Common Cause, a citizens group that advocated more openness in government, was the basis for his call for an open meeting law for any local or state government entity and other organizations that operated on public money.[11]

As Boren went one direction, his wife went the other direction to campaign or at least to become acquainted with people who expressed an interest in the Boren campaign. Boren neighbor Liz Robertson campaigned many times with Janna. Robertson remembered, "In the early months, no one knew about David or his program. All we could do was smile, get people's names and addresses, and hope that they would get on the Boren team later."[12]

Boren traveled five or six days each week and was away from the growing Boren family. Janna had given birth to a daughter, Carrie Christine Boren, on December 8, 1970. And, while Boren was making a speech to a civic club in Tulsa on August 2, 1973, Janna went into labor in a hospital in Shawnee. Boren was handed a note, cut short his speech, and rushed toward Shawnee. By the time he arrived at the hospital, a son, David Daniel Boren, already had been born.

Boren used his network of friends around the state to schedule appearances at civic clubs, neighborhood coffees or teas, and church functions. He wanted the chance to tell large and small groups about his ideas to make Oklahoma a better place in which to work and live. Because Seminole had been an oil boom town, he found former Seminole residents scattered in all four corners of the state. In addition, his parents' friends and his former students at OBU and fellow students at OU made valuable contacts.[13]

Many of his former students, only in their twenties, became county campaign managers. Most of the volunteers were in politics for the first time and were fresh and enthusiastic. Boren said, "There were church deacons and Boy Scout leaders and den mothers and young people and retired people who gave the grassroots campaign a special tenor." Often, political newcomers were the only people in town who would commit.

Very few veteran political observers gave Boren much of a chance to win and many key county Democratic leaders were committed to Governor Hall. Campaign aide Sven Holmes said, "We had political novices—feedstore operators, insurance salesmen, farmers, teachers, and retired Army colonels, all united because of some personal acquaintance who knew David."[14]

The new brand of campaign workers in cities and towns had no clout except for their reputations as citizens in their local communities. They had no campaign tools to work with except limited printed material and the grapevine of personal contact. There were no local campaign funds and phone banks.

The key leader concept evolved over time, especially with the help of Boren's father, Lyle, and his cousin, James Harlan "Jim" Boren, a veteran political operative who had managed the campaign of United States Senator Ralph Yarborough of Texas.

After a meeting in Tahlequah, Ivan Holmes, a young professor at Northeastern Oklahoma State University, volunteered to become campaign manager in Cherokee County. Boren accepted and Cherokee County ultimately became a bastion of support. Until Holmes, who became Oklahoma Democratic chairman in 2006, volunteered, Boren had visited up and down both sides of the community's long Main Street without getting a single person to publicly support him. He did have the backing of House Speaker Bill Willis and leading Democratic women's clubs in the area.

The key leader concept required a lot of maintenance, but the concept worked. Campaign staffers would call a local coordinator, such as Gail Scott in Stillwater, and hear about the progress of the campaign. If something unique was happening, other staffers passed the word to key people in other counties. Jim Boren's advice was "Keep things hopping—keep everyone pumped up."[15]

Early campaign money was raised in a unique manner. Citizens of Seminole and Wewoka were asked to contribute to the campaign and turn their lights on one night to indicate their willingness to give. Volunteers canvassed the town looking for porch lights and waiting checks and cash. More than $8,000 was raised.[16]

Boren used every contact to drum up a band of volunteers and paid staff members. He learned from visiting Ruth Sanford at her dress shop in Heavener that her son, Mike Wofford, an OU student, would like to volunteer in the campaign. Boren asked George Butner of Wewoka to contact Wofford and invite him to the Oklahoma City office where the political science major met Ann Dubler, who had been Boren's secretary in his House office for several years, Boren's father, Lyle, and Sam Hammons, who was coordinating the campaign in southwest Oklahoma.[17]

Wofford was impressed with the staff and signed on as a part-time volunteer to distribute campaign materials and accompany Boren to events in Norman and points east.[18]

After Boren appeared at several hundred civic clubs and church groups on a shoestring budget, he still believed that there was too much dissatisfaction among voters to allow Hall to be reelected. There was resistance to Hall's tax policies and even Hall's best supporters were worried about newspaper accounts of corruption. But some of Boren's advisors were pessimistic and believed he could not defeat a sitting governor who had appointed hundreds of people to boards and commissions and had run a superb campaign in 1970.[19]

David was 32, an idealistic professor and state legislator, and he was confident he could beat Hall. But, suddenly, a third candidate threw his hat in the ring. Clem McSpadden, former president pro tempore of the Oklahoma State Senate, congressman, popular rodeo announcer, and nephew of Will Rogers, Oklahoma's favorite son, announced he would run for the Democratic nomination for governor. Boren was driving down the highway and nearly "drove off the road" when he heard the news about McSpadden's entry into the race.

All at once, the campaign was no longer against a troubled incumbent governor—there was a strong opponent. After a period of doubt, Boren decided he had nothing to lose, he would continue to run. But he needed a campaign slogan or symbol to catch voters' attention.

Our county campaign managers were not veteran politicians—they were political novices who had joined us in the fight to sweep the old guard politicians out of office.

SVEN HOLMES

TWELVE

The Broom Brigade

THE FIRST PLATEAU of the gubernatorial campaign had been reached by the fall of 1973—a winning reform platform, legislative agenda, and an infrastructure of supporters in each of the state's 77 counties were in place.

By the spring of 1974, a statewide headquarters was in operation at 1701 North Broadway in Oklahoma City. It was still a meager operation. Sven Holmes and Rob Pyron both made $100 monthly and were provided a place to live. Holmes lived in a $40-a-month apartment behind the headquarters. He had the campaign telephone in his apartment, so he could answer "Boren for Governor" 24 hours a day. However, the apartment was not luxurious. Holmes, who later was appointed United States District Judge for the Northern District of Oklahoma, said, "Often I had to wrestle cockroaches to get to the phone."[1]

Boren's pledge to clean up state government did not set well with many veteran political leaders. Boren's father, Lyle, had taken a job as an assistant state insurance commissioner under his old friend, Insurance Commissioner Joe B. Hunt. After allegations that the elder Boren should not be a state employee because his son was a legislator and was running for governor, he retired.

In late spring of 1974, Boren still was running third in state-wide polls behind McSpadden and Hall. Slowly, but surely, he was gaining support all over the state, the results of dozens of speeches and appearances each week. Summer was the time for watermelon campaign parties and pie suppers in rural Oklahoma, and Boren made each one he could.[2]

In July, Boren and his staff scheduled a meeting in Oklahoma City for campaign workers from every county on the first anniversary of the announcement of his candidacy. The purpose of the meeting was to give supporters a short course in how to run a local campaign. There was instruction on a variety of topics, from how to place an advertisement in a local newspaper to how to explain Boren's stance on major issues of the campaign.

Two days before the meeting, the inner circle of staff members was evaluating the progress of the campaign and wondering if the previous year's organizational effort was paying dividends. Into the meeting burst Jim Boren, carrying a broom that he had carried with him on an airplane from Washington, D.C. Quickly, he made his case that because the theme of the campaign was getting rid of the old guard politicians, a broom would be the perfect symbol. Jim Boren had his presentation polished—he wanted brooms in the hands of volunteers, sticking out windows of supporters' cars, and even being carried by the candidate himself. He knew the history of the broom being used in the campaign to defeat the Thomas Joseph Pendergast machine that ran Kansas City, Missouri politics for many years.[3]

By the end of the day, the idea was presented to Boren. At first, Boren was reluctant—he was never one for using gimmicks—but his cousin's idea made sense. It was a strong symbol that captured the theme of the campaign. Boren remembered, "The powerful message that a simple broom made had incredible possibilities. As remote as it seemed at the moment, we all thought the idea might catch fire."[4]

Holmes saw the broom as the kick start the campaign needed, something to get free publicity to augment a steady fund raising effort that was occurring all over the state. Holmes said, "We needed something to get people interested and start asking questions."[5]

Part of Jim Boren's theory on how to make the broom symbol work was that campaign staffers had to be totally committed to the idea, even to the point of displaying brooms from their personal vehicles. That night, Holmes was scheduled to be interviewed by Dave Holliday, a reporter at KWTV in Oklahoma City, for a series the television station was running on the men behind the candidates. What an opportunity!

When Holliday showed up at the Boren headquarters, brooms were everywhere and Holmes was holding one. Holliday said, "What's that?" Holmes explained, "This broom indicates the commitment David Boren has to sweep out the old guard and it captures the sense of energy for the future in cleaning up state government." Holliday was hesitant, but agreed to ask Holmes about the broom. That night on television, perhaps the greatest symbol of political campaigns in Oklahoma history was introduced to Oklahoma City viewers.[6]

Holmes, Pyron, and volunteers bought brooms at every grocery store and five and dime within miles of the headquarters. They found enough to hand a broom to each of the 350 statewide campaign volunteers who showed up for the Sunday afternoon meeting at the Tivoli Inn Motel. The shocked volunteers were told they were now members of the Boren Broom Brigade. It was a poignant moment in political history.[7]

Brooms sprang up within a matter of days in the far reaches of the Sooner State. The Boren headquarters was inundated with calls for more brooms. To fill the mounting requests, the campaign purchased the entire inventory of the Handy Andy broom factory in Lindsay, Oklahoma. The Boren Broom Brigade was off to a quick start.

"The broom was a whole new language," Holmes said, "Supporters were trying to come up with unique ideas to use the broom to publicize Boren's candidacy. It became a contest among county campaign managers to see who could come up with the neatest ways to get brooms in the hands of supporters." The most common version of the symbol became a broom with a small blue and white Boren yard sign attached.[8]

Campaigning was focused on at least making a runoff with either Hall or McSpadden in the August 27th primary. Most observers believed McSpadden, feeding off his popularity with state senators, and David Hall, the sitting governor, would lead the field. The question was whether Boren would get enough votes to force a runoff between the other two.

A month before the primary, newspapers recognized the symbolism of the broom. On July 21, reporter Ed Montgomery wrote a story in *The Daily Oklahoman* about the campaign. The headline was, "Boren Broom Brigade on the March."[9]

That same edition of the newspaper contained a story of a most significant endorsement of Boren. Dr. George L. Cross, the retired president of OU, announced he would be the chairman of a statewide committee of educators backing Boren. Cross told reporters, "I have decided to support David Boren because I consider him to have the best combination of exceptional intelligence and integrity that I have seen in public office for some time." The educators' committee chaired by Cross included the candidate's uncle, Dr. James B. Boren, former president of Southwestern Oklahoma State College, Dr. Ollie Hatcher, former president of Northwestern Oklahoma State College, and Dr. Vance Posey, former president of Southeastern Oklahoma State College.[10]

A new series of print ads developed by Pete Rozier, the campaign advertising guru, enforced the symbolism of the broom in sweeping reform into state government. Ads told citizens, "It's time to decide what you believe in." Asking for campaign contributions, ads proclaimed, "For a few dollars, get a governor money can't buy!"[11]

The campaign staff grew. Mike Wofford, who had been volunteering for several months, was asked by Holmes to help with the campaign in southeast Oklahoma. At a salary of $200 a month, Wofford operated from his mother's home in Heavener and used her 1970 Chevrolet Impala to put up signs, distribute brochures, and buoy the hopes of the few supporters who were vocal about their support for Boren.[12]

Wofford remembered, "David's supporters in rural areas tended to be people new to politics who were excited about him personally. Their eyes lit up when they talked about his dynamic personality and his absolute commitment to being open and honest in government. They were political outsiders, but they now had a cause to be involved in the future of the state."[13]

In deep southeast Oklahoma, Wofford ran into "real characters" who had written to the Boren campaign expressing interest in helping. Sometimes, the "interested" people were anti-government and had their farmhouses posted with mean-looking dogs. Often, Wofford yelled from his car to announce his presence. He was working fulltime for Boren's candidacy, but was not willing to lose a leg to a fierce dog.[14]

Also joining the campaign staff was Dusty Martin, originally from Checotah, but attending college at Southeastern Oklahoma State University in Durant. Martin began coordinating the campaign effort in several key areas of eastern and southeastern Oklahoma.

In his uphill battle, Boren was sustained by his zeal even when close advisors thought his efforts would be futile. Boren spurned attempts to campaign negatively. Instead, he built his message on one's own merits, rather than the negative, mudslinging campaigns that had become the norm in Democratic gubernatorial races in Oklahoma.[15]

In fact, mudslinging actually backfired in the campaign when McSpadden criticized Boren's father-in-law Reuel Little, a former American Party candidate for governor. Many people believed McSpadden was off base in criticizing a member of Boren's family. Boren may not have always agreed with his father-in-law's politics, but he defended his right to his opinion and openly accepted financial contributions from the Little family.[16]

Boren refused to accept contributions from the usual special interest groups that lined up to support candidates running for governor. Even though his campaign needed an infusion of money, Boren was adamant about not taking donations from groups representing labor, education, milk producers, farmers, architects, and contractors. In fact, Boren refused contributions from any organization. He said, "I just want to be indebted to individual voters."[17]

Instead, Boren settled for nickels and dimes from the rank and file, individuals who believed in his reform candidacy. Only a few gave $5,000, the maximum under state law. When campaign coffers were low, Boren mortgaged his Lincoln County farm for a desperately needed $25,000.[18]

Boren's belief in openness of government and campaign finance did not end there. Unlike any other candidate, he opened his books to reporters and anyone who cared. Every nickel that came into the campaign was meticulously recorded by volunteer Howell Faw, a retired accountant.[19]

Boren challenged his two opponents to debate him, but they refused. No doubt, he was such a dark horse, McSpadden and Hall did not want to give him any credibility. To counter the lack of a forum to compare platforms, Boren purchased 30 minutes of television time for a program he called "The Great Debate." Boren appeared on the television set with two empty chairs, appropriately labeled for his opponents. When the moderator asked Boren a question, he responded, then tried to explain how his opponents would have answered had they been present. The Great Debate was well received.[20]

Boren also used the town-hall format to get his beliefs on the issues of the campaign to potential voters. He answered questions from the audience and succinctly made his points. Most observers believed the television programs were effective.

However, the live audience sometimes created unexpected situations. In Lawton, an elderly man stood and said he wanted to say something about the Boren family. He told the story of the Borens coming to Oklahoma in a covered wagon, how they had become educated and served as ministers and college presidents, and how much respect he had for them. Staff members were "antsy" because the man took half of the 30-minute program. Even Boren was concerned that he had lost 15 minutes in which he could explain his plan for reforming state government.[21]

Boren was surprised in the next few days in travels around southwest Oklahoma when all people wanted to talk about was the 90-year-old man and his endorsement of the entire Boren family and their contributions to Oklahoma. Boren said, "I realized that people were tired of politics, but wanted to be able to identify with an Oklahoman whose roots were deep and whose passion for the state was founded in helping those in need."[22]

Boren also recognized that Oklahomans were desperate for a fresh approach and honesty in politics. He said, "While we were a bit amateurish in our approach, the integrity of our effort struck a chord—it was clear, it was real, that we wanted to do something. It took on the feeling of a crusade to bring clean government to Oklahoma."[23]

We were so close. For a year we had hit every village, hamlet, and city. The big question was— would our efforts be enough to make the runoff?

ROB PYRON

THIRTEEN

The Final Push

BOREN USED EVERY OPPORTUNITY to convey to state voters his message of change and reform. In an address to the Oklahoma Society of Association Executives, he said Oklahomans "have lost confidence in their leaders and government." Boren challenged Governor Hall and the Oklahoma legislature to join him in awarding deposits of state funds by competitive bids, developing a new competitive process for awarding architectural contracts on state projects, structuring the merit system to diminish political patronage, have full disclosure of campaign contributions, reform the state's prison system, and record votes on all public sessions in state and local government. Boren also wanted to eliminate the state inheritance tax between spouses. Elements of the reform package were labeled as the "Boren Plan."[1]

Reorganization of state government was a major component of the plan. Boren had pre-filed for the 1974 legislative session a bill, HB 1509, that would create a special commission on state government reorganization. Boren charged that government was "cluttered" with 214 boards, agencies, and commissions, many of which overlapped in responsibility. He said, "This excessive red tape in government is a constant drain on taxpayer dollars. We need to cut red tape in government and get out of the horse and buggy era."[2]

Boren verbally sparred with old guard leaders in both parties in a speech to members of the Oklahoma County Democratic Men's Club meeting at the Boulevard Cafeteria in Oklahoma City. He said, "Neither Republican nor Democratic politicians have a monopoly on corruption in government. The legislative process in the country and our state is a disgrace." Boren said he was excited that Oklahomans were beginning to "wake up" and talk about their frustration with "government as usual."[3]

Boren was an unusually gifted communicator, and his honesty often won him support. In the midst of Democratic Little Dixie at Haileyville, Boren and campaign worker Mike Wofford were walking door to door when an elderly lady asked what Boren thought about President Nixon and the Watergate scandal. Wofford, sure that there were no Nixon supporters within 100 miles, thought, "Go on David, let ol' Nixon have it." However, rather than lambast Nixon, Boren calmly said, "I think he deserves a fair trial."[4]

Wofford looked at Boren "like he was from the moon." But the lady's response floored him. With tears in her eyes, she said, "I agree. I just hope they don't crucify him like they crucified Christ!" Wofford remembered, "I witnessed Boren's political brilliance at its best. He was honest with a lady who I thought would be blood thirsty about Nixon. The result was that Boren made a friend and supporter for life."[5]

Not all campaign stories were serious or life-changing. At a campaign debate in the open air between the Tower dormitories on the OU campus in Norman, Boren and other candidates appeared in person, but Governor Hall was represented by Richard Mildren, brother of the OU quarterback, Jack Mildren. Richard was a well-known student but had to fend off fellow students who yelled that he was subbing for Hall because the governor was afraid to appear on campus and answer charges of corruption.

After speeches, students asked questions of the candidates. Most dwelled on stories in the newspapers about the federal investigation of Hall. Time after time, Mildren arose from his chair to take the podium to answer questions. Unfortunately, each time he arose, his chair scooted back toward the edge of the platform. After a half dozen appearances at the microphone, Mildren attempted to sit down, but the chair toppled off the short stage. Mike Wofford recalled, "Richard went flying and Boren scrambled to help him to his feet. Because of the huge outburst of laughter, the program was effectively over at that moment."[6]

Pie suppers, bean and cornbread extravaganzas, and pancake breakfasts were frequent stops on Boren's campaign trail. Charlie Morgan of Prague attended a bean and cornbread supper on the campus of St. Gregory's College in Shawnee. He remembered, "Boren was a master campaigner. He held the audience in his hand. His honesty and straightforwardness captured everyone's attention. He not only had good ideas—he had the ability to convince people he could do something and change the future of Oklahoma."[7]

Radio and television ads, print ads, and position papers and brochures about the campaign adequately presented the Boren message. So did bright blue and white fence straddlers, yard signs, and billboards. The message of the ads was simple—Boren for Governor.

Change was the theme of newspaper ads. Boren and his strategists concentrated on giving the voters a clear choice—a new face with new ideas or the old guard. One popular ad was topped in large letters—DO YOU WANT A CHANGE? The ad compared the newcomer, Boren, to Governor Hall and Senator McSpadden. The ad proclaimed, "The other two Democratic candidates are like TWO PEAS IN A POD. One has already been Governor. The other has been in office 20 LONG years."[8]

But even with brilliant advertising, it was the broom that gave Boren an edge on publicity in the final months of the primary campaign. To create press coverage, Boren accepted a challenge from Roland Langford, editor of the weekly newspaper in Blair, to walk from Altus to Blair and meet prospective voters along the way. Langford reasoned that such a unique campaign tactic could generate free publicity. He was right.

Boren walked the ten miles with Altus civic leader, Dick Moore, and met dozens of people. Because press coverage of the walk had received substantial attention from the press, supporters had brooms sticking from their mailboxes or attached to barbed wire fences. Boren stayed all night with the Eddie Moss family before arriving in Blair on a Saturday afternoon when many of the residents of the area came to town for weekly shopping. Supporters carried brooms and met Boren at the center of town.[9]

Two weeks later, Boren walked from Broken Bow to Idabel in the opposite corner of the state. Television crews and newspaper reporters flocked to the area to cover this new style of campaigning. Boren spent the night at the home of David and Bea Norris and greeted a houseful of supporters. The free publicity fueled by the broom symbol ignited Boren's push to make the runoff.

The broom especially resonated with housewives. Peggy Helmerich was introduced to Boren and his call for reform at a Tulsa luncheon to which she was invited by a friend. After the luncheon, Peggy rushed home to tell her husband, Walter "Walt" Helmerich, III, about "this bright young man running for governor." At first, Walt brushed aside any suggestion that Boren could win, but quickly changed his mind when he heard Boren speak at a business meeting. Walt and fellow Tulsa leader Henry Zarrow became important advisors to Boren for the rest of his public life.[10]

An active state campaign office in Oklahoma City was staffed with hard-working volunteers such as Ann Byrd, Lynn White, Carol Hawley, Betty Replogle, and Phyllis Stough. Volunteers made sure that sacks of campaign brochures were delivered to the local post office for mailing and that county campaign workers were well stocked with yard signs and other campaign materials. Byrd was a master of organizing work that could be performed by armies of volunteers. Ann Dubler worked directly with Boren and his mother and father who often volunteered at the campaign headquarters.

Boren's association with Oklahoma Baptist University provided many campaign volunteers and full-time staff members. OBU graduates Jim Hopper, David Cox, Paul Gritz, Robert Post, Dynda Parks Post, and Gary Cook became active in the campaign along with former OBU students Rob Pyron, Sam Hammons, Gary Morris, and David Berrong.

Dr. James Marcum, associate professor of history at OBU, was active in Educators for Boren. OBU President Dr. William G. Tanner was not bashful about openly supporting Boren for governor. He wrote, "David Boren is an excellent professor, an honest and hard-working legislator, and, in my judgment, a practicing Christian. I have watched him carefully for the past four years on our campus and can recommend him for your serious consideration as our next governor without reservation."[11]

Other OBU faculty and administrators such as Dr. William E. Neptune, Karen Henson, David Jorgenson, and Dr. Daniel Holcomb publicly endorsed Boren and his mission to become the next governor of Oklahoma.[12]

Part of the campaign strategy was to personalize the campaign in each county. For example, in Coal County, Boren's cousin, attorney John B. Axton, bought ads in the local newspaper and said, "I support David, not because he is my cousin, but because I believe he is the best man for the job. He is honest, capable, intelligent, and qualified, and I believe he would make an outstanding Governor."[13]

Before the August primary, *The Daily Oklahoman* began to recognize, by conducting polls throughout the state, that Boren was gaining on Hall and might make the runoff against McSpadden. Few political observers had given Boren much of a chance before the summer and the incredible round of publicity surrounding the Broom Brigade. In an editorial titled "Untypical Fracas," the newspaper noted that Republicans Denzil Garrison and James Inhofe were unusually combative for Republican office seekers. On the Democratic side, the editorial charged that McSpadden was straddling the fence on issues such as pari-mutuel horse racing, but that Boren knew where he stood. The editorial said:

> On the other hand, State Representative David Boren
> is making his positions clear on many issues, but concen-

trates more on the future than the past. The result has not been the kind of battle royal his party has known in other election years.[14]

The broom was the central theme of the last huge campaign rally before the primary. "Sweep out the old guard!" a young man yelled. Holding a blue and white "Boren for Governor" sign stapled securely to a common household broom, the man was part of a vibrant army of 4,000 people gathered on the south steps of the State Capitol in Oklahoma City on a sultry Sunday afternoon in August, 1974.

The rousing music of the Seminole High School band gave the political rally the aura of a high school football game. Young and old alike were cheering their new hero. On their faces were looks of determination and purpose. Even retired University of Oklahoma President George L. Cross and his wife, Cleo, proudly displayed their affection for the young candidate by carrying brooms.

The Democratic faithful were caught up in the candidacy of young Boren who called for an end to corruption, abuse, inefficiency, and deception in state government. Boren, only 33 years old, was a new face in statewide politics and offered a fresh, innovative approach to the ills of Oklahoma. One elderly man in the crowd said, "Boren's a good man. And, at a time like this, that's what we need."[15]

Boren arrived at the rally on a street sweeper, another symbol for sweeping out old guard politicians. Excitement generated by brooms sweeping on that summer Oklahoma afternoon carried over into state voters' decision-making process. The results of a straw poll published in *The Sunday Oklahoman* two days before the primary showed Boren had vaulted into second place, behind

McSpadden, but ahead of Governor Hall. The newspaper poll reported that McSpadden had the favor of 46 percent of the voters, while Boren was 20 points behind at 26 percent and Hall trailing at 24 percent. Incredibly, the poll found that less than four percent of the potential voters still were undecided.[16]

In a last-minute surge of candor, Boren and McSpadden released detailed records of campaign finances. Both candidates allowed reporters to examine bank deposits and check books. For the first time, it was made public that Boren had mortgaged his farm for $25,000 which he loaned to his campaign. Also, for the first time, McSpadden released details of cattle sales orchestrated by banker Robert Earl Young to raise money for his campaign.[17]

Newspaper reporter Ed Montgomery recognized Boren's advance in popularity was definitely tied to the broom. He wrote, "The Boren Broom Brigade went on the march this week, and there's no question that people are falling in step with them. The question is how many will join the parade and whose drum they were marching to before, if any?"[18]

Montgomery's question was answered on August 27 as polls closed at 7:00 p.m. and votes were counted. As the evening wore on, it became clear that the Broom Brigade's valiant efforts had resulted in Boren unseating an incumbent governor to take the second spot in a runoff with McSpadden, the front runner.

The final official vote in the primary was 238,534 for McSpadden , 225,321 for Boren, and 169,290 for Hall. Boren trailed McSpadden by only 13,000 votes, a vastly different outcome than had been predicted by pollsters and veteran observers. On the GOP side, Inhofe defeated Garrison by slightly more than 22,000 votes.[19]

The failure of a sitting governor to make the runoff was considered one of the biggest upsets in state political history. Pundits looked forward to the three weeks ahead of what surely would be a spirited runoff between "the cowboy congressman" and the "scholarly schoolteacher from Seminole."[20]

Now that a 33-year-old college professor named David Boren has swept two of the slickest, best-financed campaign machines in Democratic history under the rug like house dust, the common domestic homemaker's broom suddenly has charisma.

THE OKLAHOMA JOURNAL

FOURTEEN

And the Broom Swept

n the Democratic runoff, Boren cast himself in the role of the underdog. He told reporters, "I've always been the underdog in every race I have run. I don't know any other way to act." Governor Hall, who had been subpoenaed the day after the primary to appear before a federal grand jury investigating his activities, refused to endorse either Boren or McSpadden. Boren and his campaign staff were confident that many Hall supporters would join the Boren Broom Brigade.

Privately, many Hall supporters and campaign workers sent word to Boren headquarters that they were ready to join the fight against McSpadden. It was not a secret that bitterness had crept into the personal attacks between McSpadden and Hall and that Boren, who took the high road, perhaps would benefit in the runoff.[1]

Boren's campaign war chest was empty, so immediate attention was directed toward fund-raising. Boren still refused to take contributions from political action committees or corporations—he strongly believed that only individuals should contribute money toward political campaigns. Boren also believed that he would gain the support of many state educators who had felt obligated to stay in Governor Hall's camp in the primary.

Boren's second-place finish vaulted him into the state's spotlight. Sven Holmes remembered, "All of a sudden, the close finish to McSpadden catapulted David into a significant position. Anyone who did not know him before suddenly was aware of his presence." Campaign headquarters were inundated with phone calls asking for bumper stickers, campaign brochures, yard signs, and offering to volunteer. It became the "chic" thing to do in Oklahoma to carry a broom and promote Boren's candidacy.[2]

Even though Boren had remained positive with his message in the primary, he went on the attack against McSpadden. He said, "There are fundamental differences between us. For 20 years McSpadden has done nothing about the inheritance tax which falls heavily on the widows of farmers, ranchers, and small business owners. He has done nothing to halt one-man control of state bank deposits." Boren told supporters that he had a better chance of defeating Inhofe, the Republican nominee, in the general election because "I am carrying the cause of reform in government."[3]

Boren's weakest performance in the primary had been in eastern Oklahoma, the heart of the Democratic electorate. Jan Cartwright, later attorney general of Oklahoma, mounted a superb effort in the Second Congressional District to turn voters to Boren. Boren also was helped by the efforts of House Speaker William P. "Bill" Willis in the area.

Even though Boren resisted name-calling most of the time, he could not resist identifying McSpadden with two well-known Democratic politicians who symbolized, in Boren's opinion, the old guard. At every stump speech, Boren rallied his troops with stories of how State Senator Gene Stipe and former House Speaker J. D. McCarty were fully behind McSpadden. Boren said, "I had to tell people about them because those were the kind of old guard leaders to whom Clem was obligated. I thought the people needed to know that."[4]

McSpadden was a famous rodeo announcer and would often be introduced to audiences at rodeos. Boren also was present, but usually was not introduced by the grandstand announcer who knew McSpadden. However, Boren would not concede even a rodeo audience to McSpadden. While McSpadden was "upstairs in the announcing platform" Boren worked the fences where cowboys and spectators gathered. He told anyone who would listen, "He's up there in the announcer's booth, but I'm down here with you because I understand the problems of the people like you and I am asking you to help."[5]

There was no shortage of dirty political tricks in the runoff. At a Democratic rally in McAlester, handbills were distributed to the elderly saying that, if elected, Boren would cut off their old-age pension checks. The handbills also were handed to elderly citizens at post offices on the first of the month when Social Security checks arrived.

The dirty tricks, the support of veteran leaders such as Stipe and McCarty, and McSpadden's attacks on Boren's family perhaps backfired. Reporter Jack Taylor observed:

> Although McSpadden contends he hasn't talked to Stipe more than an hour in the last six months and his attack on Boren's family ties was not really a switch to dirty campaign tactics, those who were close to the congressman know better. In fact, some believe that it was McSpadden's undoing, for it caused a backlash among his own supporters and a revolt from 60 percent of his own county coordinators.[6]

The attack on Boren's family made headlines. McSpadden accused Boren's relatives of trying to buy the governor's office. At his campaign headquarters in the Citizens Tower Building, McSpadden told reporters that Boren's father-in-law, Reuel Little, was raising money from right-wing groups that were trying to divide the people. He said Boren's father was loaning the campaign money and also was trying to buy the job for his son.[7]

Boren was quick to respond to McSpadden's charges. He noted his campaign had spent $120,000 less than McSpadden in the primary and that he, Boren, was the only candidate for governor who complied with the intent of the new campaign financing reporting law by reporting every single contribution, even if it was $1. Many other candidates had evaded the law by listing cash contributions which they claimed were all under $100. Boren defended contributions from his family as "the cleanest campaign money anyone can receive."[8]

Earmarking of state funds became a major issue in the runoff. Boren was opposed to designating state revenue resources to a particular project. For example, nearly one-third of state tax money was earmarked for the State Welfare Department. Instead, Boren believed that the legislature, the representatives of the people, ought to openly debate how tax money was to be spent on an annual basis.

McSpadden, a longtime legislative leader and supporter of earmarking, charged that Boren's plan to end earmarking would throw into chaos the retirement funds of police officers, firefighters, and teachers, and destroy the effectiveness of road-building programs. Boren countered, "I, too, want security for our pension funds, but any department that spends tax money should account to the people for every dollar it spends." Boren's premise was that earmarking prevented any accountability to the people.[9]

Boren also had to respond to McSpadden's charges that Boren's call to "sweep out the old guard" meant that he would fire all veteran state employees if he was elected governor. Boren's answer was that he thought all state jobs should be filled on the basis of merit and that, if political hacks were unqualified to hold certain jobs, they should be filled with hard-working Oklahomans who would work for the taxpayers, not for the bosses that appointed them.

There was no doubt that Boren, with his candor, openness, and zeal to serve the people first and his own ambitions second, was a sharp contrast to the usual brand of Democratic politicians in Oklahoma. He also was somewhat of an enigma, incapable of being branded a liberal or conservative. A reporter called him "a curious blend of conservative and liberal, a throwback to the progressivism of Woodrow Wilson where structural reform was the order of the day."[10] Boren described himself as a fiscal conservative, but acknowledged he could be classified as liberal in his support of full disclosure in government and open meetings.[11]

By the weekend before the election, the fruits of successful fund-raising were realized by the Boren campaign. Financial records revealed a virtual dead heat in raising money between the Boren and McSpadden campaigns. Between the primary and runoff, Boren had raised $79,000 to $63,000 for McSpadden. Boren's campaign was in the black by $15,000 and McSpadden's campaign was in the red by $13,000. Boren was more successful in getting backers to repeat their primary campaign contributions with additional funds for the runoff.[12]

On September 17, Boren defeated McSpadden to win the Democratic nomination for governor. The race was not as close as some had predicted. Even though Boren had trailed McSpadden in the primary, he topped McSpadden in a record turnout for a Democratic runoff 286,171 to 248,623, a difference of more than 37,000 votes. It was one of the most astounding reversals of fortune from a primary to runoff in Oklahoma political history.[13]

A year before, few observers gave either Boren or Republican Inhofe a chance to meet in the general election. Both were reform candidates. Inhofe had said many nice things about Boren during the Republican primary, including that if the Democrats were wise enough to nominate Boren he might have stayed out of the race. However, facing Boren "for all the apples" in the general election, Inhofe had to shift gears and try to point out differences between Boren and himself.[14] Boren considered Inhofe a friend. They had co-sponsored reform legislation in the legislature and agreed on many reform principles.

At a press conference after the primary, Inhofe had been asked by a reporter if he planned to withdraw since he said he would not have run had he known Boren would be the Democratic nominee. Inhofe quickly said he was not withdrawing because the Democratic primary had changed Boren. Many at the press conference laughed at the response.

Boren had to walk a fine line as the Democratic nominee. The entire thrust of his campaign was to sweep out the old guard, yet he had to be careful not to offend his fellow Democratic nominees. He sidestepped questions about his support for Democratic State Treasurer Leo Winters, Secretary of State John Rogers, Labor Commissioner Wilbur Wright, and Examiner and Inspector John M. Rogers. However, Boren had no problems supporting the candidacy of attorney general candidate Larry Derryberry and Lieutenant Governor George Nigh.[15]

Leading Democrats lined up behind Boren. United States House Speaker Carl Albert embraced Boren as "an inspiring young man who has shown what young people can do." Albert said when he looked at his party's choice of strong young men such as Boren and Derryberry, he liked the chances of Oklahoma having a great future. About Boren, Albert said, "David Boren has more education than any public official in the state of Oklahoma, and he has the common sense to go with it."[16]

Senator Denzil Garrison, who lost the GOP primary to Inhofe, endorsed Boren, the Democratic nominee. Garrison and the Boren family had many connections. When Garrison served in the Korean War, his unit chaplain was Boren's uncle, Dallas Boren.

Boren did not take the general election for granted, even though early polls in October showed him 50 percentage points ahead of Inhofe. Boren crisscrossed the state, revisiting every village and town in which he had become acquainted with Oklahomans from every walk of life during the previous 15 months. In October, he walked from Fort Gibson to Muskogee, accompanied by State Democratic Chairman Boyd Stevenson. When asked by a supporter if he believed that he was way ahead in the polls, Boren said that the surest way he could lose was if his supporters believed the polls. Instead, Boren said he was "running scared" and would continue to work 20 hours a day to carry his message of reform and hope to every corner of the state.

He accepted opportunities to debate Inhofe. Sometimes, the debates were mundane because both candidates shared common views on vital issues. For example, both supported education and were for the elimination of the state inheritance tax. Inhofe's uphill battle was to find issues on which he could trump Boren. Fortunately for Boren, those issues never materialized.[17]

Boren ultimately received the endorsement of the state's two largest newspapers, *The Daily Oklahoman* and the *Tulsa World.* The Tulsa newspaper, endorsing Boren over their own citizen, Inhofe, said Boren had "far the better chance" of turning promises of reform into reality. Boren also received the official support of the Oklahoma Education Association and many other groups.

The "non-campaign" was noticed by columnist Ray Parr, who had commented on Oklahoma elections for decades. Parr wrote in his popular column in *The Daily Oklahoman:*

> The way Boren and Jim Inhofe have got themselves trapped in this sweet feeling of friendship toward each other,

this could turn out to be such a sissy political campaign they won't even draw an audience for their TV debate.[18]

One of the few bones of contention in the general election campaign was over Inhofe's charges that Boren would not release his personal financial records to the press. Boren believed that Inhofe would try to capitalize on the issue during an hour-long debate two weeks before the election on KRMG Radio in Tulsa. Boren was prepared. Before the debate, aides Sven Holmes and Bob Burke typed out a document in which Boren gave Inhofe the authority to personally review his financial records and then report to the public if he found any irregularities.[19]

When Inhofe again charged that Boren was hiding something by not releasing his personal bank account information, Boren pulled the written authorization from his pocket and handed it to Inhofe. Boren said, "I am signing this document because I want you to personally look at all my financial records. If you find something wrong that you think Oklahomans ought to know, you tell them." Holmes remembered, "Whatever effect that Inhofe thought the issue would have, died on the spot. You could see the issue evaporating at that moment."[20]

Boren never admitted to himself or his closest supporters that he thought he had the election within his grasp. It was part of his success—the belief that he should take nothing for granted and continue to shake hands and address the issues at least six days a week.

On the Thursday night before the general election, Boren attended a fund-raising dinner at the home of Garfield County court reporter H. W. "Pete" Peters. After the event, Boren retired to the local Holiday Inn with aides Holmes and Burke. After the lights were turned out for the night, for the first time Boren recognized the significance of what all observers were seeing as a potential landslide victory for him. In a whisper, barely heard by Holmes and Burke, Boren said, "Boys, I think I might have this race won!" It was only five days until the election—and Boren was absolutely correct.

On the Sunday before the general election, publisher Edward L. Gaylord was behind an editorial prominently placed on the front page of *The Sunday Oklahoman*. The headline was, "Bellmon and Boren the Best," signifying the newspaper's endorsement of Henry Bellmon for United States Senate and Boren for Governor. Gaylord broke with his newspaper's tradition of supporting primarily Republicans to endorse the young Democrat.

The endorsement puzzled seasoned Democrats. However, Boren was not surprised. Since his days as a freshman legislator, his friendship with Gaylord had flourished. It was not a political alliance, but a close, personal relationship that gave Boren the opportunity to express his program for change to Gaylord.

On November 5, Boren carried 74 of the state's 77 counties and defeated Inhofe by nearly a quarter million votes, 514,389 to 290,459. Boren received 64 percent of the more than 800,000 votes cast in the general election. His total vote count was a new record in Oklahoma gubernatorial elections.[21]

Boren supporters were jubilant at the election watch party at the Skirvin Hotel in Oklahoma City. Before arriving at the hotel, Boren attended a victory party with Tulsa supporters. In Oklahoma City, Boren told a huge crowd, "I've been given a lot to live up to. The governor's office is a public trust. I'm going to work as hard as I can and try as hard as I can to be the governor of all the people."

Ray Parr reported on the victory in the following morning's edition of *The Daily Oklahoman:*

> Boren's victory climaxed a remarkable one-man performance that amazed long-time political observers. He

was virtually unknown outside his home district when he announced his candidacy...and had no political organization...

Boren walked county roads and city streets to carry his campaign into every section of the state, promising far-reaching reforms in state government. His reform program and promise to end old guard politics caught on with the people. Boren said he shook hands with 80,000 Oklahomans before he quit counting.

It was strictly a no-contest from the opening bell of the general election campaign.[22]

FIFTEEN

Forming a Team

FOR HIS FIRST ORDER OF BUSINESS as Governor-Elect, Boren named campaign aide Rob Pyron press secretary. Pyron had been the campaign's first paid staff member and could hardly believe all that was happening as a transition office was established in the basement of the State Capitol.[1]

Boren wasted no time in forming a transition team and going to work to carry out his campaign promises. Oklahoma City University School of Law Assistant Dean Von Russell Creel, a former Boren law school classmate, was named Executive Assistant and chief of the governor's staff. Former OBU students Sam Hammons, David Berrong, Paul Gritz, and Gary Morris joined Sven Holmes, Gail Scott, Bill Foster, and Dusty Martin as administrative assistants.

Hammons was responsible for law enforcement. Berrong was administrative assistant for natural resources and conservation, Scott was responsible for education and cultural affairs, while Holmes was administrative assistant for governmental finance, welfare, and program development, Gritz was responsible for health services and Foster was liaison with labor-related agencies. Martin was administrative assistant with responsibilities in dealing with the state legislature and other elected officials.

Robert Mitchell became legal counsel and Jan Cartwright was legislative liaison. Later Cartwright became legal counsel when Mitchell resigned. Cartwright served until he was appointed to the Oklahoma Corporation Commission. Ann Dubler, who had been Boren's personal secretary since he began service in the legislature, became the governor's personal assistant and "gatekeeper."

Other than Mitchell, most of Boren's staff were men and women in their twenties and early thirties, prompting Capitol observers to refer to the staff as the "Kiddie Corps." Ray Parr wrote:

> If you have any complaints about the way the governor's office is run the next four years you sure won't be able to blame things on my old guard politicians. They're gonna have a youth movement down there that will make J. Howard Edmondson's crew cuts look like a bunch of grandpaws. Thirty-six-year-old Bob Mitchell will stand out as an apparent old-age pensioner from the welfare mess when he moves in as legal counsel.[2]

Within a week after Boren's election, his number one legislative priority, repealing the state inheritance tax between spouses, was approved by the executive committee of the State Legislative Council. The approval cleared the way for the bill to accomplish the campaign promise to be introduced into the next session of the Oklahoma legislature. Senator Lee Cate of Norman predicted the change would cost from $10 million to $14 million per year in state revenues.[3]

Noting that the first step of approving Boren's highest priority had been taken so quickly, *The Daily Oklahoman* editorial page lauded Boren's efforts in an editorial titled "Walking on Water." The editorial reported that Boren and his staff had been working behind closed doors to abolish earmarking of tax money for the State Welfare Department. The editorial proclaimed, "If he can do those two things, abolish the hated tax and restore control over sales tax money to the lawmakers, he will indeed be a miracle worker. As one observer noted this week, if he can do that he can 'walk on water.'"[4]

When the state Christmas tree was erected at the Capitol, Ray Parr compared Boren to Santa Claus:

> We are expecting David to hang up tax cuts for everybody, along with increased appropriations for higher education, University Hospital, school teachers, and all the capitol poor children. Boy, if he gets that accomplished, he is without question gonna wind up the No. 1 Santa Claus in the entire nation, even on the UPI poll.[5]

Almost daily, press secretary Pyron had new information for the Capitol press corps about another plan that Boren intended to implement or ask the legislature to authorize. In rapid succession, announcements were made to create an agricultural advisory council to provide the new governor with a forum of ideas and a means to review problems of the Oklahoma farmer,[6] to ask the legislature to pass legislation to protect Oklahoma's scenic rivers,[7] and to support a fair program to build a series of new state highways.[8]

Just before Thanksgiving, Boren shocked Capitol observers by rejecting a $7,500 annual pay raise and leaving his governor's salary at $35,000. Boren also issued an open invitation to heads of all state agencies and institutions to turn down any salary increase above $42,500. State Welfare Director Lloyd Rader was the first to respond, accepted the challenge, and asked the State Welfare Commission to cut his salary by nearly $8,000. Rader said, "We're part of the executive branch. We have to be on the team." Within 48 hours, Chancellor of Higher Education E.T. Dunlap, OU President Dr. Paul Sharp, and OSU President Dr. Robert Kamm followed suit, expressing their desire to support Boren's personal belt tightening.[9]

To aid in planning his inauguration as governor, Boren appointed two former Oklahoma First Ladies, Mrs. Raymond Gary and Mrs. J. Howard Edmondson, to the Inaugural Committee chaired by Edward H. Cook, outgoing president of the Oklahoma City Chamber of Commerce. Thirty two other men and women served on the committee to plan the celebration set for January 13, 1975, including the official swearing-in and inaugural balls. Members of the executive committee of the Inaugural Committee were Chairman Cook, State Representative Hannah Atkins, Mrs. George Cross, Lorray Dyson, Minnie Lou Jessup, Lieutenant Governor George Nigh, Mrs. Edmondson, and Scott Orbison. Boren's instructions to the Inaugural Committee were to make it "a family affair."

As the time to take office grew near, Boren named more members of his staff. Don Coffin, former state representative from Guthrie, was named as special assistant to the governor for legislative and congressional liaison. Neal Harris of Norman was named administrative assistant for public administration and office administrator of the governor's office. Harris was a retired Army colonel. Jim Purdy became temporary administrative assistant for federal programs until Joe Glenn could assume the position several months later after his retirement from the United States Air Force. Glenn was a newsman at KTOK Radio in Oklahoma City.[10]

Boren's first test of strength in politics came in December when he objected to the Oklahoma State Troopers Association hiring a lobbyist to represent its interest before the legislature. Rumors were that the group was planning to hire Clem McSpadden who Boren defeated in the Democratic runoff. Boren told the troopers that if they hired a lobbyist, he would cancel his plans to propose for them the best raise they had ever had. After the executive committee of the troopers association considered their options, they withdrew plans to hire a lobbyist.[11]

One of the toughest campaign promises to keep for Boren was to wait until after he became governor to announce appointments to state boards and commissions. From the day he moved into the transition office in the Capitol basement, supporters and friends began putting their names into consideration for the hundreds of board and commission members a governor appoints during his term in office.

In visits with reporters, Boren outlined how he intended to govern. He believed he had a mandate for change from the size of his victory. He thought he could be more successful at bringing about change than J. Howard Edmondson was after a reform campaign in 1958. "The difference," Boren said, "is that I have been in the legislature, I know the leadership, and will listen to their advice." Boren said that some of the legislators he had clashed with most in the past had been some of his strongest advisors and supporters in the gubernatorial campaign.

Road building was a topic of hot conversation in December. Boren spoke out early in criticizing the way roads and highways were built in the state. He knew roads had been highly political over the years and that powerful legislators "brought home miles of black top." Boren favored using studies to determine where roads would be built. He also was greatly disturbed that some highways were being built with 100 percent state funds. Boren wanted state funds to be combined with available federal dollars to stretch tax money to build more miles of roads and highways.[12]

On the night before the inauguration, an Evening of the Arts delighted more than 1,000 supporters at the Oklahoma Theater Center. Among those appearing were Boren's aunt, Mae Boren Axton, composer of "Heartbreak Hotel" for Elvis Presley and the official Boren campaign song, and Boren's cousins, Altus and Keith

Boren, country and western singers. Also present was Arlo Guthrie, the son of the late Oklahoma balladeer, Woody Guthrie. Arlo was a friend of the Axton family, especially Boren's cousin, Hoyt Axton, who wrote famous rock and roll hits such as "Joy to the World," performed by Three Dog Night.

The Evening of the Arts was coordinated by Admiral John Kirkpatrick, Betty Price of the Oklahoma Arts and Humanities Council, and Minnie Lou Jessup, overall arts coordinator for the inaugural activities. Performances in the four-hour spectacular ranged from the symphonic explosion by the Oklahoma City Symphony to the romantic sounds of Spain through Ron Radford's flamenco guitar.[13]

SIXTEEN

Governor Boren

A T AGE 33, BOREN WAS THE NATION'S YOUNGEST governor when he was inaugurated on the south steps of the Oklahoma State Capitol on January 13, 1975. He was the second youngest Oklahoma governor, a few months older than when J. Howard Edmondson became chief executive in 1959.

It was a cold, blustery day as the Boren family and thousands of friends and supporters began inaugural day activities. An interdenominational religious service was held in the Raley Chapel at Oklahoma Baptist University. Boren ripped his pants as he got out of his automobile at OBU, but Eunice Short, director of the University Center, quickly made the needed repairs.[1]

At the prayer service, Boren noted how important OBU had been to his career and the fact that a majority of his gubernatorial staff would be former OBU students. Boren said the opportunity to teach at OBU was "the greatest present" he had ever received.[2]

The Oklahoma Military Band, the combined Seminole County high school bands, and the OSU band provided spirited music as Boren was sworn in by Oklahoma Supreme Court Chief Justice Ben T. Williams as the 21st governor of Oklahoma. The cold weather—38 degrees at swearing-in time—did not keep more than

4,000 supporters from braving the winds to watch their hero take the reins of the Sooner State.

It was the biggest day so far in Boren's life. It was a proud moment when his parents, Lyle and Christine Boren, watched him raise his right hand and promise to govern Oklahoma to the best of his ability. For the entire crowd, it was a day of hope and anticipation as power was passed from Governor Hall to Governor Boren.

In his inaugural address, Boren asked for an "old-fashioned spiritual renewal" and continued to emphasize the themes that catapulted him into office. Openness in government was a serious theme of his speech:

> I am determined to make Oklahoma an example to the nation in open and honest government where the people will know how every dollar is spent and about every action taken. This office is yours. I take it in trust. I will treat it as yours and not mine.
>
> You have given me the responsibility to make tough decisions, and I will make them. I cannot promise you that my judgment will always be right, but I do pledge that I will work hard to learn what is right and then always do the right as I perceive it.
>
> I will require the highest standards of public service from all who serve under my authority. Any failure to measure up to those high standards will know justice that is swift and sure.[3]

At the end of his address, Boren asked, "Will America remain great?" He suggested, "Comfort says, 'Tarry awhile.' Opportunity says, 'This is a great spot.' Timidity asks, 'How difficult is the road ahead?'" Boren answered his own question, "I know how Oklahomans will answer them. We answer, 'Stand aside; Oklahoma cares enough to lead the way.'"[4]

That evening, the inaugural ball took place in three different rooms at the Myriad Convention Center in downtown Oklahoma City. It was the first time in memory that Oklahomans were invited to the ball without formal invitations—and come they did. More than 10,000 people chose among three distinct kinds of music. Boren and First Lady Janna Boren, who had been very active in her husband's campaign, greeted them all.

In one room, Les Elgart and his band played dance music. In another room, the Oklahoma Federation of Square Dance Clubs performed while country music played. In the third room, younger supporters danced to rock and roll music. The announced dress for the ball, "wear what you like," kept few from donning the traditional tuxedo and evening gowns, although a few young people sported bib overalls, boots, and blue denim shirts.[5]

After the long day of inaugural activities, Boren arrived at the governor's office on the second floor of the State Capitol early the following morning, ready to govern. With his staff, he reviewed 15 to 20 major proposals that he intended to push in the legislature. The 35th Oklahoma legislature convened at noon under the leadership of House Speaker Bill Willis of Tahlequah and Senate President Pro Tempore Gene Howard of Tulsa. After housekeeping activities, Boren delivered his first state-of-the-state message, outlining his goals and dreams.

Boren's first priority was elimination of the state inheritance tax between spouses. He also championed a cut in state income tax, welfare reform, the elimination of earmarking state revenues, increased funding for higher education, and began the difficult process of cutting the state payroll—his announced goal was to reduce the state payroll by three percent. Among Boren's other goals were to successfully work with the legislature to resolve crises in road funding, the state prison system, and the OU Health Sciences Center, including Children's and University hospitals.

Quickly, the legislature abolished the inheritance tax and sent the bill to Boren's office for his signature. It was such a popular idea, the bill's Senate author, Senator Finis Smith of Tulsa, was joined by 40 of the 48 members of the State Senate as co-authors. The Senate passed the bill 43 to 4. The measure was sponsored in the House of Representatives by Representative Wayne Holden of Duncan. Even though some legislators called the bill tax relief for the wealthy, it passed both houses of the legislature almost unanimously—sailing through the House 95-1.[6]

Even with the tremendous pressure of presenting his programs to the legislature, Boren also had to begin the process of naming state agency directors and members of boards and commissions who served at the pleasure of the governor. One of Boren's first agency appointments was that of Jeff Laird, Sr., as director of the Oklahoma State Bureau of Investigation (OSBI). A former FBI agent and general counsel of the Oklahoma Bar Association, Laird was an old Boren family friend. As head of the OSBI, Laird brought new standards of professionalism and had his agents trained at the national Federal Bureau of Investigation academy.[7]

Since the election, Boren and his inner staff had made a detailed list of supporters he wanted to appoint to boards and commissions that controlled the activities of most state programs. He immediately began combat with old guard forces who wanted to keep their key people in power. For example, when Boren appointed William "Bill" Allford of McAlester to the powerful State Highway Commission, Senator Gene Stipe was the local state senator who had to move the confirmation. Stipe balked at giving his nod to Allford until Boren threatened to travel to McAlester and announce that Stipe was blocking the four-laning of US-69 by preventing Boren from choosing someone of his choice to serve on the Highway Commission. Stipe backed down and Allford was confirmed. Because Boren had somewhat literally run against the legislature in his successful gubernatorial campaign, the battle with Stipe was repeated in several appointments that required confirmation of the State Senate.[8]

Boren showed bipartisanship in selecting Scott Eubanks, a Republican, as director of the Office of Industrial Development. Such selection of officials on the basis of merit, not just the person's party registration, was refreshing to Denzil Garrison, chosen by Boren to maintain good relations between the governor's office and the state legislature. Garrison had served as Republican floor leader in both houses of the legislature.[9]

The national media took note of Boren's election as governor. After a trip to his native Oklahoma, Bill Moyers wrote in *Time* Magazine, "There is nothing orthodox about Boren except ambition." Moyers noted that Boren had carried both rural counties and university towns and had brought a fresh, new mood to Oklahomans who were tired of corrupt government. Moyers wrote, "There was little of the old rural-urban split. People on the farms and in the small towns are fed up just like people in the cities."[10]

The crisis in Oklahoma's corrections program begged for the attention of the young governor. He called for the immediate construction of a new maximum security unit at the state penitentiary at McAlester. There was a glaring need for a maximum security unit since a fire had destroyed most of the cells holding the worst prisoners in July, 1973. Senator Herschal Crow of Altus, chairman of the Senate Appropriations Committee, agreed in principle with Boren and introduced the necessary legislation to provide $23 million for corrections expansion.[11]

The Daily Oklahoman stood behind Boren's call for reform of the state welfare system. An editorial noted, "One of the few issues on which responsible liberals and conservatives find common ground is the state of our crazy-quilt welfare system. They agree it is an appalling mess, even though they may disagree on what should be done about it."[12]

Boren declared war against welfare waste and abuse. He wanted cheaters prosecuted, monthly pensions increased for those who desperately needed state help, and prescription drug assistance for helpless victims of inflation. The most controversial plan unveiled by Boren was to require parents of children receiving state Aid for Dependent Children (AFDC) payments to prove they were actively seeking work. Boren also called for mandatory jail terms for fathers who repeatedly refused to support their children. State Welfare Director Lloyd Rader already had agreed to transfer more than $5 million in earmarked funds to the general fund so that the legislature could openly and publicly debate the use of the money in welfare programs.[13]

Boren's mandate allowed him to win the first few skirmishes with the legislature. He won a showdown on deciding how much money to add to a supplemental highway funding bill. The mandate was recognized by an editorial in *The Daily Oklahoman*, "If Governor Boren succeeds in carrying out his pledges to the voters, which won him overwhelming approval at the polls last November, it will be because the public continues to back his program."[14]

Boren worked hard to establish a working relationship with the legislature. He invited leaders to the governor's mansion weekly during the session for conversation about the progress of his programs. The breakfast meetings caused one reporter to dub Boren "the scrambled eggs governor."

Boren had to deal with veteran legislators who had been in office nearly as long as he had been alive. When he sent aide Robert Mitchell to talk with Stipe to ask for his vote for a certain bill, Mitchell said, "What do you want to be able to support us?" Stipe replied, "I'm not sure, but I'll think of something."[15]

House Speaker Bill Willis gave strong support to Boren's proposed increase in educational spending. For three of the four years Boren was governor, Oklahoma led the nation in percentage increase in state funding of common schools and higher education.[16]

There was so much serious business being addressed in Boren's first month, he welcomed tongue-in-cheek comments on Sundays in Ray Parr's column in *The Sunday Oklahoman*. There was little doubt that the veteran columnist liked the youthful and honest new governor. His Sunday comments included:

> Speaking of receptions, Governor Boren says he has eaten so many brownies since he took office he's gonna have to start walking again to stop all his clothes shrinking. For the good of the state, folks, trot out those carrot sticks and celery and knock off the sweet stuff when he shows up…
>
> Mrs. Ira Mckinzie of Kingston wants to know if Boren has any stockpiled brooms he would sell. She writes, "There's not a decent broom left in the stores here in Marshall County. Since Boren bought up all the good ones, the flimsy things in the stores won't last. How about a broom-rebate program for the housewives, governor?"[17]

Besides the serious business of being governor, there were light moments during Boren's first year in the governor's mansion. In February, 1975, Boren and other governors were invited to visit with President Gerald Ford in Houston, Texas. Seated next to the president at dinner, Boren cut into his grilled tomato and squirted tomato juice on the president's necktie that contained the presidential seal. Ford, who was known for like mishaps, laughed loudly.

On another occasion, Boren was meeting at the governor's mansion with legislative leaders. On the day the Republican State Senate leadership was scheduled for lunch, Boren was running behind schedule and the senators were already in the mansion when he arrived. As he came in the door, four-year-old Carrie ran up to him and said, "Daddy, Daddy, Inhofe's in the house!" She obviously had remembered her "daddy" running against Inhofe the previous year and wondered why he was now sitting in "their dining room."[18]

*After just a few months in office...we know one thing...
David Boren is a realist about government and
what it should do and what it should not do.*

THE DAILY OKLAHOMAN

SEVENTEEN

Tax Relief and Yes-All-8

VEN THOUGH HE WAS THE NATION'S YOUNGEST
governor, Boren was not bashful about attending the
National Governor's Conference in February, 1975, to
challenge White House officials who had proposed national
energy reforms that, in Boren's opinion, would devastate
independent oilmen in Oklahoma.

Boren received much press attention when he targeted the
chief of the White House energy policy and other governors who
suggested that price controls on crude oil and elimination of the
depletion tax allowance might somehow solve the growing concern
over the shortage of energy. The thrust of Boren's argument was
that such moves would exacerbate the energy shortage, rather than
improve the situation.[1]

Not only did the 1975 Oklahoma legislature eliminate the
state inheritance tax between spouses, but legislators also followed Boren's call to reduce the state income tax for the first
time in 27 years. Boren had campaigned to end the "double
income taxation." Oklahomans were given no credit on state
income tax for federal taxes they had paid. Boren wanted full
credit given on state tax returns. Speaker Willis balked at the
proposal.

Boren had great personal respect for Willis and for his knowledge of the state budget. Willis worried that Boren's proposal might leave the state short of funds in the event of an emergency. Willis said, "If you will meet me half way, we'll give credit for half the federal taxes paid and you can still claim victory."[2]

Boren agreed and that is exactly what happened. Half the state income tax credit for federal income tax payments was reinstated, a savings to state taxpayers of more than $13 million. After the legislature passed the bill, Boren said both houses had set a new course by thinking of the taxpayer when considering legislation.

For weeks after taking office, Boren's staff had hinted to the press that the governor would show up at state offices on Friday afternoons to make certain that state employees were "working until quitting time." Sure enough, Boren began unannounced visits to state agencies on Friday afternoons. In early March, he and aides Rob Pyron and Dusty Martin appeared at 4:00 p.m. at the offices of the Oklahoma Wildlife Conservation Department. Fortunately, everyone was at their posts and officials gave the governor and his staff members a tour. Boren bought a combination hunting and fishing license and renewed his subscription to *Outdoor Oklahoma* Magazine.[3]

Boren's propensity to check on state workers on Friday afternoons caused at least one news organization to monitor the working habits of the governor's office. David Holliday of KTOK Radio showed up at closing time one Friday to see if the governor's staff was working. Sure enough, every staff member was at his or her post, including interns Mike Wofford and John Wampler whose offices were hidden away in former vaults in the Capitol. Holliday, who later joined Boren's staff, often told the story on himself and how he was impressed that the governor was holding his own staff members to his expectation that state workers should give taxpayers a full week's work. Wofford credited executive assistant Von

Creel and office manager Neal Harris with communicating the governor's work ethic to other staff members.[4]

Harris, a retired colonel with a flat-top haircut and a burning desire for saving tax money, was legendary for counting pencils and distributing office supplies sparingly. Once when Boren noticed Wofford and other administrative assistants were not taking notes during a meeting, he asked why. Wofford answered, "Neal won't give us pencils." Wofford remembered, "Boren's reaction was that look of rolling his eyes and turning his head to the sky while laughing. What a thing for the state's governor to have to resolve!"[5]

In April, 1975, Boren addressed a joint session of the legislature and advocated sweeping changes in the executive branch of government, including the removal of five statewide elective offices from the ballot. He asked that a special election be held on July 22 to approve eight state questions that would forever change the Oklahoma ballot and the fate of the "famous name" contests for lesser state offices.

Boren proposed that the offices of secretary of state, labor commissioner, and chief mine inspector be made appointive, rather than elective. In addition, he asked voters to eliminate the office of commissioner of charities and corrections and combine the offices of examiner and inspector and state auditor into a new elective office to be known as state auditor and inspector. Another question would strengthen the state's constitutional budget-balancing amendment and set up a reserve fund.

Boren echoed several previous governors in complaining that many secondary officeholders were unresponsive to the chief executive because the governor had no control over them. Many offices were filled not on the basis of merit, but on which candidate had the most famous name. Voters seldom knew who they were putting into office.

Boren asked his supporters to back the "Yes-All-8" campaign, to approve the eight state questions that changed the executive branch of government more than at any time since the state constitution was approved in 1907. Although a majority of the members of the legislature backed Boren, Representative John L. Monks, a Democrat from Muskogee, said Boren was seeking power and that approval of the state questions would allow one man to run the entire executive branch of government.[6]

Boren hit the campaign trail to convince voters to approve the eight state questions. He met head-on criticism that the power of the voters would be lessened by taking away the right to elect some of the secondary state offices. Instead, he said the changes would "make the governor accountable for the duties of the offices being removed from the ballot."[7]

There was a variety of reaction from office holders affected by the proposed changes. Commissioner of Charities and Corrections Jim Cook agreed with Boren that the charities and corrections job had outlived its usefulness and that the Department of Corrections had assumed all of the vital functions of the post. New Secretary of State Jerome "Jerry" Byrd had no problem with his office being appointed by the governor, rather than being elected by the people.

On the other hand, State Auditor Joe Bailey Cobb bitterly opposed the elimination of his office and called Boren "phony as a $3 bill." Cobb was upset because the proposed constitutional amendment would require the new auditor and inspector to have three years' experience as an accountant. That requirement would have knocked Cobb from seeking the new combined post.[8]

On the Sunday before the special election, columnist Ray Parr weighed in on the issue:

> Making these offices appointive won't solve all our problems. I've seen some good candidates elected to office and I've seen some good ones and bad ones appointed. The only

difference is that when you get some screwball elected you don't know just who to blame. When some nut gets appointed you will at least know who is responsible.[9]

When the votes were counted, Oklahomans overwhelmingly approved all eight state constitutional amendments. Surprisingly, there was no rural-urban split of the vote—Oklahomans everywhere wanted to shorten the ballot and strengthen the constitutional provision requiring the legislation to balance the budget—to not spend more than the state had in revenues. The approval of the state questions was seen as a solid vote of confidence for Boren's plan to reorganize government and make it more accountable to the people. Boren took the voters' approval as a mandate for further reorganization of state government.

In July, the Commission on Reorganization of State Government (Commission on Reorganization) held its first meeting. The commission was comprised of legislators appointed by the House Speaker and Senate President Pro Tempore and six citizen members appointed by the governor. Boren chose businessman Gary Cook of Tulsa, retired school superintendent Bryan Waid of Lawton, banker Bert Mackie of Enid, retired Oklahoma Gas and Electric Company Vice President Herbert Branan of Oklahoma City, oil man Douglas Wixson of Tulsa, and Shirley Weeks of Stillwater, president of the Stillwater League of Women voters. The commission's job was to make recommendations to the legislature on how Oklahoma government could be streamlined and restructured.[10]

Assisting the reorganization effort was a new Division of Planning Management Analysis attached to the governor's office. Appointed as director of the new effort was James C. Buchanan, III, of Muskogee.

Buchanan and other Boren staff members' lives were changed by their participation in his administration. Denise Bode, who worked in the governor's mail room before completing law school, serving on Boren's United States Senate staff, and upon becoming a member of the Oklahoma Corporation Commission, said, "He taught me that one person could make a difference. I saw him try his best to develop a consensus on issues. No one has ever done it better. He has an amazing ability to convince people to do what is right."[11]

Jack McCarty, Boren's law school classmate and avid supporter in the 1974 governor's race, was proud of Boren's early accomplishments as governor. He often traveled to Oklahoma City to see his old friend. Once he accompanied Boren to speak to a small group of people. "No matter how small the crowd was," McCarty remembers, "he gave them his best effort. He could be exhausted, walk into a room, and be energized by it."[12]

In August, 1975, Boren and several other governors met with President Gerald Ford at the White House to discuss federal control of natural gas prices. Boren believed in the free market system and suggested that Congress should decontrol federal price ceilings in an effort to encourage increased natural gas production in the nation. Three weeks later, Boren's gas pricing proposal was adopted by the Southern Governor's Conference meeting in Orlando, Florida.[13]

Boren's support for open meetings of agencies spending state monies resulted in the removal of the chairman of the Board of Corrections in October, 1975. Irvine Ungerman was asked to resign after he moved that the board go into executive session to discuss an architectural contract for the new medium security corrections facility at Lexington. The Board of Corrections earlier had tried to award the contract to the brother of a department employee without going through proper notice and selection channels. Boren and Attorney General Larry Derryberry "blew the whistle" on the board action and made them back up and do it correctly.[14]

It was not the first time Boren had clashed with corrections officials in his first nine months in office. Corrections reform was becoming a major headache for the state and Boren was unable to see eye-to-eye with programs pushed by Director of Corrections Russell Lash. When the differences came to a head, Lash resigned and Boren's new majority on the board chose Ned Benton as Director of Corrections. Boren believed Benton's choice was key to solving the prison crisis.[15]

Boren moved to establish new prisons at Lexington and Hominy where younger first-time offenders would be held separately from older repeat offenders. Boren also set up college and vocational technical programs behind bars, reduced overcrowding at the McAlester state penitentiary, and expanded work-release programs in which inmates worked and paid the state for part of their imprisonment costs. An additional benefit was giving real work experience to the inmate to make it easier to stay out of prison. Boren hoped the work-release program would reduce the number of repeat offenders.

Personal tragedy hit Boren in October, 1975. On October 24, he and his wife, Janna, jointly announced that they were divorcing, based solely on incompatibility. The problems in the marriage had been kept quiet from family and staff as attempts were made to reconcile. Under the terms of the divorce agreement, Janna was awarded custody of Carrie, age four, and Dan, age two, but the governor had unlimited visitation rights. Although neither Boren nor Janna ever discussed the break-up, newspaper reports suggested that Janna did not cherish her new public role as First Lady. A reporter in the *Tulsa Tribune* quoted an unidentified Capitol source, "The pressure of trying to raise two young children in a political atmosphere was too much."[16] Boren often told friends he blamed himself for not giving enough of his time to his wife and young family.

Janna married Texas oil man, John C. Robbins, the following year and lived a quiet life in north Texas until her death from cancer in 1997. She and Boren remained friends, especially during the time that children, Carrie and Dan, were completing their education.

As if the divorce did not place enough stress upon Boren, two days after the action was announced to the press, Boren faced his first crisis in the state prison system. Seven inmates armed with knives took a guard and two cooks hostage at the Oklahoma State Reformatory in Granite. The inmates were upset over their treatment at the prison, including new rules that limited the amount and type of Christmas gifts they could receive. Boren was on a hiking trip in the McCurtain County Wilderness Area in southeast Oklahoma when he was notified of the hostage situation.[17]

Prison officials feared that several hundred inmates were at risk. It had not been that long since the prison riots at the state penitentiary at McAlester and the riots at Attica, New York. When Boren was asked if state troopers and Department of Corrections officers could storm the prison and retake control, he hesitated. He certainly did not want another full-scale prison riot on his hands. It was widely believed that instant use of force is what caused the riots in New York, so Boren wanted to try negotiation first.

Boren traveled to Granite and met with Corrections Director Ned Benton and law enforcement officials. It was a dramatic scene as he arrived. Three hundred inmates were milling around the prison yard while the three hostages were held behind barricaded doors in the kitchen. Guards on the towers were equipped with machine guns.[18]

To diffuse the situation, Boren agreed to meet with inmates in the yard at the center of the compound. He, two aides, and two unarmed security officers met with the inmates who were very direct about their perceived mistreatment by prison officials. Among other complaints were about lack of exercise time, good food, and access to the library. Boren said he would try to get those areas improved, but that the hostages must be freed immediately.

The newspaper headline the following day reported that Boren said, "If you don't release the hostages, you'll fry!," an obvious reference to being sentenced to death in the state's electric chair. Boren denied using that particular word, but did use strong language to indicate the inmates would be prosecuted to the fullest extent of the law if they harmed the hostages. Even Boren's mother, Christine, called him after she read the newspaper story and said she was shocked that her son would use such language.[19]

After Boren's talk with the inmates, and the promise to set up a formal complaint system, the inmates returned to their cells, the hostages were released unharmed, and peace was restored. The hostage situation had lasted 26 hours. The seven inmates were charged by District Attorney Richard Dugger.[20] Boren kept his promise to listen further to inmate grievances. He visited the prison twice over the following months to meet with inmate representatives.

Boren's second session with the Oklahoma legislature was a challenge. Projected state revenues were down from the previous year. Building on his unprecedented success in his first year as governor, Boren kept up the pressure for reform. He had not won every battle, but was encouraged by the editorial writers of the *Tulsa Tribune* to keep up the fight. An editorial in the newspaper just before the January 6 start to the new legislative session said, "None of Boren's setbacks need cripple his efforts to reduce waste and improve efficiency in state government. He has the intellect to profit from his mistakes. He has the imagination to conceive new approaches to longstanding problems. He retains the goodwill of most of the people who helped elect him."[21]

Any observer of state politics realized that the Boren term in office would be a period of major reform. Boren's ideas sprang into a flood of legislation. Some compared it to President Franklin D. Roosevelt's first 100 days when New Deal legislation was introduced to loosen the grip of the Great Depression on America. Boren did not get all he wanted within 100 days, but he would propose more than 100 major legislative proposals during his four years as chief executive of Oklahoma. More than 80 percent of the proposals passed in some form.

The state's prison population and outdated facilities continued to be a pressing issue. In his state-of-the-state message to the 1976 legislature, Boren called for the people of Oklahoma to join him in waging a war on crime. As part of that war, Boren proposed a comprehensive corrections program that would provide salary increases for prison guards and other law enforcement officials and millions of dollars for prison construction.

In addition to needing more money in the Department of Corrections budget, new anti-crime laws were proposed. During the legislative session, bills were approved to provide restitution to victims of crimes, strengthen securities laws to halt fraudulent investment in the state, begin the process of enacting rules for uniform sentencing, increase public school counseling and vocational retraining programs for inmates, and increase funding for the Oklahoma State Bureau of Investigation (OSBI) and the Oklahoma Bureau of Narcotics and Dangerous Drug Control.

Boren's plan was to double the number of OSBI agents so that a highly-trained state law enforcement agent could be within 50 miles of any citizen to assist local law enforcement agencies. The effort was applauded by the *Tulsa Tribune,* "Not since the Lord took Gideon's army of 22,000 and trimmed it to 300 men has any general prepared for battle with such a limited fighting force. But as in the Biblical story, Boren's emphasis is on quality and strategic location."[22]

Boren continued to press for state funds to build two new prisons. Opponents argued that making the state penitentiary at McAlester larger would only make it a bigger failure. Legislators battled over the location of medium security prisons at Lexington, Tulsa, and Oklahoma City. Boren constantly was involved in both private and public debates over the necessity of new prisons. However, after the prison construction legislation went through the legislature three times, a comprehensive corrections package was passed and signed into law.[23]

It was a red-letter day when Boren spoke to a crowd of 200 at the groundbreaking of the Lexington Regional Treatment Center, the first correctional facility built by the state since the state reformatory at Granite in 1910. Boren said, "Oklahoma is turning the corner today. We are serving notice that we are going to build a model corrections system in Oklahoma." The Lexington complex included a medium security prison and a diagnostic center.[24]

The state legislature balked still at approving sweeping changes in the structure of state government, but Boren did win some concessions in 1976 and used the power of executive order to make other changes. He created five mini-cabinets made up of heads of about 20 state agencies to work with the governor to coordinate activities. The mini-cabinets were in the fields of education, law enforcement, human resources, natural resources, and economic development.[25]

Boren certainly did not equal his first year's successes with the legislature, but lawmakers passed 21 of 24 Boren-sponsored bills in the 1976 session. The governor scored well in corrections and education and suffered his only real setbacks in executive branch reorganization. One of the real victories was the passage of an $800 yearly pay hike for Oklahoma teachers and record appropriations for the state's common schools and institutions of higher education.[26]

In the area of natural resources, Boren convened a blue-ribbon forestry panel to address public concerns about clear-cutting practices by the Weyerhaeuser Company and its impact on water quality in southeast Oklahoma. Boren toured lands owned by Weyerhaeuser and saw how the forestry company giant was literally cutting all trees from large tracts of land and replanting them with tiny seedlings. It was a practice in use in other areas of the United States, but shocked local residents of southeast Oklahoma who were accustomed to selective cutting in the pine forests.

Boren met with Weyerhaeuser President George Weyerhaeuser. Each pledged constant communication to make certain Weyerhaeuser changed its practices to the extent of leaving green belts along creeks and streams and taking other steps to prevent the loss of soil into southeast Oklahoma's clear streams. Boren also dedicated a new state-funded Forest Heritage Center at Beavers Bend State Park near Broken Bow, the first museum dedicated to remembering and explaining Oklahoma's forest heritage.

Showing that government can move quickly, Boren called a special session of the legislature that enacted a new death penalty statue in just five days. The new law was necessary because the United States Supreme Court had found Oklahoma's old law allowing the imposition of the death penalty in certain criminal cases to be unconstitutional.

On the national political scene, Boren was the first governor in the nation to endorse former Georgia Governor Jimmy Carter in his bid to become the Democratic nominee for President of the United States. Boren liked Carter's energy policies and his stance on states' rights and decentralization of the federal government.

Boren had met with Carter on several occasions, the first time at a dinner honoring Jim Thorpe in Yale, Oklahoma. With Boren's backing, Carter picked up a majority of delegates at the Democratic district conventions in preparation for the Democratic National Convention.[27]

Boren urged Carter to choose Maine United States Senator Edmund Muskie as his running mate. When Carter chose Minnesota Senator Walter Mondale, Boren's enthusiasm for a Carter presidency waned somewhat, although he still supported Carter's candidacy. No doubt he believed Carter, as a former governor, would be in tune with problems of state governments.

In December, 1976, Boren was elected chairman of the Interstate Oil Compact Commission (IOCC), a politically influential platform. Immediately, Boren called on President-Elect Carter to support natural gas price deregulation. Boren was elected to the IOCC post after other governors conceded that Boren, as an energy advisor to Carter, would have substantial influence with the new president.[28]

*Even though we had passed many elements
of my reform program in the first two years in office,
there remained much to be done.*

DAVID L. BOREN

EIGHTEEN

Sunset Laws and Workers' Comp

THE GOVERNOR WAS PROUD of his first two years' efforts. Oklahoma had made record-breaking increases in education funding, from common schools to higher education. Heavy commitments had been made to special education, elementary counseling, and programs for gifted and talented students. The line had been held on growth in the number of state employees. There were 12,500 fewer people on the state's welfare rolls than when Boren took office, and the state reserve cash account was approaching $80 million.

Boren presented the 1977 Oklahoma legislative session even more reform proposals. He suggested workers' compensation reform, passage of a law that would require lobbyists to disclose who they were working for, reform of the unemployment compensation system, and state support for juvenile facilities in Oklahoma cities and towns.

A significant part of Boren's legislative proposal in this third year as governor was a sunset law designed to eliminate agencies that failed to justify their existence. Most legislators appeared to like the idea, although some suggested that if the governor and legislature used the laws already on the books, unneeded agencies could be abolished. Boren took the challenge and terminated 56 boards and commissions by executive order before the legislature could take up the question.

Senator Wayne Holden of Duncan and Representative Charles Elder of Purcell sponsored Boren's sunset legislation. Speaker Willis was opposed to the bill because he believed some agencies should never die—they were too important to the operation of state government. A House committee trimmed the original list of 184 agencies in the sunset bill to 111, but added 200 other commissions and advisory boards.

The legislature passed the sunset law which called for a staggered legislative review of the boards, commissions, and agencies beginning with 21 in 1978. The law called for the automatic abolishment of agencies unless specifically recreated by the legislature. Boren saw the sunset law as a step toward more efficient state government. At least the legislature would be required to occasionally review the purpose and duties of state agencies.[1]

The state's workers' compensation system which provided indemnity and medical benefits for injured workers had been a problem since Boren became governor in 1975. It was widely reported that Oklahoma had the lowest benefits for the injured and among the highest insurance rates for employers. Boren appointed a committee to take an in-depth look at the system and recommend changes to help the Oklahoma Industrial Court decide compensability of contested cases and award benefits. The Oklahoma Bar Association offered its help in solving the crisis.

Boren declared workers' compensation reform as his top priority in the 1977 legislative session. He was convinced that the present law was unfair to both employer and employee. He called it a "disgraceful worker's compensation system." Boren's reform plan was principally authored by Senator Bob Funston of Broken Arrow. The bill increased benefits and established a medical panel to offer a third opinion when doctors for the employer and employee disagreed on the amount of the injured worker's disability.

While Boren's bill was being heard in the State Senate, Representative Glenn Floyd of Norman was pushing his own bill that would eliminate the Industrial Court and allow workers to take their claim for benefits to district court. Floyd's bill, which he claimed would cut the size of state government and move the decision making in work-related injury cases to the local level, was supported by Speaker Willis.

Compromise came when drafters of both bills combined selected provisions into a measure that could pass both houses of the legislature. When the legislature passed the workers' compensation bill, Boren called it one of the most important reforms in recent Oklahoma history. The new law raised benefits for injured workers, provided coverage for nearly every type of employee in the state, and created a new seven-judge Oklahoma Workers' Compensation Court. A major difference was that the governor would appoint judges from a list of recommendations from a nomination commission. No Senate confirmation was required, as had been the case with the old Industrial Court.

Boren changed the tenor of the worker's compensation system by appointing new judges to the Worker's Compensation

Court as the new system took effect. Marian Opala, James Fullerton, Charles Cashion, and Chris Sturm were selected for positions on the Court. Cashion and Sturm were law school classmates of Boren. Cashion also had been involved in Boren's campaign and was intrigued how quickly Boren grasped the significance of workers' compensation reform. Cashion said, "He could read the most difficult material and immediately assimilate it. After just a short review of a complex topic, he could speak to the subject as an expert."[2]

Opala remembers Boren's interview with him before he was appointed to the Workers' Compensation Court. Boren told him, "The only thing I expect of you is even-handed treatment of all claims and an absolute commitment to the rule of law."[3]

When Boren was not busy discharging his duties as governor and pushing his legislative agenda, he was a powerful voice in the national debate about energy policy. He was kept abreast of the Carter administration's development of a national energy plan. However, early in the Carter years, Boren was troubled at the ideas proposed by national energy chief James Schlesinger.

Boren's problems with Carter's energy policy reached an early boiling point in April, 1977, when the headline in the *Saturday Oklahoman and Times* was, "President Lied to Me, Boren Says." Boren and seven other governors had met at the White House with Schlesinger to review a preliminary draft of the president's energy program. Veteran reporter Allan Cromley said someone close to Boren told him that Boren had emerged from the meeting with Schlesinger and said, "The President said he's never lied to anybody, but he lied to me."[4]

Boren was upset over what he perceived as Carter back-
tracking from a promise made during the campaign to help
Oklahoma, Texas, and other natural gas producing states to
work toward deregulation of natural gas prices. As the meeting
with Schlesinger ended, Boren handed a Carter aide a note
that, as one of Carter's earliest supporters, he expected to be
able to talk to the president before he went public with his
criticism.[5]

Boren's outrage paid off. Before the day was done, Boren
received a call from Schlesinger that "positive movement" was
being made to change objectionable provisions of the energy
policy that was to be released the following week. Boren insisted upon at least a phased program of deregulation of natural
gas, incentives for more production of oil and gas, and relief
for farmers who would be affected by any sweeping changes in
national energy policy.[6]

Boren also told reporters he had never used the word, "lied,"
when talking about his meeting the day before. Boren was summoned back to the White House to discuss the three key points
he was pushing.

Carter unveiled his new energy plan on April 20. In a 31-
minute speech to a joint session of Congress, a solemn offering that was interrupted only eight times by applause, Carter
urged consumer conservation, a tax on big cars, and an increase
in fuel taxes. Boren's reaction to the plan was mixed. He was
happy that the president had at least talked about his suggestions of natural gas deregulation and providing incentives for
new oil and gas exploration, but Boren had "grave" questions
about many areas of the plan that lacked specific goals. A bright
spot for Boren was that Carter included at the last minute

Boren's idea of discussing lifting the federal tax on intangible drilling costs.[7]

The week after Carter's announcement of his controversial plan to meet the nation's energy crisis head on, Boren called on the president at the White House for a 20-minute audience and an hour-long, follow-up meeting with Schlesinger. Boren's purpose was to come with an olive branch. He certainly was not taking back his criticism of the energy plan, but he wanted Carter to succeed in implementing a reasonable energy initiative "for the sake of the country." Boren applauded the president for penalizing energy wastefulness and rewarding conservation.[8]

In the meetings with Carter and his top energy aide, Boren reiterated the necessity for natural gas deregulation and increased prices for old oil. Many Oklahoma producers were taking oil from wells that had been drilled 50 years before. The production was small in quantity and higher prices were necessary to make it economical to continue to produce from old wells, known as "stripper" wells which produced less than 10 barrels of oil per day and had very high operating costs.

From the time Boren took office as governor, the overcrowding of the state prison system was a problem. Even though some progress had been made with appropriations for two new prisons and other reforms, including raising the pay for underpaid prison guards, the federal government got involved in the prison situation. Drew Days, head of the office of civil rights in the United States Department of Justice, threatened a federal takeover of Oklahoma's prisons. Boren, not liking the idea a bit, issued his own threat. He told Days that if Justice Department officers tried to take our state prisons, he would call out the Oklahoma National Guard to prevent such action.[9]

Boren did not believe the president of the United States would take over the prison system "for the purpose of turning dangerous inmates loose on the street." After Boren's firm threat, Days backed down and refused to recommend Justice Department intervention. Years later, Boren sat next to Days on an airplane. Days asked, "I have always wondered if you really would have called out the National Guard." Boren answered with amusement, "I am never going to answer that question. I am going to keep you wondering if I would have done it."[10]

Despite the state's efforts, in June, 1977, United States District Judge Luther Bohanon ordered Oklahoma to reduce its prison population at penitentiaries in McAlester and Granite. Bohanon found that overcrowding was unconstitutional treatment of inmates.[11]

Boren said that the federal judge's order was a gross abuse of discretion and warned that the court order would trigger "dangerous chaos" in Oklahoma prisons. The order mandated that 760 inmates would need to be shuffled from the two prisons to other prison facilities. Boren said, "The judge's order is totally unreasonable because it sets an arbitrary figure of 150 reductions per month without regard to when space will become available elsewhere."[12]

Boren directed an appeal of Bohanon's order which was ultimately affirmed by the United States Tenth Circuit Court of Appeals. However, after Boren and the legislature promised additional funds for construction to add prison beds, Bohanon issued a temporary order relaxing the inmate population levels. Boren kept his promise and launched the largest prison reform and capital improvement program in state history.

In the summer of 1977, political pundits began wondering in print what Boren would do in the 1978 election. Most writers believed he had two choices—become the state's first two-term governor or run for the United States Senate seat occupied by Republican Dewey Bartlett whose battle with lung cancer had become public. It was uncertain whether Bartlett would run for reelection.

Either way, Boren had to stay in contact with the people of Oklahoma. He conducted Main Street meetings, a series of stops in cities and towns around the state. The forum gave him a chance to talk about what his administration had accomplished and hear from the people about their concerns.

Even though the constituency was the same for running for governor or the United States Senate, Boren had different election laws to consider, especially federal laws that severely limited individual maximum contributions in comparison to state races. He knew that he needed to make a decision early in 1978 of which office he would seek.

Education always had been dear to Boren's heart and he used his power as governor and the bully pulpit of the chief executive's office to further education at all levels. He championed a program at the University of Oklahoma to bring extraordinary scholars and business leaders to spend time with Oklahoma's most gifted students. Even though the program was housed at OU, students from all over the state were allowed to enroll in intensive seminars and courses. It was known as the Scholars Leadership Enrichment Program (SLEP) and continues as a viable program today.[13]

One of Boren's visions was the establishment of the Oklahoma Arts Institute, a response to concerned parents who wanted quality arts education for Oklahoma's youth. In 1977, Boren and Mary Frates spearheaded the effort to hold a three-day pilot program for 100 high school students with intensive art training in five disciplines. Frates directed the first camp, the Oklahoma Summer Arts Institute, at Camp Eagan near Tahlequah.

The following year, the summer institute was expanded to a two-week program for students studying acting, ballet, choral music, drawing, painting, modern dance, orchestral music, photography, poetry, and sculpture. Learning from renowned artists such as Richard Thomas and Jane Alexander, students attended the institute which relocated to a permanent home at Quartz Mountain State Park near Altus. Later, the Oklahoma Arts Institute was designated by the state legislature to be Oklahoma's official school of the arts.[14]

Boren also supported a rural medical education effort that provided scholarships for students to attend medical school if they promised to return to rural areas that needed physicians. The program was part of the family medicine program at the University of Oklahoma Health Sciences Center. Additional efforts were made to train emergency medical technicians for service in rural Oklahoma.

The Health Sciences Center was a small operation in which Boren saw great potential. During a meeting with the dean of the OU College of Medicine, Boren took a sheet of shelf paper and drew his concept of what the Health Sciences Center could look like with a strong partnership between federal and state governments and the private sector.

Even though the federal government would not allow Boren and the Oklahoma Department of Human Services to require that people work in order to receive welfare benefits, Boren urged the introduction of a volunteer program. Welfare recipients were encouraged to take jobs at state hospitals and other public institutions. Surprisingly to some observers, many people drawing welfare checks volunteered for service.

One of the beneficiaries of the volunteer work was the Department of Tourism and Recreation which, with the use of volunteer labor and federal job training funds, began the construction of hiking trails at state parks and recreation areas. One of the most scenic hiking trails was named the David Boren Hiking Trail in Beavers Bend State Park near Broken Bow.

After Boren's divorce in 1975, he spent a great deal of time with his children. Nellie and Lowell McDaniel were old family friends from Seminole who lived in the garage apartment at the governor's mansion and helped Boren care for his children during times of visitation. It was not uncommon to see the governor, Carrie, and Dan on Sunday afternoons riding a special-built, three-person bicycle around the State Capitol Complex.

In 1976, Boren was introduced by his Chief of Staff, Bob Morgan, to Molly Wanda Shi, a special judge in Pontotoc County. Morgan knew Molly through her brother, A. H. Shi, a physician in Seminole County. Molly, born in Ada, Oklahoma, to Augustine Henry "Gus" Shi and Molly Wanda Shi, grew up in Stratford in Garvin County and graduated from East Central State College in Ada.[15]

After teaching English in the public schools of Byng, a small community north of Ada, Molly earned a master's degree in English from the University of Oklahoma and began law school at OU in 1971. Three years later, in 1974, she graduated from law school, passed the state bar examination, and opened a private practice in Ada next door to veteran lawyers Barney Ward and Bob Bennett.[16]

Molly was aware of Boren's candidacy of governor in 1974. She never had met him personally, but followed the campaign on television and in newspapers. She not only voted for Boren, but convinced friends such as Hope Harder that Boren was the best man for the job.

In 1976, Molly was appointed special judge and began her duties at the county courthouse in Ada. After attending the National Judicial College in Reno, Nevada, in the summer of 1976, she received a call from Morgan who said he would like to introduce her to the governor. Molly liked the idea and agreed to attend a dinner theater presentation with Boren, Morgan, and his wife, LaDean.

There were occasional dates in the fall of 1976 and spring of 1977. Both Boren and Molly were dating other people. The governor made the social news by being seen in public with news reporter Pam Henry and former Miss America Jane Jayroe. However, by the summer of 1977, Boren's relationship with Molly grew serious.[17]

The first time that the press corps saw Boren with Molly was at the National Governor's Conference held at Grand Lake, Oklahoma, in August, 1977. In October, Boren secretly planned to propose marriage to Molly after dinner with friends Dr. Ron and Lynn White following the OU-Texas football game at the Cotton Bowl in Dallas, Texas. But Molly became ill before dinner and had to excuse herself.

Within the next two weeks, Boren proposed at the governor's mansion. He had all details worked out, including a marriage date of November 27. It was decided to try to keep the event secret, although reporters began hearing rumors at the State Capitol about an impending marriage. Molly made arrangements for District Judge Ronald Jones in Ada, her former boss, to issue a marriage license after the county courthouse closed for the Thanksgiving holiday. Required blood tests were conducted by family doctors but the results were sent to the lab under assumed names. Molly's sister, Judy Connally, made her wedding dress.[18]

On Sunday, the wedding day, Molly drove with her parents and her sister to the governor's mansion where only a few family members gathered. Boren was completely calm, Molly cried. Reverend Robert Cocke, pastor of First Methodist Church in Seminole, performed the wedding ceremony. The bride and groom exchanged plain, gold bands.

Later that afternoon, Jim Mills, a friend from McAlester, flew the newlyweds in his private plane to Dallas where they boarded a commercial flight for a honeymoon at the Fairmont Towers in San Francisco, California. Only after the couple was airborne did gubernatorial press secretary Rob Pryon issue a press release containing details of the marriage.

On their way home from their honeymoon, the Borens stopped at a meeting of the Interstate Oil and Gas Compact Commission in Santa Fe, New Mexico. Jim Young, a reporter for *The Daily Oklahoman,* caught up with them in Santa Fe and dispatched a romantic story back to the state. Young wrote:

> Governor David Boren, who has had great success with wooing the voters, had the campaign of his life in convincing Molly Shi of Ada to become his wife.

"I had a hard time getting her to leave Ada," the governor said. Boren makes no secret of the fact that he decided on marriage and then spent several weeks convincing the Pontotoc County special judge to become Oklahoma's first lady. Mrs. Boren, the dark-haired, brown-eyed bride with an infectious smile, said she and the governor talked around the subject until three or four weeks before they decided to wed.[19]

We will revive the Boren Broom Brigade.
The broom hasn't done any harm in the
State Capitol and there are even more cobwebs
in Washington that need to be swept out.

DAVID L. BOREN

NINETEEN

A Crossroads

AT THE END OF 1977, Boren considered his future—he had three paths from which to choose. First, he could retire from public life, practice law, and perhaps teach. Second, he could seek a second term as governor of Oklahoma. And third, he could run for the United States Senate seat occupied by Republican Dewey Bartlett.

The first option was the path least likely to be taken, and it quickly fell from serious consideration because Boren still had a strong desire to serve the people of Oklahoma. There were positives about running for reelection. His popularity among voters was high, he had successfully passed most of his reform proposals, and there had been no major scandals in his administration. If reelected, he would be the first governor to succeed himself in office. It was not until 1970 that succession was constitutionally permissible. Two governors, Dewey Bartlett and David Hall, had the opportunity to be elected to a second term, but both failed.

On the negative side of running for reelection was the opinion of some that Boren would in a second term lose some of his luster as a "reform governor," and that he would give up an excellent chance of becoming a United States Senator. One advisor said, "If you had a meeting of all the living governors of all the states in the land, you would have to hold it in a football stadium. But, if you held a meeting of all senior United States Senators, you could have the meeting in a small conference room."[1] It was anticipated that, if elected to the Senate, Boren would serve long enough to become Oklahoma's senior United States Senator.

On the positive side of running for the Senate were Boren's strong and abiding interest in national issues, the six-year term of office, and the fact that United States Senators were not term-limited. Boren's father's service in Congress had an impact upon his decision early in life to serve in the federal government. Since he was a child, Boren wanted to follow in his father's footsteps. While a student at Oxford, Boren wrote in his diary that someday he wanted to be, among other things, a United States Senator from Oklahoma.

In addition, there was the possibility, even the likelihood that Bartlett, who had been battling lung cancer for a year, would not run for reelection. Boren considered Bartlett a personal friend, had a good working relationship with him, and did not cherish the idea of running against him. In fact, Boren so admired Bartlett's integrity, he told his closest advisors that he would not run against Bartlett. Bartlett had told Boren that if he decided not to run again, Boren would be the first to know.

As with seeking a second term as governor, running for the Senate also was not encouraging if one looked at Oklahoma history. In fact, no Oklahoma governor had ever been elected to the United States Senate while serving as governor. J. Howard Edmondson had gone to the Senate after the death of Robert S. Kerr in 1963 but was defeated in his bid for a full term the following year. Governor E.W. Marland ran for the Senate midway in his term in 1936 and lost decisively in the Democratic runoff. Marland was defeated again in 1938 when he ran for the Senate. Two other governors, Lee Cruce and Raymond Gary also lost races for the United States

Senate. Only three Oklahoma governors had been elected to the Senate after leaving office—Robert S. Kerr, Henry Bellmon, and Bartlett.

Veteran political reporter Ed Montgomery accurately assessed the situation in a December, 1977, story about Oklahoma politics. He said the office Boren would seek was the "most asked political question of the year."[2]

Lieutenant Governor George Nigh and Attorney General Larry Derryberry, potential candidates for governor, were particularly interested in Boren's decision which was complicated by Bartlett's illness. Boren had decided that he would never run against Bartlett because of their friendship, and under no circumstances could he announce his intentions before a public announcement was made by Bartlett.[3]

In mid-January, 1978, Boren's campaign structure was in place. However, it still had not been decided which office he would seek. Jack Pratt, the owner of the printing company that was ready to print blue and white bumper stickers, had the type set, except for the office Boren was running for. It was fortunate that the words "governor" and "US Senate" occupied the same number of spaces on the typeset machine in Pratt's office. He informed campaign officials that he could make the final wording and print bumper stickers with a 24-hour notice.

On January 14, 1978, Bartlett met with his family and top aides at his home in Tulsa. There was a frank discussion and many people present at the meeting urged him to run. However, at the end of the meeting, Bartlett decided that he could not stay in the Senate, run a vigorous campaign, and try to fight his battle against cancer. That night, Bartlett called Boren and told him he would not run for reelection. A public announcement was made the following day. Bartlett lost his battle with the dreaded disease after completing his term in office. He died on March 1, 1979.[4]

Within a few days of Bartlett's announcement, Boren told a Saturday morning news conference at his campaign headquarters in Oklahoma City that he would be a candidate for the Democratic nomination for the United States Senate. In his announcement, Boren said, "The job of a U.S. Senator belongs to the people, and I am applying for that job." He pledged a grassroots campaign reaching into every part of the state. Listed as primary issues of the campaign were agriculture, energy, and unnecessary and unwise federal regulations.[5]

When Boren announced, *The Daily Oklahoman* called it "the least surprising political statement of the month," and opined that Boren was "certain to face some strong rivals in the Senate race."[6] Boren recognized that his years as governor had challenged the leadership of several entrenched Democrats who surely would try to retaliate.

At first, major Democratic candidates did not throw their hats into the ring. The most likely early opponent was Robert Hefner, III, a prominent oil man and member of a highly-respected Oklahoma legal and business family. Hefner commissioned a poll and concluded that while Boren was the man to beat, "he's beatable."[7] Other possible candidates were Representative Glenn Floyd of Norman, former State Senator Bryce Baggett of Oklahoma City, and former Attorney General Charles Nesbitt. Floyd, Boren's classmate in law school, had often sparred with the governor during the first three years of Boren's service as governor, although they remained personal friends at the time and to this day. Baggett had previously run unsuccessfully for governor, and Nesbitt had failed to be elected in campaigns for governor and the United States Senate.

Boren opened a relatively small campaign office staffed by his personal assistant, Ann Dubler; gubernatorial administrative assistant David Berrong; and Bob Burke, director of the Department of Economic and Community Affairs. By April, two months after Boren entered the race, 1,000 individuals from 72 counties had contributed $217,400.

Burke, the statewide campaign coordinator, told reporter Ed Montgomery, who was visiting the campaign headquarters at 4921 North Lincoln, that it had taken Boren 15 months to raise the same amount of money four years before. As before, Boren accepted only contributions from individuals and returned checks from political action committees. Boren wanted to answer only to the people.[8]

As the campaign workers began raising money, distributing campaign materials, and revitalizing the network of supporters in each of the state's 77 counties, Boren had to spend most of his time dealing with his full-time job as governor.

In his last state-of-the-state address to the Oklahoma legislature, Boren called for a solution to Oklahoma's long-range water problems as the most significant issue of the day. He noted that many cities and towns were forced to ration water each year. It was not that Oklahoma lacked sufficient water—the water delivery system was inadequate. Boren's program was to create the Oklahoma Water Development Authority (OWDA) to offer a system of grants and loans financed by legislative appropriations and sale of revenue bonds. The money would be used to help local governments improve water delivery systems.

Creating a comprehensive state water plan had been a political football for decades. While western Oklahoma needed water, eastern Oklahomans were protective of their excess water. For more than 30 years, legislative attempts to even talk about eastern Oklahoma sharing its bountiful supply of water had been shot down.[9]

Boren's plan to create the OWDA was supported by Robert S. Kerr, Jr., president of Oklahoma Water Incorporated (OWI), the

leading water resources development advocacy group in the state.
Kerr admired Boren's leadership in water resources. Boren was the
first governor since Kerr's father, Robert S. Kerr, Sr., to truly sponsor water development legislation. Boren's plan was filed as Senate
Bill 625, principally authored by Senator Wayne Holden.

Boren had a good record of trying to solve water problems in
the state. Two years before, he had met with the governors of five
other High Plains states to form the High Plains Study Council, a
conduit for $6 million in federal dollars to study what the future
held for the Ogallala formation which provides groundwater
for more than 20 percent of the nation's irrigated lands, including the parched lands of western Oklahoma and the Oklahoma
Panhandle.

Boren tried to convince the legislature of the great need of a
comprehensive water plan. He wrote House Speaker Bill Willis
and Senate President Pro Tempore Gene Howard, "Without exag-
geration, we may see the day in which a barrel of water will be as
precious as a barrel of oil…Even in eastern Oklahoma, which is
considered relatively rich in water, it is estimated that one-third of
all rural residents lack safe, dependable community water supplies.
Yet Oklahoma continues to allow vast quantities of our water to
flow into other states."[10]

Fighting an uphill battle with legislators from eastern Oklahoma,
Boren offered to compromise his plan, limiting funding for projects which would transfer water outside a particular county where
a source existed. SB 625 was passed by the State Senate, but the
House of Representatives adjourned unexpectedly to avoid considering the bill.

The idea was narrowly defeated, but all observers predicted
that Boren's boldness in pushing for a comprehensive water plan
broke new ground in the arena. OWI Executive Vice President Ron
Cupp said, "The bill was devoured by that old green-eyed politi-

cal dragon which thrives on conflict between eastern and western Oklahoma, a dragon which must be slain forever if Oklahoma is to develop her water resources for the future."[11]

The failure of the legislature to approve Boren's water plan drew the ire of the editorial writers of *The Daily Oklahoman:*

> Further delays in implementing a comprehensive water plan imperil Oklahoma's future economic growth and progress. Every year brings a further withdrawal of diminishing groundwater supplies in many of the more arid western and southwestern counties…Failure to adopt any plan could preclude Oklahoma from having any say about how and when and where its surplus water will be used.[12]

Boren considered the defeat of his water bill as perhaps the greatest disappointment of his reform attempts while governor. However, the seed was planted, a future legislature created a comprehensive water plan, and Boren was able to use his position as United States Senator to provide matching funds for many Oklahoma water development projects.

When the legislature adjourned, news watchers speculated about which Democrats would end up in the race against Boren for the United States Senate nomination. As the dust settled and filing time came, Hefner, Floyd, Bagget, and Nesbitt were on the sidelines, having decided not to make the race.

Until the final day of filing, minor candidates Dean Bridges, Anthony Points, and Rosella Pete Saker joined George Miskovsky, the only candidate with any degree of public recognition. Miskovsky was a former county attorney in Oklahoma County and member of the state legislature. In 1958, he had made a surprisingly strong campaign for governor, placing third in the Democratic primary, principally on the issue of repealing prohibition. However, he lost his State Senate seat in 1960 and had not held political office since.

Bridges was a Claremore Junior College dean and former mayor of Tahlequah. Saker was a retired Air Force master sergeant from Altus and Points listed his occupation as "contractor" on his filing papers.

The complexion of the race changed dramatically at the last hour when Ed Edmondson and Gene Stipe paid their filing fees and entered the contest. What appeared to be an easy Democratic primary now was destined to be a serious test of political strength. Even for a governor with high approval ratings, it would be almost impossible to garner more than 50 percent of the vote against six other candidates.

From Muskogee County, Edmondson represented Oklahoma's Second Congressional District for 20 years from 1953 to 1973. His younger brother, J. Howard Edmondson, was governor from 1959 to 1963 and served the final years of Robert S. Kerr's term in the United States Senate. Boren was surprised with Edmondson's entry into the race. The Edmondson and Boren families were old friends. Boren thought Edmondson had been talked into running by old guard Democrats who were still smarting from Boren's success in the 1974 race. Also, some Democrats were upset that Boren was "too Republican," trying to accomplish good things in government with bi-partisan cooperation.[13]

An attorney from Pittsburg County, Stipe was elected to the Oklahoma House of Representatives in 1948 and had been a member of the State Senate since 1956. Although never officially elected as President Pro Tempore of the Senate, Stipe was considered by astute political observers as the most powerful member of the State Senate.

In a sense, the Boren versus Edmondson and Stipe contest was one between "old" and "new" Democrats. The political roots of Edmondson and Stipe were deeply implanted in the New Deal-Fair Deal tradition. Both candidates looked for support from organized economic groups such as labor and agriculture and emphasized paternalistic and regulatory governmental programs depending on heavy government spending. Not surprisingly, Edmondson was endorsed by the Committee on Political Education of the AFL-CIO, while Stipe was supported by the state arm of the Fraternal Order of Police and the Oklahoma Education Association.

While a great admirer of both Franklin D. Roosevelt and Harry S. Truman, Boren thought it was time for the Democratic party to move beyond the mindset of the Great Depression. He was concerned that the national party was losing the strong support of the middle class that it had enjoyed since the early days of the New Deal. In Boren's view, it was time to reduce governmental regulation of the market place and significantly reduce the federal tax burden. He also strongly advocated deregulation of natural gas prices and endorsed the Kemp-Roth bill, a Republican congressional proposal to reduce federal income taxes by one-third over a three-year period.[14]

With the campaign heating up, Boren brought more of his campaign staff from his previous race on board. Sven Holmes returned from study at the University of Virginia law school. Von Creel, who was again a law school professor at Oklahoma City University, was campaign chairman. Press Secretary Rob Pyron, legislative assistant Dusty Martin, and administrative assistant Sam Hammons all left their state-paid jobs at key junctures to guide the Senate campaign.

It was like old times. Most of the county coordinators in the 1974 governor's race were again at the helm of their county's efforts. While some observers believed Boren's grassroots support had slipped, reaction from county supporters and contributors led Boren and his staff to believe otherwise.

Even though many of the campaign staff and county workers were the same as four years previous, there was a "different feel" in this election. In the governor's race, an initial poll showed little name recognition for Boren. Now, one reporter said, "Boren is known to just about everybody who is old enough to vote."[15]

The problem with generating support for Boren was that many of his longtime supporters believed he was a sure winner. That was a danger for the Boren campaign. Pyron said, "Our biggest job was to convince people that Boren had not already won the Senate seat and that much hard work was ahead."[16]

LEFT: Boren and his mother, Christine, in their Seminole home when he was six years old.

Two-year-old David Boren poses in front of the United States Capitol in Washington, D.C., in 1943. His father, Lyle H. Boren, was a member of Congress from Oklahoma's Fourth Congressional District.

BELOW: H.B. Mitchell was the speech teacher at Seminole High School who helped Boren develop his public speaking skills.

RIGHT: Congressman Lyle Boren was a confidant of President Franklin D. Roosevelt. On a campaign stop in Oklahoma, Roosevelt spoke to supporters from the back of a train car. Left to right, Oklahoma United States Senators Elmer Thomas and Josh Lee, President Roosevelt, Roosevelt's son, Elliott, Congressman Wilburn Cartwright, and Boren. *Courtesy Western History Collections, University of Oklahoma Libraries.*

Lyle Boren was elected to Congress in 1936, having never been to Washington, D.C. before his election. He served until January, 1947.

RIGHT: Boren played saxophone in the Seminole High School band.

ABOVE: Clifford C. McKown, Boren's maternal grandfather, held one of the earliest pharmacy licenses in the state and operated a pharmacy in Maud, Oklahoma. He later in life became the community's postmaster.

BELOW: Alice Villines McKown, Boren's maternal grandmother, was of Cherokee and French ancestry. She was the daughter of one of the two founders of Maud.

RIGHT: Margaret Casey, David's high school English teacher, instilled in him the importance of writing. As president of OU, David used principles learned during Mrs. Casey's tutelage to revolutionize OU's emphasis on teaching students to write. *Courtesy Western History Collections, University of Oklahoma Libraries.*

LEFT: Vice President John Nance Garner, center, with David Boren's grandparents, Mark Latimer and Nannie Mae Boren. *Courtesy Western History Collections, University of Oklahoma Libraries.*

LOWER LEFT: After launching a successful career as a public servant, Boren returned to visit his first grade teacher, Mrs. Ruth Robinson. *Courtesy Western History Collections, University of Oklahoma Libraries.*

ABOVE: Boren, fourth from top, was a member of the rowing team at Oxford University during his time in England as a Rhodes Scholar. *Courtesy Western History Collections, University of Oklahoma Libraries.*

RIGHT: Boren as a Rhodes Scholar at Oxford University in England. He is second from the left on the third row. Over his right shoulder is Allan Taylor, who later became director of the intelligence agency for the Australian government.

RIGHT: As a professor, David Boren taught a political science class at Oklahoma Baptist University in 1971. *Courtesy Oklahoma Baptist University.*

LEFT: While at student at Yale, Boren took every opportunity to visit with longtime family friend, House Majority Leader Carl Albert. Boren was intrigued with Albert's personal stories of life in the Nation's capital. This photograph was taken when Boren was governor and Albert was Speaker of the United States House of Representatives. *Courtesy Carl Albert Center Congressional Archives, University of Oklahoma.*

UPPER LEFT: Boren making a point at an Oklahoma City Chamber of Commerce luncheon during the 1974 gubernatorial campaign while his Republican foe, James Inhofe, looks on. *Courtesy Oklahoma Publishing Company.*

ABOVE: Boren addresses interested citizens outside Democratic Party headquarters in Stigler, Oklahoma. *Courtesy Oklahoma Publishing Company.*

LEFT: Boren never missed an opportunity to stop at local stores in even the smallest of communities. In Whitefield, he took time to drink an orange drink and talk to, left to right, Lori Simon, Louis Simon, and Oscar Flood. *Courtesy Oklahoma Publishing Company.*

BOREN
FOR
GOVERNOR

David Boren
DEMOCRAT
FOR GOVERNOR

FAR LEFT: With a broom hanging on the wall behind him, Boren addresses supporters at the Skirvin Hotel in Oklahoma City after winning the race for governor in November, 1974. *Courtesy Oklahoma Publishing Company.*

LEFT: Carrie Boren with her broom, publicizing the fact that her father intended to sweep out the Old Guard of Oklahoma politics if elected governor of Oklahoma. *Courtesy Western History Collections, University of Oklahoma Libraries.*

BELOW: Students at OU were armed with brooms as they listened to Boren during a campaign stop. The Boren Broom Brigade generated excitement among many first-time voters who supported Boren in his race for governor in 1974. *Courtesy Western History Collections, University of Oklahoma Libraries.*

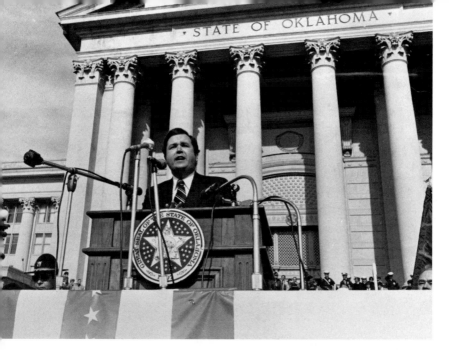

ABOVE: Boren addressing a large crowd gathered on the south steps of the State Capitol during his inauguration as governor of Oklahoma in January, 1975. *Courtesy Western History Collections, University of Oklahoma Libraries.*

RIGHT: Boren eats a hot dog during a University of Oklahoma football game in September, 1975. Saying that "we are not part of a caste system," he gave up his seat in the VIP Lounge at Memorial Stadium for a bleacher seat. *Courtesy Oklahoma Publishing Company.*

LEFT: Left to right, United States Senator Henry Bellmon, Governor Boren, and United States Senator Dewey Bartlett were selected in 1977 as Brotherhood Honorees by the Oklahoma City Chapter of the National Conference of Christians and Jews. *Courtesy Oklahoma Publishing Company.*

RIGHT: Boren met with President Gerald Ford to discuss energy policy. Boren Ford's operatives did not understand the problems facing independent oil and ducers in Oklahoma and surrounding states. *Courtesy Western History Collections, ty of Oklahoma Libraries.*

LEFT: Boren, left, was the first governor in the nation to announce his support for Jimmy Carter for the Democratic nomination for president in 1976. *Courtesy Oklahoma Publishing Company.*

RIGHT: Governor Boren signs the final 78 bills passed in the closing hours of the 1976 legislative session. *Courtesy Oklahoma Publishing Company.*

BELOW: The Oklahoma Department of Tourism and Recreation named a hiking trail for Boren at Beavers Bend State Park near Broken Bow. Left to right, Jon Burke, Nathan Burke, Cody Burke, and Courtney Bolt. *Courtesy Melissa Wilson.*

BELOW:
Governor Boren hosts former Vice President Hubert Humphrey on a trip to Oklahoma City in 1977. It was Humphrey's last trip to Oklahoma before his death in 1978. *Courtesy Oklahoma Publishing Company.*

BELOW: David and Molly were married in a private ceremony at the Oklahoma governor's mansion. The marriage was a closely held secret among the couple's closest family and friends. However, reporters had been speculating for weeks that the event was about to happen. *Courtesy Western History Collections, University of Oklahoma Libraries.*

LEFT: Molly and David on their honeymoon in Santa Fe, New Mexico, in December, 1977. They were privately married at the governor's mansion in Oklahoma City a few days before. *Courtesy Oklahoma Publishing Company.*

ABOVE: The First Couple reading the morning newspaper after breakfast in the sun room of the governor's mansion in June, 1978. *Courtesy Oklahoma Publishing* Company.

LEFT: When Molly and David rode bicycles from the governor's mansion driveway into the surrounding neighborhoods, they were accompanied by Oklahoma Highway Patrol troopers. Molly's bicycle was equipped with a book rack, used during law school. The governor's bicycle had a child carrier for when children, Carrie and Dan, visited. *Courtesy Oklahoma Publishing* Company.

ABOVE: Carrie and Dan Boren with their grandparents, Lyle Boren and Christine Boren. Congressman Boren died a decade before his grandson, Dan, was elected to Congress to represent some of the same area of Oklahoma which he represented. *Courtesy Western History Collections, University of Oklahoma Libraries.*

LEFT: A youthful Boren Broom Brigade follows Boren in a march through a shopping center in Moore. Boren is holding son, Dan, while daughter, Carrie, hoists a smaller version of the Boren broom. *Courtesy Oklahoma Publishing Company.*

ABOVE: Vice President George H.W. Bush swears Boren in as the newest member of the United States Senate in January, 1979. *Courtesy Western History Collections, University of Oklahoma Libraries.*

LEFT: Boren talks to reporters during a campaign stop in Tulsa during the 1978 United States Senate race. *Courtesy Oklahoma Publishing Company.*

ABOVE: President Ronald Reagan announces bipartisan support for legislation in a ceremony in the Rose Garden of the White House. Left to right, Senator Robert Dole, Senator Howard Baker, Congressman Barbour Conable, Senator Boren, President Reagan, Senator Harry F. Byrd, Jr., Senator Lloyd Bentsen, and Congressman Kent Hance. *Courtesy Western History Collections, University of Oklahoma Libraries.*

RIGHT: Boren with President Anwar Sadat of Egypt. Boren and other United States Senators visited with Sadat in Egypt shortly before he was assassinated. *Courtesy Western History Collections, University of Oklahoma Libraries.*

ABOVE: Boren attends a high-level national security meeting with President Ronald Reagan and members of his inner staff in the Oval Office at the White House. Left to right, General Colin Powell, Senator William Cohen, President Reagan, Boren, Secretary of Defense Casper Weinberger, and CIA Director William Webster. *Courtesy Western History Collections, University of Oklahoma Libraries.*

ABOVE: Senator Boren, left, and Republican Senator Barry Goldwater of Arizona worked in a bipartisan fashion to create legislation to reform campaign financing.

ABOVE: Boren and President George H.W. Bush had much in common. They were both members of the Skull and Bones Club at Yale and shared many political views. *Courtesy Western History Collections, University of Oklahoma Libraries.*

LEFT: In May, 1986, the Senate Finance Committee debated the removal of a tax allowance for the oil and gas industry. By a one vote margin, largely brokered by Boren with table pounding and heated debate in a backroom before the public meeting, the committee voted to preserve the allowance. *Courtesy United States Senate Historical Office.*

ABOVE: The Borens visit the Bushes at the White House. Left to right, Molly Boren, President George H.W. Bush, First Lady Barbara Bush, and Senator Boren. *Courtesy Western History Collections, University of Oklahoma Libraries.*

RIGHT: Molly Boren accompanied her husband on an official trip to Prague, Czechoslovakia. She was more than an enthusiastic campaigner during Boren's years in the United States Senate. She was perhaps his most influential policy adviser. A veracious reader, Molly constantly briefs her husband on new books and ideas. *Courtesy Western History Collections, University of Oklahoma Libraries.*

BELOW: Senator Boren speaks at a New York City dinner celebrating the 100th anniversary of the Indian National Congress political party. Seated at his left is Indian Prime Minister Rajiv Gandhi. It was Gandhi's last trip to the United States before he was assassinated by a suicide bomber during the political campaign in India in 1991.

RIGHT: Boren and four other United States Senators visited the Soviet Union in 1991 to investigate the political and economic climate of the country. Left to right, James Exon of Nebraska, Howell Heflin of Alabama, John Chafee of Rhode Island, Orrin Hatch of Utah, and Boren. *Courtesy Carl Albert Center Congressional Archives, University of Oklahoma.*

ABOVE: Senator Boren meets with Israeli Prime Minister Itzahak Rabin in Tel Aviv. Boren was with a group of United States Senators in high-level talks with the Israeli government.

BELOW: One of Boren's proudest achievements is the establishment of the Oklahoma Foundation for Excellence, an organization that annually awards Oklahoma's brightest students and most gifted and dedicated teachers. *Courtesy Oklahoma Foundation for Excellence.*

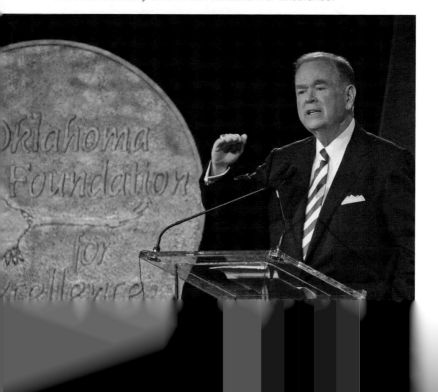

ABOVE: Boren announces his plans to become president of the University of Oklahoma in April, 1994. Left to right, Molly Boren, Senator Boren, outgoing president Richard Van Horn, and OU Regents Chairman E. Murray Gullett. *Courtesy Oklahoma Publishing Company.*

ABOVE: Boren speaks at the White House in 1993. Listening intently, left to right, are President Bill Clinton, Secretary of State James Baker, Secretary of Defense William Cohen, and Vice President Al Gore. *Courtesy Western History Collections, University of Oklahoma Libraries.*

BELOW: Senator Boren, left, and publisher Edward L. Gaylord, right, visit with former President George H.W. Bush in October, 1993, at the dedication of a new $30 million expansion project at the National Cowboy Hall of Fame, now the National Cowboy and Western Heritage Museum, in Oklahoma City. *Courtesy Oklahoma Publishing Company.*

BELOW: President David Boren and First Lady Molly Boren in 1996 at the front door of Boyd House, the renovated president's home at the University of Oklahoma. *Courtesy University of Oklahoma.*

ABOVE: President Boren, left, with his mentor, Dr. George L. Cross, center, and former OU President Dr. Paul Sharp. *Courtesy Western History Collections, University of Oklahoma Libraries.*

Boren addresses the rain-soaked crowd at his 1995 inauguration on the south oval of the OU campus in Norman. Friends and associates from all over the Nation attended the event. *Courtesy Western History Collections, University of Oklahoma Libraries.*

LEFT: At Boren's 1995 inauguration as president of OU were, left to right, his aunt, Mae Boren Axton, daughter, Carrie, son, Dan, and wife, Molly. *Courtesy Western History Collections, University of Oklahoma Libraries.*

ABOVE: In 1998, *Oklahoma Today* Magazine named Boren "Man of the Year." Boren accepted the award from Joan Henderson, left, and executive editor Louisa McCune, right. *Courtesy Western History Collections, University of Oklahoma Libraries.*

TOP: President Boren with his sister, Susan Dorman, left, and his mother, Christine Boren, right. Susan retired after decades of service at the Library of Congress. *Courtesy Western History Collections, University of Oklahoma Libraries.*

ABOVE: Former British Prime Minister Margaret Thatcher, left, was a guest at OU's second annual Foreign Policy Conference in February, 1999. *Courtesy Western History Collections, University of Oklahoma Libraries.*

BELOW: President Boren, left, and General Colin Powell at OU's Big Event in 2000. Boren and Powell worked together during the administration of President George H.W. Bush. *Courtesy Western History Collections, University of Oklahoma Libraries.*

ABOVE: President Boren driving a tractor during a cookout for OU Cousins, an innovative program to link international students with new friends at OU. *Courtesy Western History Collections, University of Oklahoma Libraries.*

Bishop Desmond Tutu, right, receives an honorary degree in humane letters from President Boren in 2000. Tutu was honored for his contributions to world humanitarianism. *Courtesy Western History Collections, University of Oklahoma Libraries.*

LEFT: President Boren congratulates Jack Valenti on receiving an honorary doctorate from the University of Oklahoma. The Borens and Valentis were good friends when David and Molly lived in Virginia. *Courtesy Western History Collections, University of Oklahoma Libraries.*

ABOVE: One of Boren's great loves is teaching his political science class at OU. It gives him a break from the rigors of the presidency and allows him to return to the classroom to fulfill his life ambition to be a teacher. *Courtesy Western History Collections, University of Oklahoma Libraries.*

INSET: Left to right, President Boren, daughter, Carrie, and wife, Molly. at Carrie's graduation from Yale University. Carrie played a role in the movie, "The Pelican Brief." After completing her education, Carrie began her career as a missioner for evangelism for the Episcopal Diocese of Dallas. Carrie believes her father is the eternal optimist. She said, "He is constantly seeking to make all things work together for the good. He sees the best in people and does not judge them. He always looks for ways to better the world around him and truly believes it can improve." *Courtesy Western History Collections, University of Oklahoma Libraries.*

ABOVE: Boren portrays Wiley Post during a presentation of the Will Rogers Follies in 1997. *Courtesy Western History Collections, University of Oklahoma Libraries.*

BELOW: Former Secretary of State Henry Kissinger, left, and President Boren at the Foreign Policy Conference on the Norman campus. *Courtesy Western History Collections, University of Oklahoma Libraries.*

RIGHT: President Boren greets President Bill Clinton at Tinker Air Force Base in Midwest City, Oklahoma. The President was visiting Oklahoma to view the destruction left by the May 3, 1999 F-5 tornado. *Courtesy Western History Collections, University of Oklahoma* Libraries.

ABOVE: Boren with Robert Gates, left, and George Tenet, right, two former directors of the Central Intelligence Agency. *Courtesy Western History Collections, University of Oklahoma Libraries.*

BELOW: President George W. Bush welcomes the OU national champion football and women's softball teams to the White House in March, 2001. To the President's left are President Boren and OU quarterback Josh Heupel. *Courtesy Western History Collections, University of Oklahoma Libraries.*

ABOVE: As OU president, Boren became a vocal supporter of OU football, even riding the Sooner Schooner during pre-game activities at a Sooner football game at the Gaylord Family Oklahoma Memorial Stadium. *Courtesy Western History Collections, University of Oklahoma Libraries.*

RIGHT: President Boren has welcomed dozens of notables to OU as commencement speakers, lecturers, and honored guests. With Boren, in the OU cap, is Tim Russert, host of NBC's "Meet the Press." *Courtesy, Western History Collections, University of Oklahoma.*

RIGHT: Congressman Dan Boren, left, and his father, President Boren. In 2004, Dan was elected to Congress from Oklahoma's Second Congressional District, representing many of the same people his grandfather represented decades before. The Borens became the first family west of the Mississippi River to serve as members of Congress in three successive generations. *Courtesy Western History Collections, University of Oklahoma Libraries.*

ABOVE: Left to right, President Boren, Dan Boren, former Soviet President Mikhail Gorbachev, Molly Boren, and Gorbachev's daughter at a Boyd House reception for the former Soviet leader who spoke to students and faculty at OU. *Courtesy Western History Collections, University of Oklahoma Libraries.*

UPPER LEFT: Much of First Lady Molly Boren's time is hosting dignitaries who visit OU. Left to right, Molly, President Boren, Mexican President Vincente Fox, and Mrs. Fox. *Courtesy Western History Collections, University of Oklahoma Libraries.*

LEFT: Former Senator and presidential contender Robert Dole, left, and President Boren at OU. Note the statue of former OU President Dr. George L. Cross between Dole and Boren. Courtesy Western History Collections, University of Oklahoma Libraries.

ABOVE: Over the years, Boren developed a strong friendship with Edward L. Gaylord, publisher of *The Daily Oklahoman.* At Gaylord's request, Boren delivered the eulogy at the publisher's funeral. During their long friendship, Boren saw how Gaylord privately, and often anonymously, helped many people. Boren said, "I only wish more Oklahomans could have known Ed Gaylord the man, not just the public personality." Courtesy Western History Collections, University of Oklahoma Libraries.

INSET: President Boren joins members of the OU band at a Sooner basketball game at Lloyd Noble Center to play "Boomer Sooner." *Courtesy Western History Collections, University of Oklahoma Libraries.*

President Boren and OU students celebrate reaching $50 million in contributions to the Campaign for Scholarships launched in April, 2005. The goal was achieved in one year. Courtesy University of Oklahoma.

ABOVE: New York City Mayor Michael Bloomberg was the OU commencement speaker in 2007. Left to right, Bloomberg, Molly Boren, and President Boren. *Courtesy Western History Collections, University of Oklahoma Libraries.*

RIGHT: Dan Boren married Andrea Heupel in a wedding ceremony in Norman in 2005. Andrea is the sister of former OU quarterback and assistant football coach Josh Heupel. *Courtesy Western History Collections, University of Oklahoma Libraries.*

LEFT: The Borens' first grandchild was Janna Lou Boren, born to Dan and Andrea Boren on October 9, 2007.

BELOW: President Boren spends much of his time speaking to community and civic groups about advances being made at OU.

TWENTY

Dirty Politics

BOREN WAS 37 YEARS OLD when he ran for the United States Senate in 1978, but he campaigned as energetically as he did four years before. He walked the main streets of cities and towns as temperatures hovered near 100 degrees in the July Oklahoma heat. He occasionally ducked into coffee shops and civic luncheons and would stop his campaign car just to shake the hand of a single highway department worker on the side of the road.

Most of the time, Boren traveled with Oklahoma Highway Patrol Lieutenant Don Rausch, chief of the governor's security detail, in a plain blue Chevrolet sedan followed by a van loaded with campaign literature and signs. Campaign aides took turns driving the van and following their boss around the state.

Everywhere Boren went in the state, his campaign signs were more numerous than those of his opponents, including the only Republican candidate, former Oklahoma State University President Robert Kamm, who won the GOP nomination without contest.

On a typical July campaign day, Boren walked the main streets of Ringold, Oleta, Rattan, Antlers, Clayton, Talihina, and Wilburton. He stopped at Snow, a Pushmataha community that had no main street, and had a "bottle of pop" with Leonard Sherrer, who had supported Boren four years before. Boren was an hour late for a luncheon in Antlers and wedged in his speech between two visits to senior citizens' centers in Rattan and Antlers. Boren told supporters, "I won't forget who pays my paycheck, where I came from, or who sent me."[1]

For a time, the primary campaign was essentially a contest between competing philosophies of government—the old guard and the Boren Broom Brigade. It was a campaign based upon issues, not personalities, even though occasional jabs were launched at Boren by his opponents.

At an American Legion convention in Oklahoma City, a convention that Boren was unable to attend, Stipe, Miskovsky, and Edmondson "chatted like school chums at a class reunion," then took potshots at Boren. Miskovsky said, "Our part-time governor, 'Porky' Boren, has snubbed the American Legion." Miskovsky said he called Boren that because he was "the greatest pork barrel politician ever." Miskovsky not only criticized Boren, but called Edmondson the "AFL-IOU" candidate because of his strong support from the AFL-CIO and other labor groups.[2]

The "politics-as-usual" campaign changed on August 10, 1978, when Miskovsky shook the political landscape with an offhanded comment in a speech to a Democratic Women's Club meeting. Miskovsky reported that another candidate for the Senate, Anthony Points, had accused Boren of being a homosexual and of frequenting homosexual bars in Oklahoma City. Miskovsky, playing the coy role of "just asking a question," said Boren ought to respond.

Miskovsky was quick to point out that he was not accusing Boren of being homosexual and that he was unaware of any evidence to support Points' claim. But, Miskovsky sent a letter to Boren asking him if he knew the definition of the terms bisexual and homosexual and whether or not he had ever been engaged in such conduct.[3]

Boren was on the campaign trail in Woodward when Miskovsky raised the homosexuality question. Boren released a statement through his press secretary, Rob Pyron, which called the accusation "utterly ridiculous and categorically untrue." The press release stated that Boren did not know Points and that if Points had repeated the unfounded and vicious lie, "he did not care to know him."

Boren then flew to Oklahoma City where he was met at Wiley Post Airport by his wife, Molly, and hundreds of supporters. Standing under the wing of the airplane, with his hand on a Bible, and his wife by his side, the governor vigorously denied any homosexual involvement.

Reaction to Miskovsky's unsubstantiated charges two weeks before the primary election was universally negative, even from opponents. Saker said a person who raised such questions was "riding a dirty trail." Edmondson called the charge "unworthy of comment." The *Tulsa World* editorialized that the comments were "a voice from the sewer." Radio station KTOK in Oklahoma City called for the names of Miskovsky and Points to be stricken from the ballot.

The *Shawnee News-Star* wrote, "These cesspool allegations have no place in the political arena. We believe George Miskovsky has no place in it any longer either." The toughest criticism of Miskovsky's underhanded tactics came in an editorial labeled "Miskovsky and Mud" in *The Daily Oklahoman:*

> George Miskovsky has sunk to a new low in Oklahoma political rhetoric—and for him that takes some doing... Were it not for the fact that American law and tradition make it virtually impossible to libel or slander a political figure, Miskovsky's words would be actionable. As it is, they are merely despicable and stupid...

Of the other candidates in the race, not even the wily State Sen. Gene Stipe, the wheeler-dealer from Little Dixie, has stooped as low as Miskovsky has…

Miskovsky should save his gutter theatrics for the next time he is defending some scoundrel in criminal court. [4]

The rumors about Boren's sexual orientation were not new. After his divorce in 1975, his political opponents had hired private investigators to check out rumors of homosexual activity. At the time, Boren told his friends, "The private investigators must have a pretty boring life, following me around with my kids."[5]

After candidate Points' unsubstantiated allegations against Boren became public, investigators began looking at Points' past, wondering how an unknown self-employed carpentry worker in south Oklahoma City could cause such a stir in the important United States Senate election. Jack Taylor, investigative reporter for *The Daily Oklahoman,* began uncovering unsavory facts about Points' shadowy past.

Taylor's investigation found that Points, whose real name was Antonio Reyes, Jr., was born in 1946 in Corpus Christi, Texas, and had used at least ten different names, five different dates of birth, and four social security numbers in the previous six years. He filed for the United States Senate and paid the hefty $1,000 filing fee even though he had testified under oath less than a year before that he could not afford a doctor or medicine after allegedly being hurt while working as a cook at a Pizza Hut restaurant. He said in sworn testimony in a workers' compensation claim that he earned money by painting house numbers on curbs and mowing lawns.[6]

Points claimed that he had changed his name to Reyes and later to Determan. All of his aliases had been variations of those three names. Officials of the United States Marine Corps revealed that Points had served four months in a naval prison for desertion after jumping ship in Hawaii on his way for active duty Marine service in Vietnam. He also was wanted for past due traffic tickets and was charged with writing bogus checks. Among his arrests were incidents involving swearing at a policeman and disorderly conduct.[7]

After obtaining a driver's license and registering to vote under various names, the mysterious man began using the Points name a few months before he filed as a candidate for the Senate. However, during the campaign, he paid for a newspaper advertisement under the name Tony Determan, and less than two weeks later voted under the name Points. In the same month, he obtained a new driver's license in the name of Anthony Reyes. Reporter Taylor said it was the first time, according to available records, that Points had used three different names in a single month.[8]

When Points rented a vehicle from an Oklahoma City car rental agency, he reserved it under the name Points, but had to change the paperwork when he arrived to pick up the car because his drivers license showed his identity as Anthony Reyes. Both state and federal authorities began investigation of whether Points had fraudulently filed for office using an assumed name. Ultimately, the investigations were dropped when Points disappeared and was never heard from again.[9]

As for Miskovsky, he had little to do with Boren in the years after the election. But a dozen years later, both men walked out of a funeral and briefly talked. Miskovsky apologized and told Boren he regretted ever bringing up the sexual orientation issue. Boren told Miskovsky he both appreciated and accepted his apology.[10]

In the three decades following the Points' allegations, Boren tried to piece together the little information known about his opponent to determine why he asked the questions about his sexual orientation. Boren was later told by Jack Taylor that telephone records obtained from Southwestern Bell Telephone Company showed Points made more than 200 telephone calls to a pay phone in New Orleans, Louisiana, during the months of the United States Senate campaign. It was strange for Points to spend so much money on telephone calls when he had no visible means of support. Observers wondered how he even paid the rent on his apartment.[11]

Some people believe that Points, or Reyes, or Determan was placed in the race for the sole reason to try to discredit Boren and cause his defeat. Points' actions were not amateurish—there was much evidence that a sophisticated plan had been hatched.

Boren believes that Points' candidacy could have been related to elements of organized crime. Two years prior to the campaign, Boren had denied the attempts of a Louisiana man to take over a bankrupt insurance company. When Boren told the Louisiana man he would not be allowed to assume control of the defunct insurance company, the man told Boren, "I will get you!"[12]

Another possible reason criminal forces wanted Boren defeated was because of his strong stance on reforming law enforcement efforts of the state government. After the Oklahoma State Bureau of Investigation was raised to new professional levels and a new agency was created to handle investigations of drugs and narcotics-law violations, Boren began receiving threatening telephone calls. On one occasion, the OSBI intercepted a man who arrived in Oklahoma City with a rifle and telescopic sight in his luggage. The man stayed at a motel on Lincoln Boulevard, near the State Capitol and governor's mansion, until he was interviewed and then disappeared.[13]

Boren's feelings were hurt by the accusations of Points, but he looked at them philosophically. He said, "Once the charges were out in the open, we had an opportunity to refute them. Time has been my champion. Never once has a single person come forward with any evidence whatsoever to support the allegations."[14]

In elections since 1978, Boren always had to answer the questions raised by Points. He said, "Even when there is no evidence to support an accusation, there is no way to prove a negative for those who want to believe something bad about you." The sleepless nights caused by the Points scheme solidified Boren's feelings that personal attacks have no place in American politics. He has always had sympathy for those being attacked and sought to campaign positively even when opponents used negative tactics.[15]

In later speeches, Boren often included references to the destructive force of intolerance in American life. He has been quick to condemn intolerance because of race, religion, gender, or sexual orientation. "Having been on the receiving end of unfair attacks, I know how it feels," he reflected. For example, when Boren later presided over the confirmation hearings of Robert Gates to be director of the Central Intelligence Agency, it was suggested that the President withdraw the nomination in favor of someone less controversial. Boren said he did not care how long it took to generate sufficient information to clear Gates. Boren would not allow Gates to be denied a fair chance for a job for which he was well qualified just because he had been the subject of personal attacks. No doubt, many of the painful lessons learned at the hands of the unknown Anthony Points made Boren a stronger, more tolerant, and more patient leader.[16]

When the furor caused by the Points' allegations waned, Boren completed the last days of his primary campaign. When Oklahomans went to the polls on August 22, there was no serious disagreement among political observers that Boren would lead the field of seven Democrats. The major question was how large the lead would be and whether Boren would win without a runoff.

From the first returns, Boren led, with Edmondson running second, and Stipe third. At times, Boren's vote total was above the magic 50 percent plus one needed to avoid a runoff. When all the votes were counted, Boren garnered nearly 46 percent of the vote, making him clearly the front runner, but throwing him into a runoff against second-place finisher Edmondson who bested Stipe by nearly 40,000 votes.

The final primary tally was 252,560 for Boren; 155,626 for Edmondson; 114,423 for Stipe; and less than one percent of the votes for the other four candidates. Interestingly, Miskovsky received less votes than Dean Bridges, the Claremore Junior College dean.

The runoff campaign against Edmondson was a gentlemanly contest. Boren and Edmondson stuck to the issues. Boren worked hard because his campaign advisors could not predict who Stipe supporters would vote for. Conventional wisdom would say that Edmondson would do better than Boren with Oklahomans who voted for Stipe in the primary. There was no guarantee that Boren would hold the wide lead he enjoyed over Edmondson in the primary. Edmondson, referring back to Boren's oath that he was not homosexual, swore on a Bible that he was not a Republican. Throughout the runoff campaign, Edmondson's major attack on Boren was that Boren was really a Republican and that Democrats should not vote for him.

As in all his campaigns, Boren continued to stress issues—energy, taxation, governmental regulation, economic growth, and steady development. However, he also called Edmondson "too liberal for Oklahoma Democrats." He hammered away at Edmondson's financial backing by organized labor and continued to link the former congressman to the national Democratic party's constituency. Boren called himself "an Oklahoma Democrat."

Boren ran television ads that showed Edmondson was receiving substantial campaign contributions from outside Oklahoma. One ad asked why the Seafarers Union of New York would contribute to an Oklahoma candidate. The ad concluded that

Oklahomans, not New Yorkers, should pick Oklahoma's United States Senator.

First Lady Molly Boren was a vigorous campaigner for her husband. Traveling with aide Barbara Webb, Molly crisscrossed the state. Because of her rural background, she enjoyed visiting with supporters in the smaller cities and towns in the state. She was greeted warmly by Oklahomans who believed in her husband's cause. She remembered, "People were so warm and wonderful. When we came to a town, they brought baked goods for me to take back to the mansion." In return, Molly gave them a recipe card that had been carefully designed for the campaign.[17]

In the closing days of the campaign, Boren and Edmondson participated in two televised statewide debates. Boren was less on the offensive in the first encounter, and the consensus among political observers was that Edmondson won the debate. In the second meeting, however, Boren took the offensive from the opening statement, and never yielded it. In an inexplicable decision, Edmondson, who had won the coin toss, chose to make his closing comments first. This gave Boren the final word, and he used it to great advantage taking Edmondson to task on matters dear to the heart of Oklahoma voters.

When Oklahomans voted on September 19, Boren easily defeated Edmondson by nearly 100,000 votes, 281,587 to 184,175. Boren received more than 60 percent of the total vote. A headline the following morning in *The Daily Oklahoman* read, "Boren Ballot Blitz Buries Edmondson."[18]

Boren carried every congressional district except the Second. Edmondson carried only 14 counties, none west of Interstate 35. Eleven of the counties, Adair, Cherokee, Craig, Delaware, McIntosh, Mayes, Muskogee, Okmulgee, Rogers, Sequoyah, and Wagoner, were in Edmondson's old congressional district. The three other counties, Haskell, Latimer, and Pittsburg, were in the

Third Congressional District and included Gene Stipe's home area. While the vote was close in Tulsa County—Boren carried it by only 4,000 votes—he carried Oklahoma County by a substantial margin of 23,000 votes.[19]

While they had been competitors in the 1978 election, Boren remained friends with Edmondson and their friendship grew closer until Edmondson's death. Boren supported Edmondson's son, Drew, in his campaigns for Oklahoma Attorney General.[20]

TWENTY ONE

Senator Boren

ITH THE RUNOFF WON, Boren turned his attention to the general election race against Republican Robert Kamm. On the surface, Republican chances of retaining the Senate seat in Oklahoma should have been good. Democratic President Jimmy Carter was less than popular in the Sooner State. Indeed, Carter had not been able to carry Oklahoma in 1976 even with Boren's help. Since that time, however, Boren had distanced himself from the national administration, particularly with regard to energy policy.

Boren's campaign clearly sought to portray him as an Oklahoma Democrat, one not comfortable with the national party's liberal wing. Boren's platform called for less federal spending, a strong military, an energy policy that would encourage exploration and development, limitations on tenure of federal judges, abolition of the federal inheritance tax between spouses, and support for the Kemp-Roth tax reduction bill.

Throughout the campaign, Boren ran as the frontrunner, paying as little attention as possible to Kamm. The former Oklahoma State University president's attempts to hold joint debates regularly were rejected. As Boren's press secretary, Rob Pyron, said, "We don't see any reason to stir up something."[1]

At one point in the campaign, Kamm accused Boren of lying about his alleged involvement in an effort to create a vice presidency for agricultural studies at OSU for Dr. James Plaxico, a well-known faculty member who happened to be a Boren supporter. Boren said he was simply responding to suggestions from agricultural leaders who were concerned about Kamm putting less emphasis on agricultural courses at OSU. Kamm went so far as to challenge Boren to take a polygraph test, a suggestion rejected by Pyron as "ridiculous."

While nothing approaching the Points-Miskovsky episode marred the general election campaign, two matters were seized upon by the Kamm campaign in an effort to snatch victory from the certain jaws of defeat.

One was a proposal made by Boren as a member of the Oklahoma Turnpike Authority to build an exit on the Turner Turnpike at Wellston. Boren and his sister, Susan, owned 160 acres within a few miles of the proposed exit. The land had been given to them by their father who had used the property for cattle ranching for years. Boren made no attempt to conceal ownership of the acreage. He even listed the property on campaign finance reports.

In supporting construction of the exit, Boren said, "Wellston should not be punished just because I own land in Lincoln County." Boren also noted he had promised an exit to Wellston residents when he ran for governor in 1974. Wellston civic leaders, in a town known for its Republican leanings, spoke out strongly in favor of Boren's actions and the need for the exit. In time, members of the Turnpike Authority unanimously approved the proposed exit.[2]

The other matter involved a vacancy on the Oklahoma Supreme Court when Justice William A. Berry announced his retirement. Under Oklahoma law, the Judicial Nominating Commission (JNC) would interview applicants and submit three names to the governor from which the successor to Justice Berry would be selected by the governor. One of the applicants was Von Creel, who served as executive assistant to Boren from 1975 to 1977.

Homer Smith, a district judge in Oklahoma County, wrote Boren suggesting that he was attempting to influence members of the JNC to include Creel's name among the three applicants sent to the governor. According to Smith, he had "heard rumors" to that effect. Republican nominee Kamm then called for an immediate investigation by the Oklahoma Bar Association. Boren characterized the action as "unprofessional" and denied any involvement in the nominating process. Creel, a highly-regarded lawyer and law professor at Oklahoma City University, was never appointed to the bench. Boren always maintained that Creel would have made a great judge.[3]

Irritating as these matters may have been, nothing slowed the momentum of the Boren campaign. Every poll before the election indicated a Boren victory of landslide proportion. And, in this election, the polls were correct. Boren won more than 65 percent of the votes cast, 493,953 to 247,857. Boren carried 74 of the state's 77 counties, losing only Beaver, Major, by 9 votes, and Payne counties. Boren's margin was approximately 23,000 votes in Tulsa County and 35,000 in Oklahoma County.

On November 8, 1978, Boren made history. He was the first Oklahoma sitting governor to win a United States Senate seat. As he prepared to move his base of action to Washington, D.C., Boren reflected on his four years as governor. He had presented more than 120 detailed legislative proposals, and more than 80 percent of them had been enacted into law. He felt good about what he had accomplished as governor.

The Daily Oklahoman summarized "The Boren Years" in an editorial:

> Boren won some battles, lost others. Equally important as his legislative batting average, however, was the integrity and openness Boren brought to the governor's office. No major scandals rocked the state government during Boren's term. Taxpayers were spared the addition of any further burden. His was an administration that was free of corruption, and

the size of his Senate election victory majority attests to the fact that he hasn't lost his ability to communicate effectively with Oklahomans.[4]

Looking back, Boren was proudest of advances made in education funding, making Oklahoma the first state in the nation to fund programs for gifted students from kindergarten through high school, opening the legislative process to public scrutiny, adding visible voting boards for members of the legislature, mandating full disclosure of campaign contributions, developing mechanisms for the preservation of natural resources, raising the pay for members of the Oklahoma Highway Patrol and Oklahoma State Bureau of Investigation, and establishing the Oklahoma Arts Institute.

In December, Boren announced he would leave the governor's office early to gain seniority in the Senate. Though his term as governor officially ended on January 8, 1979, Boren resigned one minute after midnight on January 2, thus assuring himself of a more favorable ranking in the Senate. Seniority had everything to do with office and committee assignments.

With Boren's resignation, Lieutenant Governor George Nigh, who had been elected to a full term in the general election, completed Boren's term of office. For Nigh, it was the second time he had been governor for a few days. In 1963, Nigh was governor for nine days when J. Howard Edmondson resigned and was appointed to replace the late Robert S. Kerr in the United States Senate.

When Boren and his wife visited the residential areas around the nation's capital, they were shocked at real estate prices. Nancy Whorton George, a longtime friend of Molly, helped the Borens find a perfect, new townhouse in Arlington, Virginia, close to Washington National Airport. Being close to the airport was convenient for the Borens who would split their time between their home in Arlington and Oklahoma. In 1981, they purchased a two-bedroom home in Seminole, their home in the district for the years Boren served in the Senate.[5]

It was the first time the Borens had purchased furniture. Living in the governor's mansion, they used only a few items of personal furniture. They went furniture shopping in Oklahoma City and Norman and bought everything they needed for their Virginia home. Molly was at first "a little scared" of her husband's "instant" furniture-buying technique. He would ask her, "Do you like it?" If she said, "Yes," Boren quickly replied, "We'll take it!"[6]

From their new home, it was only a ten-minute drive to the Capitol. It was a bit difficult at first because Boren had been driven around Oklahoma by state troopers for four years and the District of Columbia traffic was less than hospitable. They had to buy two cars, one for Boren and one for his wife. Boren drove a 15-year-old Chevrolet station wagon with wood side panels that were peeling.

Boren took his place in the United States Senate as his reputation preceded him. The *Congressional Quarterly* wrote, "Boren's reform impulses got him into the governorship, and his conservative stands launched him into the Senate. These two streaks in his personality will make him a man sought after by both sides to many contests."[7]

Boren was among 20 freshmen senators, the second-largest group of first-time members of the body since the beginning of popular Senate elections in 1914. He was fortunate enough to be assigned office space in the Russell Senate Office Building. Built in 1903, it was the oldest of the Senate office buildings, later named for Senator Richard Russell, Jr., of Georgia. At first, Boren was assigned space that had been occupied by Senator Bartlett. He used the desk Bartlett had used during his term and asked that he be allowed to keep the desk in his permanent office space.[8]

The United States Senate was created by the federal constitution as the upper house of the Congress. Each state is represented by two senators who serve six-year terms, three times the length of terms for members of the House of Representatives. The idea of the framers of the constitution was that the Senate would be the more deliberative body of Congress and, by their longer terms, be more insulated from changing public opinion. One third of the senators are chosen in elections every two years, thereby assuring consistent leadership.

The Senate, named after the ancient Roman Senate, has several powers enumerated in Article One of the constitution. Most treaties signed by the President must be ratified by the Senate. Ambassadors, cabinet members, and members of the federal judiciary, including the United States Supreme Court, must be confirmed by the Senate after nominated by the President. Senators were selected by state legislatures until 1913, when passage of the Seventeenth Amendment to the constitution required them to be elected by popular vote. The Vice President serves as President of the Senate and casts a vote in the event of a tie.

The Senate is a special place. President Harry Truman said his best years were spent in the Senate, and he returned there for his 80th birthday celebration. One hundred desks are arranged in a semi-circular pattern in the Senate chamber in the United States Capitol. By tradition, Democrats sit on the right and Republicans on the left, separated by a wide aisle, giving birth to senators from opposite parties being "on the other side of the aisle." Sessions are opened with prayer and are open to the public. Senate procedure is guided by rules and by a vast body of tradition.

As a United States Senator, Boren was immediately labeled a moderate. Frosty Troy wrote in the *Oklahoma Observer,* "Boren obtains the dream of every politician—almost everyone thinks he is on their side, and he is about half the time." Boren did not object to being called a moderate. He believed that his willingness to work with Democrats and Republicans would allow him to forge coalitions to accomplish his objectives.

As a freshman senator, Boren's desk on the Senate floor was in the far right in the back of the chamber. With time, he moved closer to the center aisle and toward the front as he gained seniority. It is a tradition in the Senate for senators to carve their names in the drawers of the desk at which they sit. For a time, Boren used the desk of Thomas P. Gore, one of Oklahoma's first United States Senators at statehood and grandfather of novelist Gore Vidal. Gore was the only blind person to ever serve in the Senate.[9]

At different times, Boren sat at desks previously occupied by Huey Long of Louisiana and Harry Truman of Missouri. The history of the Senate inspired Boren. "I never walked up the steps of the Capitol or into the Senate chambers," he said, "without feeling some sense of being part of something that was much larger than any individual. I was part of history and proud to be there. The Senate was an institution that had been there nearly two centuries before I arrived and would be there long after my service."[10]

As Boren settled into his new position, he reflected on how fortunate he was to carry on the family tradition of the Borens being stewards of the great values of the past and to hopefully give service that would build a better future for the nation. He relished the fact that he was able to walk the same halls as his mentors and heroes such as House Speaker Sam Rayburn. He also was able to serve in the Senate with great leaders who had been friends of his father when he served in the House of Representatives—friends such as Warren Magnuson and Henry Jackson of Washington and Jennings Randolph of West Virginia. Many of the veteran senators took Boren under their wing.[11]

Texas Senator Lloyd Bentsen and Oklahoma's other United States Senator, Henry Bellmon, also were very helpful in Boren's first months and years in the Senate. Bellmon had been a friend for a long time and "was unfailingly kind" to Boren. Another close friendship was established with Senator Sam Nunn of Georgia.

The more time Boren spent with Nunn, the more he found what similar views they had on the purpose and operation of the federal government. Nunn, a fellow conservative Democrat, was impressed with Boren from the beginning, "My first thought was this was a young man with unbounded enthusiasm and energy that he conveyed in everything he did. There was no doubt he was a leader, was positive, and was looking forward."[12]

When Boren's service began, there still existed a huge tradition of bipartisanship in the Senate. It was normal to work across party lines and "reach across the aisle" to forge legislation that would better the country and remedy a wrong. One of Boren's best Republican friends was Howard Baker of Tennessee who said, "It is the senators that play between the 40-yard lines of the chamber that determine the outcome of things here."

There was a warm circle of friends among the freshmen senators from both parties. Nancy Kassebaum of Kansas, the daughter of presidential nominee Alfred M. Landon, was the first woman elected to the Senate without being preceded in Congress by her husband. There was a broad ideological spectrum among the freshman class—Democrats like Paul Tsongas of Massachusetts and Carl Levin of Michigan; moderate Republicans like David Durenberger of Minnesota, William Cohen of Maine, and Thad Cochran of Mississippi; conservative Democrats like Boren and James Exon of Nebraska; and far-right Republicans like Roger Jepsen of Iowa and Gordon Humphrey of New Hampshire.[13]

Other new senators included former basketball star Bill Bradley of New Jersey, Howell Heflin of Alabama, Alan Simpson of Wyoming, John Warner of Virginia, and David Pryor of Arkansas. Boren knew Pryor as the governor of the neighboring state of Arkansas.

Senator Robert Byrd of West Virginia was the Majority Leader of the Senate and spent a great deal of time with Boren talking of Senate tradition. The two senators developed a strong bond of friendship that continued after Boren left the Senate. Byrd and Senator Russell Long of Louisiana were the only members of the Senate that Boren had asked to campaign for him in the 1978 election. Boren returned the favor to Byrd by hosting a successful fundraiser in Oklahoma in Byrd's difficult 1980 reelection contest.

Assisting Boren on his staff was Charles "Charlie" Ward, a veteran of congressional wars. A former newspaper publisher from Poteau, Ward had served as the top aide to House Speaker and Oklahoma Congressman Carl Albert for many years. Boren tabbed Ward as his top assistant and immediately made available decades of experience.

A familiar joke told in Washington circles demonstrated how well Ward was known. The joke told of a group of people looking at two men standing on a balcony at the White House. One man in the group of onlookers said, "Who is that man standing next to Charlie Ward?" It was an implication that Ward was better known than the President of the United States.

Other members of Boren's initial Senate staff were David Cox, Ann Dubler, Denise Bode, Jim Hopper, Rob Pyron, Dusty Martin, Bettie Hastey, Delores Jackson, Beth Garrett, Kellye Eversole, Barbara Webb, Opal Norvell, Ann Byrd, Peggy Wilhoit, Michael Fogarty, Dave Holliday, and Boston Smith.

Later Senate staffers in the Washington, D.C. office and in field offices in Oklahoma City, Tulsa, and Seminole included Brett Wesner, Ken Levitt, David Hoffman, Dan Webber, Cody Graves, Tripp Hall, Will Batson, Paul Gaines, Josh Galper, Nick Hathaway, Joe Harroz, Lucy Rooney, Bruce Robertson, Mike Morgan, Alyson Stanfield, Sean Burrage, Adair Wolfe, Jeff Rabon,Rebecca Cooper, Patti Mellow, Charles Atkins, Blythe Thomas, Phyllis Kreis, Carolyn Quinn, Elizabeth Byrd, Shreese Wilson, Greg Kubiak, Megan Hardwick, Mike Boyd, Pete Glavas, Peter Reagan, Nita Adams, Mary Tharel, and Marolyn Sauls.

Fresh from his campaign that won him the Senate seat, Boren had to immediately launch another campaign, to vie for open seats on Senate committees on which he wanted to serve. Because of the interests close to Oklahoma needs, he wanted to serve on the finance and agriculture committees, with a second choice of the Energy Committee and the Senate Armed Services Committee, because of the presence of major military installations in the state.[14]

Senators Long, Bentsen, and Byrd very much wanted Boren to serve on the Senate Finance Committee, one of the original standing committees of the Senate that had far-reaching power over everything from Social Security, Medicare, and Medicaid, to taxation, including energy taxation, international trade, and the bonded indebtedness of the United States. Major social programs such as Social Security and Medicare had been born in the Finance Committee.

Oklahoma had enjoyed the fruits of membership on the Finance Committee. Senator Robert S. Kerr became known as the uncrowned king of the Senate, largely due to his influence on spending and tax policies that came from his role as ranking member of the Finance Committee. Boren knew Oklahoma leaders wanted him on the committee because of its influence on taxes that directly affected the petroleum and agriculture industries, the top two components of Oklahoma's economy.

There were two open seats on the Finance Committee, but liberal and conservative wings of the Democratic Party battled for position. Senior senators on the Steering Committee of the Democratic caucus decided which senators were assigned to specific committees. Senator Edward Kennedy did not want an overload of conservative Democrats on the committee and supported Senator Max Baucus of Montana and Senator Bradley of New Jersey for the two open spots. Nor did Kennedy want a senator from an oil and gas producing state on the Finance Committee.[15]

It appeared for awhile that Senator Baucus would withdraw from consideration and that Boren, a conservative, and Bradley, a liberal, would be awarded the seats, leveling the conservative-liberal playing field. Senators Byrd, Long, and Bentsen thought they had worked out an informal agreement to that effect. However, Baucus stayed in the race and Boren was shut out of the Finance Committee, at least temporarily.

During a meeting with Senators Byrd, Long, and John Stennis of Mississippi, Boren was informed that he lost his bid for the seat on the Finance Committee by one vote. Senator Stennis confessed that he had voted against Boren because he wanted him on the Senate Armed Services Committee of which he was chairman. Stennis said he had known Boren since he was a teenager and wanted to serve alongside him. Boren told Stennis he would enjoy serving on the Armed Services Committee, but that Oklahomans wanted him on the Finance Committee, where he believed he could do the most for the people of his state.[16]

Stennis said he would change his vote and reconvene the Steering Committee to reconsider committee assignments. It was agreed that Boren would have a spot on the Senate Agriculture, Nutrition, and Forestry Committee and that attempts would be made to clandestinely slip Boren's name into a third slot on the Finance Committee, moving a Democratic seat from the Armed Services Committee. Without incident, Stennis changed his vote, and Boren gained membership on the powerful Finance Committee.

With positions secured on two of the most powerful committees in the United States Senate, Boren went to work. He studied the federal budget during every spare moment—he knew that if he absorbed details of the massive budget, he could rapidly build his influence with his colleagues and with the agencies which are funded by Congress.

Because reform ideas had been so successful in Oklahoma,
I set out to introduce reform to the national government,
but was met with stiff resistance from an entrenched bureaucracy.

DAVID L. BOREN

TWENTY TWO

Reform at the National Level

URING HIS FIRST YEAR in the United States Senate, Boren was given the rare opportunity of recommending four nominees for federal judgeships. The appointment of federal judges is one of the most lasting influences a senator can leave as part of his legacy. Federal district judges serve for life, absent impeachment for serious constitutional wrongdoing, and assume a position of power and authority unparalleled in our society.

The significance of a senator picking four federal judges in one year was unheard of. For example, Boren was able to choose more federal judges in his first few months in office than Senator Robert S. Kerr did in a dozen years. There also was a vacancy for an Oklahoma judge on the United States Court of Appeals for the Tenth Circuit. With that vacancy, five federal judgeships would be filled at one time.

It was traditional for the most senior United States Senator of the same political party as the President to recommend federal judges for appointment by the President. Because Oklahoma's senior senator, Henry Bellmon, was a Republican, Boren, a Democrat like President Carter, was handed the chance to fill half the federal judicial posts in Oklahoma.

A series of events had created the vacancies. Judge Joseph Morris left the federal bench in Muskogee and Judge Allen Barrow of Tulsa died. Congress added an Oklahoma slot on the Tenth Circuit Court of Appeals and gave Oklahoma two new federal judgeships.[1]

Anticipating that he would be asked to fill judicial posts, Boren appointed a 13-member advisory commission, the United States District Judge Selection Advisory Commission of Oklahoma, to screen and recommend finalists from which Boren would pick the names he would submit to the President. The commision was led by Fred Gipson and Henry Zarrow. Once Carter made the appointments, the nominees were required to go through the confirmation process in the United States Senate.

The significance and long-lasting effect of Boren's decision of who he would recommend to Carter was brought home by an editorial in *The Daily Oklahoman,* "No matter how long he may serve in the U.S. Senate, David Boren will never be confronted with a more important set of decisions than the federal judgeship selections he will make."[2]

Boren was inundated with letters of recommendations from supporters of many lawyers who made application for the vacant federal posts. Most letters were from political leaders or attorneys. However, the nomination of Lee West was trumpeted by Ellis Freeny, president of the Oklahoma Cattlemen's Association, who had grown up with West in meager circumstances in southeast Oklahoma. Freeny wrote, "I don't know anything about judges or judging. But, Lee and I for two years hunted rabbits on the halves with a borrowed dog and he ain't ever cheated me yet."[3]

At the end of the advisory commission process, Boren was presented with 13 candidates. He sent to the President the names of Thomas R. Brett, a Tulsa lawyer and former president of the Oklahoma Bar Association; West, a former chairman of the Civil

Aeronautics Board and state district judge in Ada; James Ellison, a Tulsa attorney; and Frank Seay, a former prosecutor in Seminole and longtime Boren family friend. Stephanie Seymour of Tulsa was nominated by the President for the new position on the Tenth Circuit.

Boren introduced all five judicial nominees at their confirmation hearings before the Senate Judiciary Committee. The process was largely procedural and without controversy. Senator Howell Heflin, sitting in for Judiciary Chairman Edward Kennedy, noted that it was a rare hearing in which no objections whatsoever had been filed. A few days later, all five judges were approved for service by the Judiciary Committee and the full Senate.[4]

It did not take Boren long in the nation's capitol to "tee off" on the red tape of the federal bureaucracy. When a group of citizens attempted to obtain a few hundred dollars in federal funds to winterize homes in Pryor, they were faced with filling out a 15-page form. They took one look at the mountain of paperwork and decided it was not worth the effort.

Boren cited page 5 of the grant application that required a citizen to "calculate the floor area from above in square feet and multiple the number by the floor exposure factor and then multiple that number by the district heating factor and then divide by the R factor" in order to determine how many potential heating units would be paid for. Boren blasted federal officials, writing, "The irony of all this is that the federal funds—tied up in red tape—are monies sent to Washington by the citizens of this land…including the folks at Pryor."[5]

When a Republican leader suggested Boren was trying to make a name for himself by criticizing the bureaucracy, a newspaper editorial said, "Well, if the senator could succeed in cutting out even half the bureaucratic problems foisted on Americans, he will make a name for himself all right—a name that would go down in history."[6]

Boren and Oklahoma's other senator usually voted together on many issues affecting Oklahoma. However, in April, 1979, they found themselves on opposite sides of a sensitive issue—prayer in public schools. Bellmon did not support congressional attempts to overturn previous decisions of the United States Supreme Court that banned prayer in classrooms as a violation of the constitutional separation of church and state. On the other hand, Boren voted to allow voluntary prayer. Boren said, "The Supreme Court decisions have forced public schools to be almost hostile to religion." He agreed that tax dollars should not be used to promote any one religion, but the right of voluntary prayer in school should be retained.[7]

Boren was thrown into the midst of complicated negotiations with the Soviet Union on armament control in the summer of his first term. He and five other senators, all uncommitted on whether or not to ratify the Strategic Arms Limitation Treaty II (SALT II), traveled to Moscow to meet with Soviet President Leonid Brezhnev, Foreign Minister Andrei Gromyko, Premier Alexei Kosygin, and other Soviet officials. With Boren were Senators Pryor of Arkansas, Joseph Biden of Delaware, Levin of Michigan, Bradley of New Jersey, and Richard Lugar of Indiana.[8]

SALT talks began in 1969 and were focused on the two countries controlling their stockpiles of nuclear weapons. The SALT II treaty had been negotiated by top level officials of both governments for seven years with the goal of curbing the manufacture of nuclear weapons.

Boren's objection to ratifying the treaty was based upon recent decisions by the Soviets to place 3,000 combat troops in Cuba, just 90 miles off the American coast. Boren did not want the United States to agree to limit its own production of strategic weapons unless significant improvements were made in our own defense posture. He urged President Carter to respond strongly to the Soviet action in Cuba. He also recommended that the Senate refrain from any vote to ratify SALT II until the administration worked with Soviet officials to remove what he considered dangerous provisions such as one that would prohibit the United States from deploying and flying its cruise missiles more than 600 kilometers.[9]

In September, 1979, the American Conservative Union (ACU) released its rating of members of Congress as to how they voted on traditional conservative issues. Surprisingly, Boren, a Democrat, received a higher rating than Senator Bellmon, a Republican. The ACU said Boren voted conservatively 68 percent of the time while Bellmon's conservative rating was at 60 percent.[10]

Boren spent a lot of time back home in Oklahoma, making speeches and shaking hands with the Oklahomans who had sent him to the Senate. Because Oklahomans' lives were affected so much by energy prices, Boren's stump speech often turned to America's energy policy. He decried the fact that Saudi Arabia was providing half the oil imported into the United States. Boren said, "When we bought 5 and 10 percent of our oil from them, they didn't raise prices. But when we bought 50 percent, they realized they had a seller's market."[11]

Boren consistently sparred with the president's advisors on the country's energy policy. He did not believe simple fuel conservation programs and additional gas taxes were the answer. Boren echoed opinions of his energy constituents in Oklahoma that American oil and gas producers needed to be given every incentive and as much help as possible by the federal government to increase domestic petroleum production.[12]

Energy policy was not the only area in which Boren disagreed with the Carter administration. An analysis by the *Congressional Quarterly* of Boren's voting record in his first year in the Senate found that Boren voted in favor of Carter's position only half the time. Oklahoma's Republican Senator Bellmon supported the Carter agenda six percentage points more than Boren. The same analysis found Boren voting with the Democrats only 33 percent of the time. He scored low in supporting special interest groups such as organized labor and Americans for Democratic Action, but voted with the position of the United States Chamber of Commerce on 82 percent of contested bills coming before the Senate.[13]

Boren teamed with Senator Levin to author an amendment to restrict the activities of the Federal Trade Commission (FTC) and to establish a procedure for Congress to annually review the thousands of regulatory actions in which the FTC was involved. The Levin-Boren amendment gave the Commerce Committee of either house of Congress 20 days to either approve or reject a rule promulgated by the FTC. Boren and many other members of Congress believed that the FTC had overstepped its bounds in controlling actions of American companies.[14]

Boren again found himself at odds with President Carter in the fight over passage of the windfall profits tax on oil (WPT) in March, 1980. Almost a year after Carter requested the huge tax increase on the oil industry, the Senate gave final congressional approval to the tax, the largest tax ever levied on American industry. It was in response to high fuel prices caused by the Arab oil embargo and the large potential profits to be reaped by oil companies. Carter argued that the tax on windfall profits of oil companies could recover for public purposes part of the extra $1 trillion consumers would pay for oil as price controls were lifted from domestic production.[15]

Boren called the WPT "a tragic mistake." He told the Senate, "We will have more taxes and more government instead of oil." Before the Senate gave its approval to the WPT, Boren and Kansas

Senator Robert Dole urged the Senate to hold more hearings on the effect of the tax on independent producers, royalty holders, and future American production. But, senators from non-oil-producing states outnumbered the senators from Oklahoma, Texas, Kansas, and other states that produced oil, and the windfall profits tax became law.[16]

Boren did not spend all his time on energy legislation. He was active in his membership of the Senate Agriculture Committee. When the Senate was considering farm legislation, he spent many late-night hours reading voluminous provisions of farm subsidy bills and pieces of legislation that controlled agricultural exports and sought to include farmers in labor protection laws.

While Boren spent long hours at his office, on the Senate floor, or in committee hearings, Molly carved a career of her own. "The incredibly long hours spent by the husband is a real challenge for every wife of a member of Congress," Molly said. She admittedly was unprepared for the major change in their young marriage as he began service in the Senate. She had become accustomed to being First Lady of Oklahoma, but being wife of a freshman United States Senator took no formal role. She was left to fend for herself in a strange city—but fend well she did.[17]

Molly met with Shirley Bellmon and other Senate wives each Tuesday. Mrs. Bellmon also had been First Lady of Oklahoma and knew well the rigors of life as a Senate wife. She told Molly, "You have to make your own friends, you have to make your own life much of the time, your husband will be in session until 2:00 a.m. some nights, and you may end up going alone to a social engagement."[18]

Mrs. Bellmon invited Molly to her first meeting of Senate wives. The group was made up of the wives of both Republicans and Democrats—neither were exempt from the special situation in which they were placed by their husband's service. Some of Molly's best friends were Ann Simpson, Barbara Pryor, Ann Bingaman, Pat Exon, and Shirley Bellmon. The wives had potluck dinners, taking turns hosting meals at each other's homes. They planned special trips to eat in the Senate dining room and to other cultural and social events. Often the wives accompanied their husbands to dinners at foreign embassies.[19]

Molly spent considerable time in Oklahoma, especially after she and her husband bought their home on Harber Court in Seminole. She served on the board of the First National Bank of Tulsa and was active in several cultural efforts in Oklahoma. She later served on the board of the Baltimore Orioles baseball team, owned by Eli Jacobs, a friend of the Borens.

Molly entertained often in their Arlington home. She consulted her *Southern Living Cookbook*, given to her by her mother, and made exquisite and beautiful food for dinner parties. Many times, guests were among their new circle of friends, including neighbors. They enjoyed spending time with DeVier and Shirley Pierson. DeVier was a former congressional aide to United States Senator Mike Monroney. Monroney's widow, Mary Ellen, was also a frequent guest of the Borens. Other close friends during the Senate years were Kate and Jim Lehrer. Jim anchors the "NewsHour" on public television. On other occasions, guests were unique, such as actress Elizabeth Taylor, the wife of Senator John Warner of Virginia. On some Sunday afternoons, the Borens were invited to lunch with a small group of senators and their wives at the home of Senator Harry Byrd and his wife, Gretchen.[20]

Another close friend of the Borens was Katharine Graham, the famous publisher of the *Washington Post*. "Kay," as Mrs. Graham was known to her closest friends, brought people of different opinions together at dinner parties. She would say, "Come, let us reason together." Mrs. Graham was very kind to Molly and David.

A dear friend of the Borens in Washington was Jack Valenti, president of the Motion Picture Association of America, and his wife, Mary Margaret. Valenti, a Harvard-trained Texan, had created the system to provide ratings for movies produced in the United States. Valenti, a former top aide to President Lyndon Johnson, had fascinating stories to tell when he and his wife dined with the Borens.[21]

*David Boren was able to communicate effectively
with the most liberal and conservative members of the Senate.
He could calm fears, point out common ground, and
encourage compromise as well as anyone I ever served with.*

SENATOR SAM NUNN OF GEORGIA

TWENTY THREE

Bridge Builder

T
HERE WAS A NEW PRESIDENT of the United States
for Boren to work with after the general election in 1980.
Ronald Reagan defeated President Carter and brought
with him a mandate for more conservative government
in the nation's capital. The new president certainly knew
how to charm members of Congress, even Democrats like Boren.
On Boren's 40th birthday in April, 1981, Boren received a call from
Reagan wishing him happy birthday. Reagan told Boren that at 40,
the best years of his life were ahead of him.[1]

Republicans also regained control of the Senate on the coat-
tails of the Reagan victory. The new Republican majority in the
97th Congress disrupted nearly a quarter century of Democratic
control.

The new Majority Leader was Senator Howard Baker of
Tennessee, known as the "Great Conciliator." Baker was an expert at
brokering compromises, enacting legislation, and maintaining civil-
ity in the Senate. Senator Byrd still led the Democrats as Minority
Leader. Even though the balance of power in the Senate had shifted
to the Republicans, there remained a good working relationship
between Baker and Byrd. Both trusted Boren and sometimes asked
him to sit in on leadership meetings between the two.

Baker and Byrd knew Boren had a line of communications with almost all factions of the Senate. Later, when Baker retired and was replaced by Senator Bob Dole as Majority Leader, cooperation was not as good between the leaders of the two parties. During that time, Boren often was called upon to act as a witness to their meetings and to keep a record of their agreements so that bills could be called up for consideration on the Senate floor by unanimous consent. After several months, Byrd and Dole worked much better together and Boren's role as a conciliator in meetings between the two was lessened.[2]

Boren's role as a bridge builder on legislation took on added significance with the election of Reagan. In May, 1981, Boren and Senator Sam Nunn met with moderate Democrats in the House of Representatives to build bipartisan support for Reagan's tax cut bill and help move it through the Senate Finance Committee, the full Senate, and then through the House.

Boren was one of 14 members of the unnamed caucus of "moderate-to-centrist" Senate Democrats who wielded a real balance of power. They announced their formation but noted that they were not necessarily opposed to Democratic leadership—they just wanted to give Reagan's tax cut policies fair consideration. There was an underlying goal of moving the Senate's balance of power toward the moderate end of the spectrum. Privately, Boren and other moderates hoped that their group could "reshape the Democratic Party to reflect their philosophy and to barter their votes for a voice in the administration."[3]

In addition to Boren, members of the special group included Lloyd Bentsen of Texas, Harry F. Byrd, Jr., of Virginia, Lawton Chiles of Florida, Dennis DeConcini of Arizona, James Exon of Nebraska, Howard Heflin of Alabama, Ernest Hollings of South Carolina, Bennett Johnston of Louisiana, Sam Nunn of Georgia, David Pryor of Arkansas, John Stennis of Mississippi, and Edward

Zorinsky of Nebraska. Harry Byrd actually was elected as an independent but was a member of the Senate Democratic Caucus.[4]

Boren's group not only expressed its positions on tax policy to the Reagan administration, members met regularly to discuss many areas of legislation. On one occasion in the spring of 1981, the 14 senators went as a group to the White House to express its plan to the President for crime control legislation.[5]

Reagan recognized he needed support from House and Senate Democrats to push through his tax cut plan. He asked Boren, Bentsen, Byrd, and Representative Kent Hance of Texas to stand with several Republican congressional leaders and him before television cameras on June 4 when he unveiled his compromise tax cut plan. Hance was one of 47 conservative Democrats in the House who called themselves the Conservative Democratic Forum, the counterpart of the Senate's conservative group.

After Reagan's tax cut was approved by Congress, Boren introduced Senate Bill 2219 to eliminate cumbersome tax reporting requirements in the new legislation. He told a Senate committee that small businesses would have to hire a fleet of accountants and lawyers to fill out all the forms for the federal government. Boren was successful in getting the Senate Finance Committee to modify the new reporting requirements.

Boren accompanied Majority Leader Baker on a trip to the Middle East in the summer of 1981. A highlight of the visit was time spent with Egyptian President Muhammad Anwar Sadat. The small American delegation of a half dozen senators and their wives was invited to Sadat's home at Mirages in the middle of the Nile delta. Sadat and his wife were gracious hosts.[6]

After dinner, Sadat led a captivating discussion of the complexity of the Middle East and how often Americans were prone to over simplify their perception of the region. He told the story of the turtle and the scorpion. The scorpion came up to the turtle and said, "I want to ride on your back across the Suez Canal." The turtle said, "How can I trust you not to sting me and kill me?" The scorpion replied, "If I were to sting you, I would of course fall into the water and drown." The turtle agreed to transport the scorpion who stung him half way across the canal. The turtle said, "Why did you do this? You're going to take your own life?" The scorpion answered, "Because this is the Middle East."[7]

Sadat told the Americans of the danger of trying to impose values of freedom and individual rights too quickly on an area of the world that had no fertile soil in which these values could take root. Ahead of his time, Sadat worried about radical elements of Islam taking over moderate governments in many countries in the region, including Saudi Arabia. He was concerned that millions of young people in the Middle East were being taught to hate America in order to divert their attention from international problems.[8]

Boren often said that Sadat was one of the most remarkable leaders he had ever met. He became acquainted with Sadat during his several previous trips to the United States. Boren said, "You felt his warmth and kindness when you were with him. During our last visit, he literally gave us a tour of the world and what was needed to maintain stability through a balance of power. He explained in detail how he had spent a decade trying to bring peace to the Middle East."[9]

When the American delegation prepared to leave, Sadat shook Boren's hand and said, "I am not sure I will see you again." Sadat, who had been president of Egypt since 1970, was in extreme danger because of the olive branch he had extended to Israel and because of other turmoil within his country. A few months later, on October 6, 1981, Sadat was assassinated during a parade in Cairo.[10]

After Boren had been in the Senate only a few years, he began to see a change. The team spirit that had permeated the body for decades had given way to the rule of individual senators and individual personalities. Many of the senators could recall the days when political enemies acted like gentlemen and socialized together. One photograph from earlier years showed three senators, John F. Kennedy, Mike Mansfield, and Henry Jackson, playing an informal softball game. Even though none of the three totally agreed on major issues, they enjoyed each other's company and formed genuine friendships.

Boren saw that senators were so busy, there was little time to think, to develop close personal relationships, and to work on community feeling to move the country forward. There was a serious policy implication of the new Senate where the individual was in control. If the administration and leadership had to spend more time satisfying individual members for a law to be enacted, chances increased there would be gridlock and no policy would come forth. The more that senators insisted on offering their individual points of view, the less chance that the institution could present a consensus on any issue. The use of the filibuster to stop or slow the progress of bills increased exponentially.

It seemed to many people that senators were interested in talking about issues to keep them electorally safe at home, but would not spend the time to build coalitions to actually parlay an issue into a law. Senator Baker appointed two former senators, James Pearson of Kansas and Abraham Ribicoff of Connecticut, to spend a year to look into the ways the Senate conducted business. Pearson said, "Senators are thinking like individuals and not team members. We need to find a way for these people to read and study and think and deliberate. The Senate is an absolute squirrel's cage. It's every man for himself. Every senator is a baron. He has his own principality."[11]

Boren was alarmed by the sharp decline in personal interaction between senators. One senator recalled having taken a foreign trip just so he could have time to work on a bill he was co-sponsoring with another senator. Minority Leader Byrd convinced 40 of the 46 other Democrats to spend a weekend retreat in West Virginia. "That was healthy," Boren said, "but it showed that the senators needed to set aside time in West Virginia to talk to each other." Very often, when Boren tried to meet with another senator about an important issue, that senator's response was often, "I will have someone on my staff talk to someone on your staff about this." The unfortunate result of an 18-hour-per-day schedule with senators each serving on a dozen or more committees was less personal contact.[12]

Another unfortunate consequence of the reduced personal contact in the Senate was a perceived increase in open confrontation and hostility on the Senate floor. Senators had long been known for their courtesy in public. They may have fought an issue tooth and nail behind closed doors, but they were civil in debate. Senator Dale Bumpers of Arkansas joked, "We now have pairs of senators who have to have bulletproof vests when they deal with each other"[13]

In 1984, Boren expressed his concern over increasing federal budget deficits in a newsletter sent to his constituents in Oklahoma. He said, "The runaway budget deficit is like a ticking time bomb. If we do not get tougher and defuse it, the explosion could well halt our economic recovery and plunge us back into real trouble."[14]

Boren was tired of leaders in both parties playing political games with the budget, "behaving like kids arguing on the school yard." He said it was time to stop blaming each other and "get on with the business of solving the problem." The problem was that the federal government was spending beyond its income in increasingly larger amounts. During the four years that Lyndon Johnson was president, $46 billion was added to the national debt. During the terms of Richard Nixon and Gerald Ford, another $225 billion was added. During the Carter administration, the debt rose by $194 billion. Boren's call for action came when the Reagan administration predicted a $700 billion increase in the deficit by 1985.[15]

With the government borrowing more money to stay afloat, Boren requested the General Accounting Office (GAO) study and audit the massive portfolio of loans to foreign governments. He was concerned that little information was available to the Senate on which countries were behind on their payments for past loans. When he received the information, he was appalled by the long list of countries that were in default.

During Boren's first term in the Senate, he and Molly spent about half their time in Oklahoma. When the Senate was not in session, Boren kept his campaign promise of keeping in touch with the people. In 1983, he appeared at 254 public meetings in 92 towns in 65 of the state's 77 counties. During his first years, he had personal contact, either by letter, personal visit, or telephone call, with more than 700,000 Oklahomans. His office helped another 15,000 people work out individual problems with some governmental agency.[16]

In 1984, President Reagan asked Boren to travel to El Salvador in Central America as an official observer of the presidential election. The United States feared that a strong communist element in the country would use violence and intimidation to prevent the election of moderate candidate Napoleon Duarte who had a constructive relationship with the American government. While in El Salvador, Boren began a close friendship with Ambassador Thomas Pickering who later would become Undersecretary of State. Pickering would become an important advisor to Boren on foreign policy matters.[17]

In El Salvador, Boren was sent to an area in the interior where opposition forces were armed and used guns to attempt to disrupt the elections. Boren was issued an M-1 rifle and a flak jacket. When he safely returned to Washington, he kidded the President about "sending him to the jungles to try to get rid of him."[18]

Boren was so popular in Oklahoma that he drew no serious opponents in his bid for reelection in 1984. He defeated Marshall

Luse 432,534 to 48,761 to win the Democratic nomination and captured nearly 76 percent of the general election vote. Boren polled 906,131 votes to 280,638 votes for the Republican nominee, William E. "Bill" Crozier, and 11,168 votes for Libertarian Party nominee Robert T. Murphy. Boren carried every county and all but four precincts in the state.

Remembering the importance of mentors in his own educational journey, Boren brought together of group of Oklahomans in 1985 to talk about their common goal of improving education in Oklahoma. With an annual battle in the legislature over appropriating more of the state budget to education, most agreed that private investment was necessary to help public schools achieve excellence.

The result of the meeting was the formation of the Oklahoma Foundation for Excellence. Its formation sent a strong and clear signal that Boren and the founding trustees valued great educators and outstanding students. From the beginning, the foundation has recognized and encouraged academic excellence in Oklahoma.

Part of Boren's motivation for establishing the foundation was his memory of a ceremony he attended years before to honor the state's outstanding teacher. Only 50 people attended the event at which the teacher received a $100 gift certificate. Boren was shocked that great teachers who change lives should receive such little recognition. He said, "Symbols are important because they show what we value as a people."

In establishing the Oklahoma Foundation for Excellence, Boren wanted outstanding teachers and students to receive the recognition they deserve. Each year the foundation sponsors a ceremony attended by 1,000 state leaders and is broadcast statewide by OETA, the Oklahoma Network. Four leading public school educators at the elementary, secondary, and university levels are recognized and receive a work of sculpture and a $10,000 prize. The top 100 public high school graduates, who must be in the top one percent in national test scores just to be nominated, are recognized as Academic All-Staters and receive a $2,000 prize.

The honorees are featured in special sections of state newspapers and receive attention on the same scale as All-State athletic stars. The home schools of the educators and students are allowed to fly the academic all-state flag at all school buildings. Because of the recognition, schools have begun to compete more intensely in academic acheivment.

In addition, the foundation has sponsored more than 200 local private foundations which set up endowment funds to provide grants to their schools for academic recognition programs. Oklahoma now ranks per capita first in the nation in private local foundations for public schools. Tens of millions of dollars have been received in local endowments. Thousands of community leaders have donated to these local foundations and have become much more involved in monitoring the academic standards of schools in their communities.

By 2008, the Oklahoma Foundation for Excellence had a Board of Trustees of 190 citizens from across the state who have joined together to improve the quality of education through increased public support and awareness. The foundation has had five executive directors—Betty Huckabay, Brett Wesner, Polly Nichols, Jenny Hendrick, and Emily Stratton.

Stratton said, "It was always Boren's idea to help duplicate the wonderful experience he had in his school days for other Oklahoma students." Boren is the permanent chair of the foundation and remains very active in its operation. Stratton said, "He has been able to impart his vision to others, his vision of what quality education can do for Oklahoma. He inspires us with his passion for education and his love for teachers who made a difference in his life."[19]

*The agenda of Congress was not being driven
by the importance of policy issues or changes in the world—
it was being driven by political fund raising.*

David L. Boren

TWENTY FOUR

Campaign Finance Reform

BOREN HAD SPENT HIS FIRST TERM in the Senate dealing with Oklahoma matters and firming up his base in the Sooner State. However, as he entered his second term, he believed it was his duty to turn to pressing national issues. He and his staff had a clear mandate from the huge reelection vote. He told a potential staff member, "This term will be a lot different. The emphasis will be on national issues of lasting importance."[1]

Boren believed that campaign financing laws had to be changed in order to ensure that the voice of the average citizen was heard within the halls of the United States Capitol. He strongly believed that political power should come from rank and file citizens at the grassroots. However, that noble idea had become skewed, with billions of dollars needed for incumbents to stand for reelection.

Campaign costs had raised dramatically in the 1970s and the first half of the 1980s. Fundraisers often cost $1,000 for a supporter to attend. Candidates spent more time with major donors and not with the average voters who sent them to Washington. Campaign finance reform had not even been an issue until the 1970s. President Richard Nixon signed the Federal Election Campaign Act in 1972, the most comprehensive campaign finance reform ever enacted. Part of the legislation created the Federal Election Commission (FEC) to curb what the public saw as disturbing new trends of the rich and powerful buying influence in Congress.

Since Boren entered the Senate in 1979, Congress had considered several campaign finance reform bills, but none became law. By 1985, members of the United States Congress were often receiving more campaign dollars from lobbyists and special interest groups in the nation's capital than from voters in their home state or district.

Shortly after he began his second term in the Senate, Boren began pushing legislation to limit the amount of contributions that members of Congress could receive from political action committees (PACs). There had been a rapid growth of PAC money showing up in both federal and state campaigns. For years, legislators had tried to control the maximum contribution by individuals. But Boren knew that funneling contributions through a PAC was a legal way around the maximum individual contribution limits.

Boren was concerned about PAC contributions that were detailed in an alarming memo from Boren aide Greg Kubiak. In the 1984 congressional races, PACs pumped nearly $105 million into House and Senate races, compared to $12.5 million to congressional campaigns a decade earlier. Nearly three-quarters of the PAC contributions went to incumbents. Boren said, "The massive involvement of PACs in federal elections is distorting the entire election process."[2]

Boren and his staff spent countless hours looking for the right language and the right circumstances under which the out-of-control campaign spending could be curtailed. The Senate was not known for changing its ways easily. Because incumbents were receiving the majority of PAC contributions, Boren met stiff resistance in the Senate. He knew most senators did not want to give up their fund raising advantage. Big donors wanted to carry favor with those already in Congress who were voting on taxes and other issues that affected them. Boren was also concerned about polling data that showed worsening public cynicism about politicians. More and more, the people at home felt that Congress no longer represented them. He said, "I think it's time that the Senate focuses on campaign reform. I am ready to just throw some bombshells. I don't care if I only get 15 votes."[3]

Boren's bill was co-sponsored by Senator Barry Goldwater of Arizona. Under the bill, a candidate for the House would be limited to $100,000 in PAC contributions, with another $25,000 available if the candidate had both a primary and general election. Ceilings for PAC contributions for Senate races would range from $175,000 to $750,000, depending on the size of the state. The limits on special interest donations assured that a majority of campaign contributions would come from individual contributors in the home state of the members.[4]

When Boren's legislation came to the Senate floor, it surprised many senators. Senator Gary Hart, who would run for president three years later, asked to be a co-sponsor. But as the idea gained steam, it caused concern for Senate leadership. Majority Leader Robert Dole was clearly against Boren's plan. Minority Leader Robert Byrd requested a hurry-up meeting with Democratic leadership. Byrd and others, including Senator George Mitchell and Senator Lloyd Bentsen, "felt that the amendment was putting the Democrats on the spot."[5]

Democrats wanted to maintain their image as champions of clean and good government, but they also were becoming proficient at raising PAC money and did not want to harm their party's efforts. Boren had scored a victory for campaign finance reform by getting his amendment considered, but he clearly had upset leadership. If there was any chance his idea would become law, he had to try to create public pressure to pass it.

Common Cause, a national lobbying group that for years had tried to stem the tide of PAC dollars going to congressional campaigns, stood behind Boren's effort. Fred Wertheimer, Common Cause president, said, "PACs are at the center of stopping people from changing the political system." Common Cause tentatively agreed to support the bill but wanted still further reform to limit the amount of soft money, contributions that could be used to promote issues, rather than candidates, being infused into congressional campaigns. Some observers believed that soft money was just another way to hide special interest group contributions.

In the end, Boren found too many obstacles to meaningful campaign finance reform. Many influential lobbying groups that raised PAC money in attempts to influence Congress were against the Boren-Goldwater proposal. Among the groups that vehemently and successfully fought to kill the idea were the American Medical Association and various labor unions. Unusual alliances were formed by groups that were normally at odds. However, they were united to protect the influence of their political action committees.[6]

Even though Boren was able to attract bipartisan support from senators such as Goldwater and Senator John Stennis of Mississippi, he often was pressured to drop his bill. The *Congressional Quarterly* said, "Boren has conducted a lonely crusade to force Senate action" on creating a limit on how much each Senate and House candidate may accept from all PACs in any two-year election cycle.[7]

Boren saw partisanship on the rise in his second term. As a moderate, he was able to step above his party and work with Republicans to hammer out solutions. During the farm crisis of the mid-1980s, Boren worked with Senator Rudolph "Rudy" Boschwitz of Minnesota, the ranking Republican on the Farm Credit Subcommittee, on an important piece of legislation that temporarily halted the increasing number of bankruptcies and foreclosures affecting America's farmers. The Farm Credit Act was the first major reform in that area in 40 years.

Congress passed an emergency farm relief bill, only to have it vetoed by President Reagan. Even though Boren had an excellent working relationship with the President, he believed Reagan had bad advice before he vetoed the farm bill. At the time, Reagan had sent the name of Edwin Meese, III, to the Senate to be confirmed as Attorney General of the United States. With Meese's nomination pending, Boren saw an opportunity for some political trading.[8]

Boren went to the White House to explain the devastation that the farm credit crisis was causing on America's farms. Boren also told the President that he and other farm-state senators would not support Meese's nomination unless the President would reconsider his position on the farm bill should it be approved by Congress again.

Boren and other senators staged a filibuster during debate over Meese's nomination on the Senate floor. Boren refused to allow the nomination to leave the committee until Reagan agreed to sign the farm legislation. When Reagan relented, the bill was signed into law and Meese was confirmed by the Senate as attorney general.[9]

In 1986, Boren introduced a series of proposals to help Oklahoma's economy. "Operation Bootstrap II" was unveiled at a joint meeting of the classes of Leadership Tulsa and Leadership Oklahoma City. Boren believed that much had to be done to allow Oklahoma to emerge from the economic recession into a position of leadership in the decades ahead. He said, "We have always shown that Oklahomans are not quitters when times are tough."[10]

Two thirds of the Operation Bootstrap II proposals dealt with education. Boren wanted local educational foundations to flourish to assist public schools. He proposed additional state-private funding of university professorships, the publication of comparative student test scores for every school district, and the establishment of summer institutes for gifted high school students. He also favored special programs to lower the high school dropout rate, what he called, "the tremendous waste of our state's talents."[11]

The Oklahoma Center for the Advancement of Science and Technology (OCAST) was created to help transfer technology and start new businesses and expand existing ones. OCAST also promoted the use of state university facilities for private sector research programs.[12]

Boren's plan for economic recovery also included doing more to promote the state's significant potential for tourism. He reminded others that Guthrie had more square blocks of buildings on the National Register of Historic Places than any city in the nation. He said, "With our rich Indian heritage, the beauty of the Wichita Mountains Wildlife Refuge, our many lakes, the tallgrass prairie, many significant historical sites, and museums with the greatest collections of western art found anywhere in the world, we can attract visitors from around the globe."[13]

Also in 1986, Boren broke tradition and became active in another politician's campaign. He called Robert Henry and suggested he run for governor or state attorney general. Boren said he could not officially get involved in the primary, but he could help with a "list of names" of people who could contribute money and wield influence. Henry remembered, "When he offered the help, I grabbed my yellow pad and began writing down names."[14]

Henry won the Democratic nomination for attorney general and turned his sights on the Republican nominee, Brian Griffin. Boren agreed to make speeches for Henry on tours of the state. When Vice President George Bush agreed to tape a commercial on behalf of Griffin, Boren told Henry, "Well, if Bush can run a television commercial for Griffin, I can make a commercial for you." Although Griffin was a personal friend, Boren had committed his support to Henry before Griffin entered the race, and Boren honored his commitment.[15]

"We would give David a proposed script," Henry remembered, "and he would sit somewhere and think about it for a few minutes, then appear before the cameras and speak without a script and with great knowledge and passion about the subject." Henry's media experts were startled by how quickly Boren could become familiar with a script and how well he could deliver the intended message in his own words.[16]

On the campaign trail, Henry continued to be impressed by Boren's ability to speak without a written text. "He sometimes would have scribbled notes available, but frequently tackled the toughest questions of the day with no notes," Henry said, "He could pull accurate figures out of the air to back up his position on almost any subject. Even in that political situation, he was a gifted teacher who perfectly knew how to communicate tough lessons. He sometimes had to tell people something they did not want to hear, but they listened."[17]

Back in Washington, D.C., Boren's gentle working relationships with others paid dividends during the debate in 1988 over the repeal of the windfall profits tax that had saddled oil producers since the Carter administration. Boren was the principal author of legislation to repeal the tax. With the help of Senator Bentsen of Texas and senators from other oil-producing states, the entire windfall profits tax was repealed. It was an issue that affected the majority of the nation's oil and gas producers and royalty owners.[18]

Boren had opposed the windfall profits tax on oil production from its beginnings in the Carter administration. He thought the tax was unwise and could never raise the huge amount of tax revenue its supporters had claimed. Boren was right. At its pinnacle, the windfall profits tax had disappointed its supporters in revenues raised, yet its existence had a chilling effect on domestic petroleum production. The tax had hit hard small producers in Oklahoma. Small stripper wells were being prematurely shut in. Boren said of the windfall profits tax, "It was a very wasteful legislation that caused the abandonment of thousands of wells that could have been productive in the future with enhanced recovery methods."[19]

As a member of the Senate Finance Committee, Boren introduced a bill to impose a $5-a-barrel import fee on crude oil to provide additional protection for America's oil producers. As world oil prices dropped, Boren believed that American producers needed a cushion. He also was concerned about state governments in oil-producing states whose tax coffers were receiving much less revenue from oil and gas production. "It is not just a regional problem," Boren said, "If the price of oil drops to $12 a barrel, it will cause chaos—and it won't stop in Houston or Dallas, but will extend all the way to New York!"[20]

Boren joined forces with Senator Bentsen of Texas in pushing the oil import fee, although both recognized that congressional leaders and members of the Senate from non oil-producing states would not support the idea. In addition, some major oil companies with large production in other countries opposed it. To attract broad congressional backing, Boren produced estimates from the Treasury Department that a $4-a-barrel fee would raise more than $40 billion dollars during a five-year period.[21]

As expected, senators from the Northeast argued against an oil import fee for fear that it would raise the price of oil and heating oil for their constituents. Senator Claiborne Pell of Rhode Island, along with 13 other senators, introduced a "sense of the Senate" resolution opposing any oil import fee. When House Speaker Thomas P. "Tip" O'Neill, Jr., announced his strong opposition to the import fee, Boren and his co-authors dropped their fight. Boren said, "It was a great idea that would have provided great support for America's domestic oil producers, but interests in the more populous states created a hurdle we could not get over."[22]

Boren's victories outnumbered his defeats in the Senate. He

offered and won passage of the first major cost savings reforms in federal unemployment laws in 40 years. He was a powerful spokesman for bi-partisanship in foreign policy and was one of the major leaders in getting improvements in the Intermediate-Range Nuclear Forces Treaty (INF) between the United States and the Soviet Union that made it possible to achieve ratification in the Senate. The treaty eliminated nuclear and conventional ground-launched ballistic and cruise missiles with intermediate range.

After his efforts on the treaty, Senator Sam Nunn said, "Boren puts country and state above party and is respected on both sides of the aisle. We need more David Borens in public life in the United States."[23]

Boren also was the first Oklahoma congressman ever to chair simultaneously a full Senate committee and two different sub-committees. When Democrats regained control of the Senate in the 1988 election, Boren became chairman of the Senate Select Committee on Intelligence, commonly called the Senate Intelligence Committee, and was chairman of the Farm Credit Subcommittee of the Senate Agriculture Committee and the Energy Taxation Committee of the Senate Finance Committee.

_I am giving Senator David Boren a standing ovation
for his stand on human rights in South Africa._

NELSON MANDELA

TWENTY FIVE

The World of American Intelligence

BOREN HAD BECOME A MEMBER of the Senate
Intelligence Committee when the Democrats were in the
minority in 1986. He had been summoned to Minority
Leader Byrd's office to be told he was being appointed to
the committee a few minutes before Senator Bill Bradley
was appointed. Byrd's idea was that if the Democrats regained
control of the Senate in the future, Boren would be the Democrat
with most seniority and someday could become chairman of one
of the Senate's most important committees.

The Intelligence Committee is a standing committee in
the Senate that oversees the United States intelligence community—the agencies and bureaus of the federal government
that provide information and intelligence for the executive and
legislative branches. The committee was established in 1975 by
the 94th Congress. Boren was only the fourth chairman of the
Intelligence Committee. Senator Daniel Inouye of Hawaii was the
first chairman and was followed by Senator Birch Bayh of Indiana
and Senator Barry Goldwater of Arizona. The committee always
is composed of eight members of the majority party and seven
members of the minority party.

As part of its oversight responsibilities, the Intelligence Committee annually reviews the intelligence budget submitted by the President and prepares legislation to appropriate funds for the operation of various civilian and military agencies and departments that make up the intelligence community. The committee oversees operations of the Central Intelligence Agency (CIA), the National Security Agency (NSA), and intelligence-related components of the Department of State, Department of the Treasury, Department of Energy, and the Federal Bureau of Investigation (FBI). The committee recommends to the Senate Armed Services Committee elements of appropriations for intelligence activities for the American military. These appropriations are classified and not made public.

Boren was elated with his membership on the Senate Intelligence Committee. His service for his first decade in the Senate was on committees outside the foreign policy arena which had been close to his heart since his days as a Rhodes Scholar in England. Boren knew he should make the most of his service on the committee because of a special Senate rule that allowed a senator to serve only eight years on the panel. The idea was that no senator should serve a longer term in fear of developing too cozy a relationship with the agencies of the intelligence community.[1]

Boren's rise to the chairmanship of the Senate Intelligence Committee came at a critical time in the nation's capital. In November, 1986, the Reagan administration had been shaken when it was revealed that the United States government had illegally sold arms to Iran to try to influence the release of American hostages.

In 1985, a second phase of what became known as the Iran-Contra Affair developed. The profit from the sale of arms to Iran was funneled to the Contras, a right-wing guerilla organization trying to overthrow the leftist Sandinista government of Nicaragua. The plan had been the brainchild of Lieutenant Colonel Oliver

North, a military aide to the United States National Security Council.

By the time Boren became chairman of the Intelligence Committee, the Iran-Contra controversy was in full bloom. The President at first denied American involvement with the Contras, but later had to admit that the American government was supplying money to the Contras, although he vehemently denied he knew of Colonel North's clandestine activities. The story filled newspapers and was exploited by Reagan's enemies on radio and television.

Boren was a member of a special congressional committee that looked into the federal government's role in Iran-Contra. Boren had supported Reagan in trying to help the Contras in Nicaragua in years past. However, once the Congress had approved the Boland Amendment that banned direct funding of the Contras, Boren strongly opposed any violation of such law. He saw the actions of Colonel North as a covert attempt to get around the constitution. He was concerned that a lower-ranking officer in the American military could subvert the constitution and act for the federal government in direct opposition to a law passed by Congress.[2]

At televised hearings of the Iran-Contra Committee, Boren asked tough questions of administration officials. He wanted to gain enough information to be able to prevent such illegal activities in the future. He believed Reagan did not know about North's actions, even though many Americans did not share that trust in the President. Reagan's approval rating plummeted to less than 50 percent.

Another investigation of Iran-Contra had been completed in February, 1987, by the Tower Commission, headed by former Senator John Tower of Texas. The report concluded that the actions of North and his superiors at the National Security Council were contrary to the federal constitution, federal law, and the public statements of the President. The Tower Commission report did not accuse Reagan of having foreknowledge of the passing of money to the Contras, but the report laid full blame at the feet of the President for not properly supervising his subordinates.

Boren was instrumental in convincing the President to take full blame for the breach of trust, apologize to the American people, and move on to focus on arms control. Boren truly liked Reagan and his devotion to his country. He also recognized that Reagan could overcome Iran-Contra and make a positive mark on world peace.

After promising his cooperation in a handwritten letter to Reagan in August, 1987, Boren watched Reagan speak to the nation with an apology and a plan to make the United States and the world safer. Reagan, responding to ideas put forth by Boren in his personal letter, called for a renewal of trust between the White House and Congress. After the speech, Boren told reporters he believed in Reagan and would cooperate with the President to further arms control treaty negotiations. Boren also helped draft an executive order that hopefully would prevent in the future any secret actions by low-ranking military officers in the National Security Council.[3]

Congress also passed a bill by Boren which included the most sweeping reforms of intelligence oversight since the congressional committees were first established. It required the president to provide the intelligence committees more details of secret, covert programs. Boren also set up a new unit in his committee which could oversee and audit secret CIA bank accounts around the world.

After Congress renewed authorization for aid to the Contras, Oklahoma Congressman Glenn English accompanied Boren on a fact-finding trip to Nicaragua in 1987. The trip was necessary to assess how well the Contras were doing and to determine what they needed to maintain their fight against the Sandinista government of President Daniel Ortega.

Despite Ortega being elected in an election of questionable validity in 1984, the Reagan administration maintained that Ortega was influenced by the Soviets and that the United States' best interest was to support the Contras. The President also had ordered a total embargo on United States trade with Nicaragua.

In Nicaragua, Boren observed how Ortega and his leadership were living in the same mansions and building fortunes in the same manner as President Anastasio Somoza Debayle, whom they had overthrown in 1979. Boren said, "Our intelligence reports were clear that the top officials of the government were very corrupt at the time."[4]

Boren met with leaders of the Catholic church who had openly opposed the government. Because of their opposition, Cardinal Obando y Bravo and other opposition leaders were under house arrest after Ortega suspended civil liberties in the country. The leading opposition newspaper in Nicaragua, *La Prenza,* also was censored or closed at various times. Ironically, the same newspaper had also opposed the Samoza dictatorship.

Boren found Cardinal Obando to be brave and passionate about helping the poor and oppressed people of his country. Boren also met with Violeta Chamorro, who became publisher of *La Prenza* when her husband was killed. In 1990, she was elected president of the country.[5]

As with any trip to a foreign country, Boren kept the President and Secretary of State fully informed on his trip to Nicaragua. He did not believe that members of Congress should conduct foreign policy on their own. He also always included the American ambassadors in his talks with foreign leaders. That policy ran into difficulty when Boren scheduled a visit with Nicaraguan President Ortega who had refused to see the American ambassador for two years.

When Boren arrived at the president's office, an aide to Ortega said the president would see Boren, but not the ambassador. Boren got up to leave and said, "That's fine. This is his country, but I will not see a head of state without the ambassador of my country being present." The aide asked Boren to "sit back down" and wait a moment. After 30 minutes, Ortega consented to the presence of the American ambassador and even allowed other American embassy staff, including Boren's driver, to attend the meeting.[6]

After he met with Ortega, Boren used secure communications equipment at the United States Embassy in Managua to communicate directly with CIA Director William J. Casey. Even though State Department officials would not approve of Boren's plans to visit a Contra training camp near the Nicaraguan border with Honduras, Casey arranged for CIA operatives to secretly fly Boren to an island off the coast where Contras were in training. Wearing a flak jacket and being handed an M-1 rifle, Boren and his delegation were then airlifted by helicopter into Nicaragua to a heavily-forested region where there was active fighting against government troops. It was not the first, nor last time that Boren had been issued an M-1 rifle for his own protection while on a congressional junket, often criticized by the public as trips where members of Congress took their golf clubs.[7]

As Intelligence Committee chairman, Boren led congressional delegations to many points on the globe. In 1987, he and other members of Congress toured the Philippines, Australia, and New Zealand. In the Philippines, Boren and the American delegation sought the truth about the presidential election of which there were two completely different stories. President Ferdinand Marcos claimed he won the election by 1.6 million votes. However, the National Movement for Free Elections, an accredited poll-watching organization, showed Corazon Aquino, the widow of an assassinated Filipino leader, the winner by 800,000 votes.

Amidst accusations of vote rigging from both sides, the Catholic Bishops Conference of the Philippines and the United States Senate condemned the action. While Boren and fellow congressmen were in Manila, the capital, protesters took to the streets. Boren even saw Americans who were members of the local Rotary Club demonstrating in support of the call for Marcos to leave the presidency.

In a telephone call, Boren reported personally to President Reagan, a long-time ally of President Marcos. Reagan was especially impressed that American Rotarians had joined the masses to call for Marcos' resignation. He said, "You mean even the Rotarians want Marcos gone?" After Boren's call to Reagan, the President sent word to the Philippines that the United States would no longer support the Marcos government. Reagan also suggested that Marcos leave the country.[8]

Quickly, the military defected, Aquino became president, and Marcos and his wife, Imelda, went into exile in Hawaii where Marcos died in 1989. As they were whisked from the country, President and Mrs. Marcos were housed at Clark Air Force Base in the same suite where Boren and his wife, Molly, had stayed a few days before.

Boren accompanied Senator Carl Levin of Michigan, Senator Orrin Hatch of Utah, and Senator Bill Bradley of New Jersey on a trip to visit with President Muhammad Zia-ul-Haq of Pakistan. Zia had agreed privately with American officials to help fund an anti-Soviet effort in Afghanistan. "He was a very stoic figure," Boren remembered. Zia was highly intelligent and shared with Boren and his companions his insights into balance in the region.

Zia was in a position to demand billions of dollars in aid from Western countries, including the United States. Behind the scenes, American intelligence agencies supplied huge amounts of money to assist Zia in financing the efforts of Afghan rebels.

On one occasion, Boren was able to secretly cross the border into Afghanistan near the Khyber Pass and meet with rebel soldiers at a base camp. He found a group of fierce fighters who were willing to give their lives for an Afghanistan free from Soviet control. At one such camp, Boren was asked to speak to the Afghan fighters. He said, "It was like making a political speech. With the help of an interpreter, Senator Hatch and I gave a stump speech full of encouragement."

The forays into Afghanistan were never made public.[9]

It made sense to Boren to support the anti-Soviet effort in Afghanistan, although there was an unintended consequence. Later, during the United States war against the Taliban in Afghanistan, some of the equipment paid for by American dollars in the previous decades was used against American soldiers.

When Boren returned to the United States, he reported to the President on his visits with President Zia and the Afghan rebels. He particularly remembered one story of how a $10,000 stinger missile made in America was used by Afghan fighters to destroy a $300-million Soviet weapons depot. Reagan, who desperately wanted the Soviet Union to pay dearly for its communist expansion efforts throughout the world, gleefully retold the story on several occasions. "That's cost effectiveness!" Reagan said.[10]

Boren's association with President Zia ended when Zia was killed, along with several of his top generals and the American ambassador, in a mysterious airplane crash in August, 1988. The circumstances of the crash remain unclear, but some observers believe Zia's death was a well-planned assassination by Soviet agents.

World travels enabled Boren to develop relationships with leaders of other countries. Rajiv Gandhi, the prime minister of India, and Boren developed a warm friendship while trying to better relations between the two countries. In India, Boren met many members of the Parliament, some of whom looked him up when they came to Washington.

When Prime Minister Gandhi appeared in a New York ballroom to speak to Indians to celebrate the 100th anniversary of India's Congress political party, he asked Boren to introduce him. The room was filled with 2,000 Indian men in white Nehru jackets and white hats. Unfortunately, it was Gandhi's last trip to the United States. He was assassinated by a man carrying a bomb at a political rally in India.[11]

Among world leaders with whom Boren became acquainted

was Nelson Mandela of South Africa. Boren and Senator Sam Nunn, chairman of the Senate Armed Services Committee, made a joint trip to South Africa, a country strangled by apartheid and embroiled in controversy. The Reagan administration was trying to bring pressure upon the white minority in South Africa to have free elections. In preparing for the trip, Boren relied heavily upon information from Edward Perkins, the first African American to serve as United States Ambassador to South Africa.[12]

The black majority in South Africa was not allowed to vote and the country was totally segregated. Boren, Nunn, and other congressional leaders made their opposition to the repressive regime known. They had meetings with a cross section of the South African people, many of whom were upset that Nelson Mandela was still in prison after 25 years. There were meetings with Johan Haynes, a moderate leader of the Dutch Reformed Church, who had been the first church leader to publicly proclaim that apartheid was a sin. "We met some remarkable people," Boren remembered, "I was impressed by the lack of bitterness of those who were pushing for change. They had tremendous courage and a remarkable human spirit."[13]

Boren and Nunn caused quite a stir when they attended the trial of a famous South African soccer star, Mosiuoa Lekota, nicknamed "Terror Lekota." The trial was known across the country as the Delmas Treason Trial, a prosecution of 22 anti-apartheid activists. Lekota and his fellow defendants were innocent, but their opposition to apartheid had caused local officials to charge them with terrorism. It was a fascinating experience for the senators to attend the trial before the appeals court in Pretoria. Their purpose was to let the judge know that the eyes of the world were focused upon the trial.

One of Boren's most disturbing meetings with a foreign leader came in South Africa. He, Senator Nunn, and Ambassador Perkins met with South African President P. W. Botha, a staunch supporter of apartheid and entrenched segregationist. Botha was rude to the American delegation and used the word "nigger" in front of Ambassador Perkins, an African American. Perkins sat with great dignity with no change of expression on his face. However, Boren was infuriated.[14]

After listening to an anti-American tirade for 15 minutes, Boren shook his finger at the South African president and said, "You have no right to be rude to my country and our ambassador. I at least expected you to be courteous and have good manners. Justice will come to your country. I will not sit here any longer and have you insult my country and our ambassador."[15]

Boren and Nunn decided not to repeat their impressions of President Botha to the press, especially while in South Africa, but pledged to repeat their conversation to President Bush. Before the congressional delegation could leave the country, their military aide, Colonel Bo Bloodworth, a man with a huge sense of humor, was repeatedly asked by the South African press about the senators' impression of their president. Not wanting to tell the real truth, Bloodworth said, "They thought he looked well-fed." The press picked up on the comment and embarrassing headlines read, "Senators say president well-fed." It became a code word among Mandela supporters to call Botha, "the man that the senators called well-fed." Any direct criticism would have been censored by the government and not allowed to be printed by the South African press.[16]

Throughout Mandela's imprisonment, international pressure mounted on the South African government to release him. When F. W. de Klerk became president of South Africa, the United States and other countries continued an economic boycott and called for other measures to force Mandela's release.[17]

Boren and Nunn met with Albertina Sisulu, wife of Walter Sisulu, one of Mandela's top assistants, who was in prison with him. Mrs. Sisulu was a leader in her own right. She had been particularly involved in improving educational opportunities for black students in South Africa. She had been under house arrest for many years and had been humiliated and strip-searched on many occasions. The Boren delegation met with her in a small three-room house. She had been invited by former President Carter to visit the United States to receive a humanitarian award, but had been denied a visa for travel to America.[18]

During the visit with Mrs. Sisulu, Boren told her, "Things are changing. Someday, you will have tea with my wife and me in our home in America." Mrs. Sisulu smiled, but Boren could not blame her for not believing his optimistic outlook on the future of the people of South Africa. She said, "That is a wonderful dream, but it will never come true."[19]

After George H.W. Bush became president in January, 1989, Boren argued for increased pressure and enhanced sanctions against South Africa. One of Boren's suggestions was that Bush should ask President de Klerk to allow Mrs. Sisulu to visit the United States to show a change in policy of the South African government. One of Bush's first actions was to demand that Mrs. Sisulu be granted a visa by the South African government. To everyone's surprise, the visa was granted.

Finally, Mrs. Sisulu was able to come to the United States and receive her award from the Carter Center and meet with President Bush. While in America, she had dinner at the Boren home with Senator Nunn and his wife, Colleen, and a few other guests. Boren remarked at the dinner that less than one year before, he had predicted Mrs. Sisulu would someday be able to have tea in his home in the United States. Tears of joy were shed by all present.[20]

Within time, Nelson Mandela was freed from prison and began a policy of reconciliation and negotiation, helping lead the transition to multi-racial democracy in South Africa. When President de Klerk allowed a free election, Mandela was elected president. Because of the cooperation between de Klerk and Mandela, they were jointly awarded the Nobel Peace Prize.

Boren was involved in a sensitive situation involving Mandela and de Klerk. Before Mandela became president, both he and de Klerk had been invited to the United States. President Bush was concerned that if de Klerk, whose trip had been planned first, came to Washington before Mandela, it would cause him to receive an unfriendly reception. However, Bush also did not want to offend the president of another nation by asking him not to visit the United States at the time scheduled.

Behind the scenes, Boren contacted the South African foreign minister, P. K. Botha, and explained the situation. Although the foreign minister was angry and considered the request an insult to de Klerk, the South African president's trip was delayed until after Mandela had visited Washington. No one except President Bush and his top aides ever knew about Boren's talks with the South African government.[21]

When Mandela arrived in the United States, Boren met him in New York City. Mandela, still a private citizen, was one of the world's most admired people. ABC's Ted Koppel asked Boren to appear with Mandela on the stage of a school auditorium in Harlem where ABC's "Nightline" program featured Mandela in a town hall meeting with more than 1,000 African American leaders.

During the program, Koppel asked Boren his position on economic sanctions that had brought about Mandela's release. After Boren expressed his strong support for sanctions and racial equality in South Africa, the audience gave him a standing ovation. Mandela, who knew of Boren's work with Ambassador Perkins, also stood, clapped his hands vigorously, and told Koppel, "I am giving Senator Boren a standing ovation for his stand on human rights in South Africa."[22]

In the following days, Boren and his wife, Molly, along with Senator and Mrs. Terry Sanford, hosted a special dinner for Mandela and his wife in the Senate Caucus Room. It was an opportunity for a small group of senators and congressmen to meet the Mandelas in an informal setting.

Boren and the CIA were concerned for Mandela's safety. There were reports that extremists in South Africa would try to have him assassinated when he returned home. That threat caused American officials to work overtime to provide protection. There was the additional concern that some of the internal security forces within the South African government were still tied to old white supremacists and might be involved in efforts to murder Mandela.

Even without Mandela's knowledge, Boren worked with the FBI and other agencies to blanket Mandela with protection during his American visit. Boren even gave Mandela his home telephone number. A photograph appeared in news services of the moment when Boren was handing Mandela an envelope that contained all his personal information. Boren made certain that if Mandela ever felt threatened, even from his own security forces, all he had to do was call Boren and American intelligence authorities would be activated.[23]

Later, when de Klerk visited the United States, the Borens hosted a reception for him. Many people still had a negative image of the South African leader, although Boren admired him for running for president in an election in which he knew he could not win. He ran in order to give legitimacy to Mandela's presidency.

Boren could not have successfully maneuvered through the South African situation without the help of Ambassador Perkins who literally scripted sensitive meetings with President Bush and officials of the South African government. After Boren became president of OU, he asked Perkins to head the international program center at the university.

We were on a yacht in the middle of the Congo River and I was not sure whether or not we might be thrown overboard to be fed to the alligators.

DAVID L. BOREN

TWENTY SIX

World Traveler

OREN AND SENATOR NUNN WERE DISPATCHED by President Bush in 1990 to the Republic of Zaire, now the Democratic Republic of the Congo, to deliver a stern message to President Mobutu Sese Seko. Mobutu had seized control of the country in 1965 and had served as its only president since that time. It had been rumored for years that American intelligence forces had assisted Mobutu in his rise to power.

The President's message was that if Mobutu did not stop embezzling foreign aid and resources of the Zaire government, the United States would withdraw its support from him, including personal physical protection. Bush and congressional leaders also were concerned about widespread reports of Mobutu's violation of human rights. As the Cold War came to a close, internal and external pressure mounted against Mobutu. Not only did the charges of outright stealing impact the world's view of Mobutu, a faltering economy and government corruption caused him major internal political problems.[1]

Boren and Nunn delivered their message to Mobutu on the presidential yacht which held 200 passengers. "It was an incredible scene," Boren remembered. Before Mobutu arrived, Boren and

Nunn, along with their wives, were left in a lounge on the yacht in which television screens blared photographs of the Zaire president in leopard-skin robes exhorting his people. They were intrigued by the fact that Mobutu had two wives, twins, who looked almost identical.

Boren, as chairman of the Senate Intelligence Committee, had reliable knowledge that Mobutu was skimming millions of dollars from his country's bank accounts and placing them in personal accounts in banks around the world. American intelligence operatives were doing their best to track the embezzlement.[2]

America was caught in a difficult situation. The stealing and human rights violations needed to cease, but the CIA was concerned about what would happen if Mobutu suddenly left power and was replaced by someone who could not control the stability of the impoverished country.

When Mobutu arrived, surrounded by body guards, the Borens and Nunns were ushered into a dining room where dinner was served on exquisite porcelain china with unbelievable silver service. But, oddly, in the middle of the table was a small bowl filled with plastic flowers, something that looked like it came from a five and dime store. Later when Boren reported on the meeting to the President, Bush laughed about the flowers—he too thought the plastic arrangement looked out of place when he had visited Mobutu as vice president.[3]

Boren and Nunn met alone with Mobutu with the local CIA station chief serving as interpreter. They delivered a strong message that was not well received by the dictator who became angry during the conversation and denied embezzling funds. It was a conversation that Boren will never forget. There were times when Mobutu was so mad and defensive, Boren sincerely thought he and Nunn might be thrown overboard into the Congo River.[4]

Mobutu totally ignored the message delivered by Boren and Nunn. He continued his heavy-handed rule of Zaire until his government was overthrown and he was forced to leave the country. He died of prostate cancer in 1997.

Boren also secretly met with anti-communist leaders in Angola where a disastrous civil war had raged since the end of the war for independence from Portugal in 1975. There were two warring factions in the conflict—one communistic, the other anti-communist. Both the United States and the Soviet Union considered the Angolan Civil War to be critical to the global balance of power. The Angolan rebels were reportedly financed clandestinely by the American government, with the existing government heavily influenced by the Soviets.

In Zaire, after meeting with Mobutu, Boren met with Jonas Savimbi, leader of the anti-communist UNITA. He was a military leader who fluently spoke seven languages and was becoming one of the most vocal anti-communist voices in the Third World. Boren needed to know if Savimbi was truly someone the Americans could trust. Boren thought, "Is he legitimate and acting out of principle, or is he another Mobutu trying to line his own pockets with any funds that might be made available to him?"[5]

Savimbi , who spoke perfect English although he had never lived in an English-speaking country, had made friends in Washington spanning a decade. He had been welcomed and supported by President Reagan. He also was strongly supported by the influential, conservative Heritage Foundation whose operatives often met with Savimbi in his clandestine camps in Angola.

In meetings in Angola and later in Washington, Boren, while not completely convinced of Savimbi's legitimacy, recommended to the CIA and the Senate Intelligence Committee that it was necessary for the United States to continue to assist him in fighting Marxist influences in the government. The Angolan Civil War continued until shortly after Savimbi was killed by government troops in 2002. The civil war spawned a humanitarian crisis that still haunts the country. The United Nations has estimated that more than 500,000 people were killed in the strife, four million people, one-third of Angola's population, were displaced by the 27-year civil war, and that 30 percent of Angola children would die before the age of five.

In October, 1989, Boren became embroiled in a high-level controversy with the Bush administration over a failed overthrow attempt of Panamanian strongman Manuel Noriega. Boren had long been aware of intelligence reports that Noriega was engaged in drug trafficking and other criminal activities. It was near the time when the United States would be turning the Panama Canal over to Panama and Boren was concerned that America could not afford to have a corrupt leader in power to control the important waterway.

The United States had been secretly providing pro-democracy forces, including some military officers, with support to overthrow Noriega and bring about free elections in Panama. Boren was fully aware of the Bush plan to dethrone Noriega and had pushed through support of the idea in Intelligence Committee closed-door sessions.[6]

On October 3, Boren received an urgent telephone call from George Tenet, Boren's staff director for the Intelligence Committee. Tenet, later the director of the CIA, was at the National Security Agency and was able to monitor communications from Panama that Noriega had been captured by a young military officer and another 15 to 20 soldiers. The capture had taken place at an outpost on top of a hill in Panama City.

Boren saw the capture as an excellent time for the United States to send troops that were stationed a few miles away in the Canal Zone to assist the Panamanian officers. Radio communications between military leaders in Panama indicated that they would have provided no resistance to the Americans had they sent a small group to arrest Noriega.[7]

Boren learned that the Department of Defense had no contingency plan to take advantage of such an overthrow attempt from within the Panamanian government. He later learned that Noriega was not rescued by his own military for three hours while the American government did nothing. President Bush was meeting at the White House with the president of Mexico and Secretary of Defense Dick Cheney was showing a visiting Russian general around the Gettysburg, Pennsylvania battlefield. Colin Powell had been Chairman of the Joint Chiefs of Staff for only two days and was not aware of any contingency plan to allow the military to act.

Tenet, who later would call Boren his "old boss and mentor" in his book, *At the Center of the Storm: My Years at the CIA*, was frustrated because the American intelligence community and the military did not move quickly to capture and arrest Noriega.[8] That frustration was shared by Boren.

Unfortunately, the President was never interrupted in his meeting with the Mexican president and the chance was lost. No order ever came from Washington and other military forces in Panama overtook the small band that had captured Noriega and freed him. Noriega reportedly murdered the leader of the coup with his own pistol. Many of the other officers also were brutally killed.

Boren remembered, "By swift action, we could have, without a shot being fired, accomplished our stated goal of removing Noriega." In his outrage, Boren released a statement to the press later that day that blamed the administration for "missing a chance for democracy in Panama." He said administration officials would have blood on their hands because of the lack of courage to reach out to the officers who were doing what they thought America wanted. Boren told the *Washington Post,* "It was wrong for the United States to stand by while the people of Panama tried to rid themselves of a drug dealer and thug who's taken over their country."[9] Boren's tongue-lashing over the inaction of the American government was the top story on the nightly news.

Predictably, President Bush was very unhappy with Boren's remarks. Boren had a strong record of supporting Bush and the President thought the intense criticism was not typical of Boren. Later that day, Boren flew to Chicago for a Democratic fundraiser. When he arrived at his hotel after the fundraising reception, he was approached by Secret Service agents who told him the President was trying to reach him by telephone. Boren went to his room and picked up the telephone to hear an "agitated President."[10]

Bush said, "How dare you say what you did? You know I support the freedom fighters, I would never leave anyone in a lurch like that." The President insisted that Boren be in the Oval Office at the White House the following morning at 8:00 a.m. to "iron things out." Boren said there was no way he could take a commercial flight and make the appointment. There were no more commercial flights available that night.

Bush countered, "Okay, you will be taken to an Air Force base and be brought back now!" Boren resisted, saying that it would not look good for a military airplane to transport him home from a party fundraiser. The President said, "You let me worry about that!"[11] The following morning, Boren was at the White House.

Also at the White House breakfast meeting were Vice President Dan Quayle, Joint Chiefs Chairman General Colin Powell, and Scowcroft. Conspicuously absent was Secretary of Defense Cheney who had complained loudly that congressional interference had undermined the administration's ability to handle the crisis. Similar charges had been made by Scowcroft in confronting Boren on ABC's "Issues and Answers" the previous Sunday.[12]

At the White House meeting, Scowcoft apologized to Boren for saying that he had ever blocked administration requests for assistance for Bush's goal of removing Noriega from power. In fact, Boren had supported every component of the administration plan to use the CIA and other government agencies to legally funnel money to the opposition in Panama.

Boren was not bashful about laying out the reasons for his strong feelings to the Bush administration officials.[13] Boren told the President that he would cease his criticism if he knew that the President himself had made the decision not to act. He said that he suspected that the President had never been interrupted during his meeting and told of the opportunity to arrest Noriega without any opposition. All at once, Boren felt the sofa moving. Bush's face turned red and his expression was angry.

The President suddenly changed expression, smiled at Boren, and apologized for making him fly late at night. The President said, "You have helped me on so many pieces of legislation. I am sorry I have been so harsh." Bush patted Boren on the back and ushered him from the room. Later, Boren learned that after he left the Oval Office, Bush began planning for an invasion of Panama to topple Noriega.[14]

Two hours later, a statement was released by the White House. In part, it said:

> The president has the highest respect for the judgment and integrity of…Senator Boren…and wanted to take this occasion to reaffirm the close working relationship with Senators Boren and Cohen and the Senate Select Committee on Intelligence.
>
> The president expressed his particular appreciation for Senator Boren's leadership on behalf of bipartisanship in foreign policy, and his support for necessary presidential authorities in foreign policy matters.

Boren was equally conciliatory in his remarks to reporters. He said, "Any difference the President and I have on Panama will not hinder our bipartisan cooperation on other matters." Boren was obviously truthful. Ed Kelley, Washington bureau chief for *The Daily Oklahoman,* wrote, "Apparently it's true. Boren immediately left the session to huddle with Sununu and budget director Richard Darman to discuss strategy over a reduction in the capital gains rate."[15]

Noriega's time as ruler of Panama was short. In December, 1989, the Panamanian legislature declared a state of war with the United States. After a Marine was shot and killed by Panamanian soldiers, President Bush launched an invasion of Panama. Twenty three American soldiers were killed and several hundred civilians died in the fighting. Property damage totaled several hundred million dollars. Had the Americans acted when Noriega was being held prisoner by pro-democracy officers, there would have been no casualties or cost.

Noriega fled during the attack and sought refuge in the Holy See's embassy in Panama. American troops, prevented by customs of international law and the Vienna Convention from storming the building, used psychological warfare on Noriega, playing loud music night and day. After thousands of Panamanian citizens demonstrated against the dethroned president a few days later, Noriega surrendered. He was flown to the United States and prosecuted for drug trafficking and racketeering. In 1992, he was sentenced to 40 years in prison. His sentence was later reduced to 30 years.

Later, Boren was able to quiz the general in charge of the Panamanian invasion during a closed-door meeting of the Senate Intelligence Committee. The general admitted that the Pentagon began planning a military invasion of Panama within three or four hours of Boren's meeting with the President at the White House.[16]

Boren's bipartisan approach was nothing new. During the Reagan administration, he and Senator Nunn often met privately with General Colin Powell, then the National Security Advisor, to discuss sensitive components of several treaties the United States was negotiating with other world powers, especially the Soviets. As Democrats and members of the Senate that constitutionally were required to ratify the treaties, Boren and Nunn were often used to help get the Soviets to agree to American proposed provisions.[17]

On occasion, Boren, Nunn, and Powell would agree upon a provision that needed to be in the treaty to avoid rejection by the Senate. The three would draft a letter from Boren and Nunn demanding that the provision be in the treaty or the Senate would not confirm it. The ploy worked. It strengthened the American bargaining position.

Boren enjoyed the bipartisanships displayed by Powell and Nunn. Boren said, "It was a great example of how we were all Americans first. We were on the same team. Instead of Congress undermining the negotiating position of the President, we were strengthening it."[18]

Boren worked well with Intelligence Committee co-chairman Senator Cohen. When Boren first became chairman, he and Cohen sat down together and decided that the staff of the committee would not be Democratic or Republican, but simply united. At first, Sven Holmes, who had been a key staff member of Boren's first race for governor in Oklahoma in 1974, led the Intelligence Committee staff.

When Holmes resigned, Boren selected Tenet as chief of staff. Tenet, from a Greek immigrant family in New York, was shocked to learn of Boren's decision because he was much younger and had less experience than several other staff members. Some staff members had been on the committee for many years, but Boren was very impressed by Tenet's ability and quick mind.[19]

Boren holds the record for serving as chairman of the Senate Intelligence Committee longer than any senator in history. During his service, there was never a single party-line vote on any issue. Even though the members of the committee were widely divergent in their ideological views, they were statesmen and hammered out what they thought was best for the country. Members ranged from a liberal Democrat such as Howard Metzenbaum of Ohio to a conservative Republican, Orrin Hatch of Utah.

"We were not there to exercise our own political views. We were there to act as trustees for the American people," Boren said, "We were privileged to hear the secrets of the nation, mountains of information that other members of Congress did not have access to." Boren believed that members worked together closely and left their political leanings at the door because they recognized the heavy responsibility of dealing with intelligence and literally the security of the nation. In his six years at the helm of the Intelligence Committee, only three roll call votes were taken. In fact, the closest roll call vote was 12-3. There was great bipartisanship in one of the most important committees of the United States Senate.

Boren said, "We were the watchdogs over the intelligence community. We were to make sure that policies being followed were sustainable, that the American people would support them if they knew about them, and that the policies did not violate our basic values."[20]

Most Senate Intelligence Committee meetings were held behind closed doors in a huge vault encased in concrete and steel. Because of the sensitive nature of information discussed in the chamber, the encasement was necessary to prevent any eavesdropping.

During Boren's tenure as chairman of the Intelligence Committee, the technological world was changing. Because of satellite photography and high-tech listening devices, huge amounts of information flowed into American intelligence operations and ultimately to the Intelligence Committee. From the time Boren assumed the chairmanship to the time he left the Senate, he estimates that the amount of intelligence information increased by perhaps 50 times.[21]

The mountain of information gathered was not necessarily improving the quality of intelligence. Boren saw that Boorstein's Law, named for Oklahoma native, historian Daniel Boorstein, "The more information you have, the less knowledge you have," was at work in intelligence gathering. CIA and national security analysts were overwhelmed at the sheer volume of the information. Unfortunately, the number of skilled agents with necessary language and cultural skills to infiltrate subversive groups and collect information had declined, a situation that would later haunt the United States. While he was chairman, Boren, with vice chairman Cohen, and Tenet pushed American intelligence agencies to work to increase human resources.

The problem was that recruiting human agents takes time and requires picking the right people. Boren said, "You can't send a fair-skinned blonde-haired Scandinavian to infiltrate an enemy cell group in the Middle East." People of Middle Eastern heritage had to be found to join the American intelligence force, train them in language and culture, and insert them into the region. It often took years before they were accepted into organizations dangerous to the United States. Boren said, "Rebuilding our human intelligence pool of experts is not as easy as turning on a water faucet."[22]

*What we do in the last decade of this century
will largely determine our role in the next.
We must never forget that those who mill around
at the crossroads of history do so at their peril.*

DAVID L. BOREN

TWENTY SEVEN

Winds of War

OREN DID NOT SPEND ALL HIS TIME on congressional trips to the far corners of the earth. He kept true to his constituency in Oklahoma, appearing at civic clubs, philanthropic events, and political gatherings each year. He took an active role in the management of the Oklahoma Foundation for Excellence and he and Molly spent much time helping make the programs of the Oklahoma Arts Institute successful and Molly served as chair of its board.

Assisting him in operations in the district were field representatives such as Robert Dick Bell, now a judge of the Oklahoma Court of Civil Appeals. In 1989, Bell spent hours writing an outline for a speech Boren was to deliver at the University of Oklahoma. When it came time for the speech, Boren looked at the outline for 45 seconds and then "commenced to rattle off an unbelievably articulated speech" that encompassed not only Bell's outline, "but improved it tenfold." Bell said, "The man's memory and intellect is beyond anyone I ever met."[1]

In Washington, Boren's staff had much contact with constituents and federal agencies. Boren wanted to use the influence of his office to help Oklahomans with their problems with federal bureaucrats, from Social Security and Medicare to military and tax questions.

"Boren was not beyond horse trading," said former legislative assistant Dan Webber. In 1990, Senator Kent Conrad of North Dakota wanted to amend the Farm Credit Act which Boren had principally authored in 1986 to allow farmers who had fallen behind on their payments additional time to attempt to restructure their loans. When it came time for the Conrad Amendment to be voted on by the Senate Agriculture Committee, Boren was absent. Committee Chairman Senator Patrick Leahy of Vermont thought the amendment would open the flood gates to similar amendments. Leahy's staff indicated to Webber that the chairman expected to have Boren's proxy. When Conrad asked Webber how Boren stood on the amendment, he was informed that Leahy had his proxy. Not accepting that fact, Conrad said, "Let's get David on the phone."[2]

Senators Conrad and Boren spoke on the telephone for several minutes. Then, a grinning Conrad handed the phone to Webber. In the conversation that followed, Webber was instructed to tell Chairman Leahy that Senator Conrad had his proxy. Webber learned later that the reason Boren was not in attendance at the Agriculture Committee was that he was busy lining up votes to make certain Tinker Air Force Base in Midwest City, Oklahoma, would be assigned a new squadron of Navy Reconnaissance aircraft to be based with the Air Force AWACS planes. Boren needed Conrad's vote to win the battle for the squadron over competing Air Force bases in Georgia and Hawaii. The "horse-trading" phone call helped make that happen.[3]

Boren was afforded the opportunity in January, 1990, to write a guest column on the editorial page of *The New York Times*. He predicted that with the end of the Cold War and the lessening of Soviet influence, America's allies would recognize they needed less military protection from the United States and would be less willing to follow our lead in the international arena. He pointed out that economically the allies no longer needed the United States in the way they did in 1950 when two thirds of the world's assets and nine of the 10 largest banks were located in America. "Today," he wrote, "we have none of the 10 largest banks. Our share of the world assets is now half of what it was in 1950."[4]

To develop a new world strategy, Boren suggested rebuilding the United States economy, developing new trade markets in Eastern Europe, increasing student exchange programs with other countries, and improving the ability of Americans to deal with the new international environment. On trade, he suggested that a large share of future aid be in the form of "Buy American" credits, especially to encourage consumption of basic capital goods that lead to long-term economic relationships. He also advocated partnerships so the United States would not have to bear the entire cost for world stability.

Boren had practical solutions for developing a new strategy in preparation for a new century:

> The study of foreign languages and international studies in schools and universities must be markedly increased. The Peace Corps should be increased ten-fold, both to raise the international sensitivities of the next generation and to build strong ties with nations that we have neglected because of our past focus on large bloc and superpower relationships.[5]

Boren's strong support for the Peace Corps was in part because of his close working relationship with Peace Corps Director Paul Coverdell, later elected to the United States Senate from Georgia. Boren so believed in the Peace Corps' work at establishing American relationships in other countries, he often helped increase the Peace

Corps appropriations over what had been recommended by the administration.

Boren's feelings about the importance of strong international relationships was expanded in his 2008 book, *A Letter to America.* Boren suggested the formation of an international peace corps as a way to build bonds between young people from different countries. Boren said, "Some of those young people will be the leaders of their countries in the next generation and our future leaders need to establish relationships with them."[6]

Boren's popularity on the national scene and in Oklahoma translated into an easy reelection campaign in 1990. In the August 28 Democratic primary, he overwhelmingly defeated political unknowns, Virginia Jenner and Manuel Ybarra. Boren, with 445,969 votes, polled 84 percent of the primary vote. Jenner received 57,909 votes and Ybarra received 25,169 votes.

In the general election in November, 1990, Boren faced Republican attorney Stephen Jones of Enid. Boren defeated Jones 735,684 to 148,814, and won all but two of the state's 2,359 voting precincts. Boren's 83 percent majority was the highest of any United States senator elected or reelected that year. There was no doubt that Boren was the most popular statewide office holder in Oklahoma history. Back in Washington, that popularity and Boren's reputation for building bi-partisan coalitions caused the *Almanac of American Politics* to list Boren as one of the ten most powerful members of the Senate.

Shortly after the 1990 general election, the international crisis surrounding Iraq and its aggressive leader, Saddam Hussein, became the focal point of the President and Congress. For years, the United States, Soviet Union, Germany, and France had supported Hussein in his fight against Iran. The Iran-Iraq War had concluded in 1988 and Hussein began flexing his muscles built upon a growing treasury from oil sales and putting hundreds of thousands of Iraqi men in uniform.

On August 2, 1990, Hussein invaded and annexed neighboring Kuwait, thus sparking an international crisis. American leaders were concerned about the stability of the region. President Bush met with British Prime Minister Margaret Thatcher who was concerned about British investment in Kuwait. The Soviet Union had perhaps the best relations with the ruling monarchy in Kuwait, but also was troubled by the fact that Hussein's invasion might cause havoc with oil prices and the world economy.

The United States and the Soviets helped pass a resolution in the United Nations Security Council giving Hussein a deadline for leaving Kuwait and approving the use of force if the Iraqi leader did not live up to the timetable. The Security Council also imposed economic sanctions upon Iraq.

Boren, as chairman of the Senate Intelligence Committee, heard top-secret assessments from the CIA and the American military that Hussein might be considering invading Saudi Arabia, a close ally of the United States. With blessings from the United Nations, the United States, and other countries such as Egypt, Syria, and Great Britain, deployed massive troops along the Saudi border with Kuwait and Iraq in order to circle the Iraqi Army, the largest in the Middle East.

When it appeared that Hussein would ignore the United Nations mandate to remove his Army from Kuwait, the Bush administration began considering sending combat troops to force Hussein's hand. Boren received frequent briefings from the military and intelligence community.[7]

Boren had strong misgivings about sending troops into battle in Iraq. Much of his feeling about supporting continued sanctions rather than going to war was based upon what turned out to be erroneous information from the intelligence briefings to the

Intelligence Committee showed that Iraq had a huge Army and nearly as many tanks as the United States could put into combat. However, later it was revealed that analysts had failed to assess the fact, for example, that Iraqi tanks had far less range than American tanks that could simply "sit back and destroy the Iraqi weapons."[8]

Also, it was learned later, that the intelligence analysts had grossly exaggerated the size of Hussein's Army and certainly did not consider the fact that many of his troops would defect if defeat was imminent. Hussein was hated by many of his country's ethnic groups because of human rights violations toward them, including mass killings and economic oppression.

Boren's primary reason for opposing an invasion of Iraq was the potential casualties that America might suffer at the hands of what he perceived to be a well-equipped and motivated massive Iraqi Army. Often, CIA officials told the Intelligence Committee that Hussein's forces would put forth a major resistance to advancing coalition forces.[9]

On November 14, 1990, Boren was called to the White House to visit with the President who knew that Boren opposed his imminent plan to invade Iraq. It was an open and candid meeting. Boren was trying to allay the fears of many members of Congress who wanted a special session to rebuff Bush's obvious move toward an invasion. Boren left the White House after asking the President to keep the Congress better informed on his plans.[10]

In early January, 1991, days before the United Nations deadline for Iraqi withdrawal from Kuwait, President Bush delivered a secret letter to Hussein through Foreign Minister Tariq Aziz. The communication indicated that if Iraq would remove its troops from Kuwait, war could be avoided, but if that action did not occur, war was inevitable.

On the day that the letter was to be delivered personally to Aziz by Secretary of State of State James Baker in Geneva, Switzerland, Boren received a telephone call from National Security Advisor Scowcroft who asked Boren to meet with the President. Scowcroft said, "The President is having a bad day, thinking about the heavy responsibility of perhaps sending young Americans into battle. Could you come down and spend some time with him as a friend?"[11]

Boren canceled his office appointments and immediately left for the White House. He found the President in the Oval Office, pacing back and forth, considering the heavy decision he had to make. Rather than discuss the world crisis, Boren and Bush talked about their families and what was going on in each other's personal lives. But occasionally, Bush would interject, "Do you think I'm doing the right thing by sending troops to Iraq?" Boren replied, "Mr. President, let's don't talk about that. You don't need any doubts in your mind if you have to make that decision."[12]

For two hours, the conversation among old friends continued. Often there was 10 minutes of silence as Boren saw what a toll the crisis was taking on the President. Later, Boren reflected, "We tend to dehumanize people in public office, especially our presidents. We forget that they are human beings with human needs and there are times when they just need a friend." To Boren, that meeting in the Oval Office was a great privilege for him perhaps to provide comfort for the leader of the free world.[13]

Within the next few hours, Boren learned that the letter to Hussein had been rejected and he knew the President's next move would be to invade Iraq. Meanwhile, Congress began debating how far the country should go in its dealings with Iraq. Members of Congress were greatly divided on whether or not to use force against Iraq.

Oklahoma Congressman Glenn English joined Boren in resisting an invasion to give sanctions more time to work. Both were concerned that Bush would not guarantee that any invasion would remove Hussein from power. Boren thought that any "band-aid" approach to only remove Iraqi forces from Kuwait and leave Hussein running Iraq would not solve the "Saddam Hussein problem."

Boren met again with the President and Scowcroft. Boren told President Bush, "You need to go all the way to Baghdad and take over Iraq." Bush, who was very knowledgeable about the history of Iraq, said he could not take over all of Iraq for fear of America becoming embroiled in a civil war among the Kurds, Sunnis, Shiites, and their various interests. The President told Boren, "Senator, you are wrong! We will never get out of a civil war in Iraq. We have to bring Hussein down some other way." Boren would later write in his book, *A Letter to America,* that Bush and Scowcroft were right, and he was wrong.[14]

On January 12, 1991, Congress gave the President authority to wage war if Iraq did not relinquish Kuwait by the deadline that was only three days away. Boren, English, and Congressman Mike Synar were the only members of the Oklahoma delegation to vote against the resolution to allow Bush to use force to expel Iraq from Kuwait. There was still much opposition to going to war in the Congress. The war resolution passed the Senate by a narrow 52-47 vote and the House of Representatives 250-183.

On January 16, Boren was notified by CIA Director William Webster that a United States-led coalition was poised to strike Iraq. Hours later, an around-the-clock barrage of missile and aerial attacks, dubbed Operation Desert Storm, began inflicting massive damage to the Iraqi war machine that turned out to be nearly defenseless. Many Americans stayed up all night to watch live action of the mighty force of the American military. The over-manned and under-equipped Iraqi Army proved unable to compete on the battlefield. Eighty five thousand Iraqi soldiers were killed and nearly 200,000 more were taken prisoner.

By the end of February, Hussein's Army was defeated and ejected from Kuwait. The fighting stopped as coalition forces occupied the southern portion of Iraq. Unfortunately, in Boren's eyes, Hussein was still in power. He promised as part of a cease fire to scrap all poison gas and germ weapons and allow United Nations observers to inspect the sites. Trade sanctions would remain in effect until Iraq complied with all terms of the cease fire. Even though he was clearly defeated in what history calls the Gulf War, Hussein publicly claimed victory.

Later, Bush and Boren in a private conversation learned that they had been given very different assessments of the likely effects of the war in Kuwait. Bush's information had come largely from the military and Boren's assessment had come from the Intelligence Committee. Both Bush and Boren were making decisions based upon two different sets of projections. Because Boren and the Intelligence Committee had been given such incorrect information about the fighting ability of Iraq, Boren opened a major review of the American intelligence community in March, 1991. He called the CIA's assessment of conditions in Iraq "inadequate." He received a promise of full cooperation from CIA Director Webster.[15]

After meeting with Webster and officials from the Defense Intelligence Agency and the Joint Chiefs of Staff, Boren raised questions about what Hussein might do next. "We're in a high state of alert." Boren told reporters, "Because Hussein has been beaten on the battlefield in his own country, he must now resort to terrorism to strike back at us." Boren feared that the Arab World was "angry beyond belief" at the United States and that evil radical forces were at work to use terrorism to punish America for its attack of Iraq. Unfortunately, history later proved the correctness of his fears.[16]

After the Gulf War, some political pundits mentioned Boren's name as a potential candidate for the Democratic nomination for President in 1992. Some admiring fans began wearing "Boren for President" buttons. Boren told reporters, "I am not saying no, I am leaving the door open."

Two Oklahomans were the subject of political rumors in connection with the upcoming presidential election. In addition to Boren, Congressman Dave McCurdy, chairman of the House Intelligence Committee, was considering a run for the White House. A story about the potential political ruckus was headlined "Shootout at the Oklahoma Corral" in a feature article in *U.S. News & World Report.*

Even *The Daily Oklahoman* published a story that implied that Boren and McCurdy had personal animosity and professional disagreements that seemed beneath the surface. When McCurdy read the newspaper story, he telephoned Boren to arrange a private lunch. McCurdy said he and Boren were longtime friends and that the friction was a "media creation." Boren had been of major help in McCurdy's first race for Congress. In off-the-record interviews, McCurdy said that he had not been critical of Boren's oversight of intelligence agencies, a fact reported to Boren staffers. In addition, McCurdy said he was not considering being a candidate for the presidency.[17]

Oklahoma's top Democrats urged Boren to seek the highest office in the land. Governor David Walters, former United States House Speaker Carl Albert, former Governor George Nigh, Congressman Wes Watkins, state Democratic Chairman Pete White, Democratic National Committewoman Senator Vicki Miles-LaGrange, National Democratic Committeeman George Krumme, Oklahoma House Speaker Glen Johnson, and Oklahoma Senate President Pro Tempore Robert Cullison sent a telegram to Boren urging the campaign for the presidency. The Democratic leaders said Boren's "record as a national leader for political reform, education, and bipartisanship in foreign policy" would make him a fine candidate.[18]

National Democrats also asked Boren to consider the race. Senators Lloyd Bentsen of Texas, Howell Heflin of Alabama, and Ernest Hollings of South Carolina all suggested Boren would make a great President. Boren said their comments were "humbling" to him.

At a family meeting with his wife and children at the Boren home in Seminole, a vote was taken as to whether or not Boren should run for president. The vote was 3-1 against entering the race. The one vote for the candidacy came from son, Dan, who said, "I sincerely wanted him to run. I think he would make an incredible president in the mold of Lincoln and Truman."[19]

In late April, 1991, recognizing that his friend, President Bush, would run for reelection, Boren ended speculation that he might run for the White House. Boren told others that he would never run against Bush because they shared a close friendship and he could never breach that relationship. He said his chairmanship of the Senate Intelligence Committee was too important to give up in order to become a presidential candidate. He called his chairmanship "a position of trust that should not be used politically." However, he held out the chance that he might run for President in the future, giving that likelihood a "50-50 chance."[20]

In addition to his Intelligence Committee responsibilities in the Senate, Boren spoke out on a variety of issues. In 1991, he differed with the Bush administration on national education reforms. The President proposed new federal guidelines to permit parents to send their children to public or private schools outside their own neighborhoods. Boren thought it was a mistake to include private schools in any school choice plan because it would deprive public education of vital support."[21]

Boren also was concerned with recommendations made to Oklahoma educators that courses in American and Oklahoma history be dropped from the list of required courses in Oklahoma high schools. Boren wrote a letter to the editor in *The Daily Oklahoman:*

> I am constantly alarmed by the erosion of the spirit of community in our nation. We are a very diverse country and justifiably proud of our diversity. At the same time, we have been bound together by common values including a commitment to democracy and to individual rights.
>
> To understand American values and to have a sense of community, it is critical that the next generation fully understand how we have evolved as a nation. It is also very important to understand the rich heritage we enjoy in our own state of Oklahoma…
>
> I appeal to you not to allow schools to deprive students of an understanding of their own heritage and the roots of the state and nation of which they are a part.[22]

TWENTY EIGHT

In the Eye of the Storm

BOREN FOUND HIMSELF IN THE MIDDLE of another international crisis in March, 1991. Soviet President Mikhail Gorbachev had made changes which would provide for greater political freedom and more private economic activities, but he had not yet come to terms with a true transition away from communism. Shortages of food and other basic commodities resulted in massive demonstrations. An unintended consequence of Gorbachev's loosening of press censorship was the reawakening of long-suppressed nationalist and anti-Russian feelings in other Soviet republics that longed for independence.

Fierce demonstrations were occurring all over the Soviet Union. From the balcony of the Metropole Hotel overlooking Revolutionary Square in Moscow, Boren and his wife observed plainclothes policemen beating and kicking demonstrators who had massed near the Kremlin in defiance of President Gorbachev's ban on demonstrations.[1]

From his vantage point, Boren had a better view of what was going on than did reporters who mingled with the demonstrators. He said, "We could see them grab people and drag them to buses. In between buses, they started punching them and hitting their heads against the doors and sides of the buses." Some of the police-men used sticks, but most beat people with their fists.[2]

Boren could see clearly that the plainclothes KGB agents were trying to force the crowd of demonstrators into a confrontation with police and soldiers. It was obvious that the professional KGB operatives were pushing the crowd so the demonstrators would surge forward unintentionally into a direct conflict with police. Boren said, "It turned ugly and violent. Tear gas smoke rose into the air as people were hauled away in police wagons."[3]

Boren was in Moscow as a member of a six-member Senate delegation examining the political and economic situation in the Soviet Union. With him were Senators Pell, Hatch, Exon, Heflin, and Chaffee. Boren, as Senate Intelligence Committee chairman, co-chaired the delegation with Senator Pell, chairman of the Senate Foreign Relations Committee.

The Americans were confined to their hotel because of the unsafe conditions created by the thousands of demonstrators marching in Moscow streets. Boren witnessed the beatings less than an hour after meeting with KGB Chief Vladimir Kryuchkov and after seeing a fire at the American Embassy which was con-tained in its damage but suspicious in nature. Boren strongly urged Kryuchkov to stop repressing dissent. Boren said, "If your country continues to turn to repression, it will have a grave, grave impact on future relations between the United States and the Soviet Union." It was clear to Boren that Kryuchkov was using the riots to stir up opposition to Gorbachev's reforms.[4]

Boren also met with Eduard Schevardnadze, who recently had resigned as foreign minister as a protest of Gorbachev's con-cessions to hard-line communists, and Alexander Yakovlev, the head of a new Kremlin advisory council. Schevardnadze, later president of his native republic of Georgia after the breakup of the Soviet Union, had been one of the authors, with Gorbachev, of Glasnost, the opening of society that pushed the end of the Cold War.

Boren's assessment was that Gorbachev was trying to move the people in the Soviet Union to favor a slowing down of reform. Most of the leaders Boren talked to believed that Gorbachev had made a tragic mistake by calling troops into Moscow for the first time since World War II and denying the people the right to have a demonstration.[5]

The meeting with KGB Chief Kryuchkov was fascinating to Boren. First of all, it was unusual for a United States Senator to meet with the head of the sprawling national agency that served as the state police and intelligence agency in the Soviet Union. It perhaps was the first time a KGB chief had met with a chairman of the Senate Intelligence Committee.

Second, Boren was surprised that Kryuchkov was so disrespectful and outspoken in his opposition to Gorbachev. "Surely," Boren thought, "the country is on the verge of a coup." During the meeting, an aide slipped Kryuchkov a note that President Gorbachev was on the telephone and needed to talk to him. Kryuchkov was so contemptuous of Gorbachev that he did not even leave the room and was "short and dismissive" with the Soviet president. Boren knew at that moment that Gorbachev's hold on the country was tenuous at best if the head of the KGB was so arrogant to not even change his schedule to take a call from the president of the country.[6]

To get a full understanding of what was happening in the Soviet Union, American Ambassador Jack Matlock arranged for a series of meetings with both supporters and opponents of the current leadership. In speaking with another former Gorbachev ally, Alexander Yakolov, Boren was given an insightful view of Gorbachev. Yakolov said, "Gorbachev is like a person standing on a boat dock with one foot on the dock and another in a boat. The dock is the old Communist party. The boat is democracy." The former close

Gorbachev advisor was describing Gorbachev's inner struggle of hanging on to the apparatus of the Communist party that had brought him to power or stepping fully into the boat to lead a new democracy. As the boat began to pull away, Yakolov said that Gorbachev tragically stayed on the dock. Yakolov predicted that Gorbachev would ultimately be forced out as Russian leader.[7]

While visiting with other dissidents and supporters of Gorbachev, Boren learned of the rising influence of Boris Yeltsin who was an elected leader in the Russian Republic. Some of the keen observers inside the Soviet Union told Boren that Yeltsin was the man to watch while Gorbachev was losing his grip on the country. Yeltsin also was known to leaders in Latvia, Poland, Czechoslovakia, and Hungary, which the delegation also visited.[8]

The first name that Boren mentioned when he reported to President Bush about the state of affairs in the Soviet Union was Boris Yeltsin. Boren also predicted that Gorbachev probably would not stay in power for another year and that the collapse of the Soviet Union was imminent. The Bush administration had emphasized its closeness to Gorbachev, but heeded Boren's recommendation that the administration begin to develop relationships with other leaders in the Soviet Union, especially Yeltsin. Bush soon invited Yeltsin to visit the United States. Boren told Bush that it would be a mistake to put "all our eggs" in Gorbachev's basket.

Former Senator Howard Baker visited Moscow a few weeks later and telephoned Boren to tell him of his experiences and feeling that Gorbachev's future was tenuous. He also called Bush to urge him to reach out to Yeltsin.

Boren told reporters after his meeting with the President, "We must know more of the leaders because one of them will replace Gorbachev. He is now a transitional figure." Boren called the Soviet Union a tinderbox. He said, "They are sitting on a powder keg and it could explode anytime."[9]

Within a few weeks, Yeltsin came to the United States for a brief visit. While at a meeting at the Soviet Embassy in Washington, Boren had occasion to speak privately with him through an interpreter in a small closet off the main ballroom where Yeltsin was greeting visitors. Boren went straight to the point and said, "Do you think the KGB and other hardliners will attempt to overthrow Gorbachev?" Yeltsin said, "It is a not a question of if—it is a question of when." Yeltsin believed a coup would be attempted within weeks.[10]

Yeltsin was correct. While on vacation in the Crimea, Gorbachev's government unraveled as many of his top leaders instigated a coup. After three days of house arrest by the KGB, Gorbachev was restored to power temporarily while the "Gang of Eight" that had led the coup was arrested. Included among them was the KGB chief who had been so defiant in his private conversations with Boren a few months before. Two of the former Soviet leaders lost their lives—one was shot and the other was found hanging in his Kremlin office.

As the Soviet republics began to declare their independence and fly their own flags, Gorbachev lost further power. Yeltsin, who had been elected as the president of the Russian Republic in July, gained power and attention. Gorbachev resigned and the Soviet Union was formally dissolved the day after Christmas, 1991. Two days later, Yeltsin became the first president of the new Russian Federation and moved into Gorbachev's old office in the Kremlin.

As the Soviet Union was falling apart, Boren assisted the President and the intelligence community to establish intelligence connections and formal relations with the new independent republics.

An important part of the adjustment to a Soviet Union that was breaking apart was Boren's 1991 effort to create the National Security Education Program (NSEP), part of the intelligence authorization bill and known as the David L. Boren Security Education Act. NSEP was created to provide scholarships and fellowships to students specializing in foreign languages and international studies. It also provided grants to educational institutions to make such courses available. It concentrated its resources on sending students to countries where American students seldom studied. These countries included the new nations that had been part of the Soviet Union.

Boren pushed the creation of NSEP to improve the pool of applicants for American intelligence and diplomatic jobs. He also wanted to increase the number of qualified teachers in these fields. He was aware of complaints that American students were often ill-equipped to deal with and understand other cultures, a trait that was absolutely necessary.

NSEP awards David L. Boren Scholarships to outstanding American undergraduates through a competitive national merit-based process. By 2008, NSEP had awarded more than 2,000 Boren Scholarships. Each Boren Scholar goes abroad to a critical country to study its language and culture. Awards are for up to one academic year. Boren Scholars demonstrate their merit for an award of up to $20,000 in part by committing to work for the United States government for at least one year.[11]

The NSEP is the largest international education initiative established by the United States since the Fulbright Scholar Program was signed into law by President Harry S. Truman in 1946.

Boren Fellowships are awarded to outstanding graduate students on a merit basis. More than 1,200 Boren Fellowships have been awarded to degree-seeking masters and doctoral students. Boren Fellowships are awarded to motivated individuals who develop independent overseas projects that combine language and cultural study with professional practical experiences. Awards of up to $30,000 over two years are given to applicants who demonstrate the highest intellectual and professional capacity along with a commitment to serve in the federal government or as a teacher for at least one year.[12]

NSEP has supported study in more than 100 countries. Scholarship and fellowship recipients have traveled to a wide variety of Asian, African, East European, and Latin American nations. NSEP is administered by the National Defense University in the Department of Defense under the guidance of a 12-member board which includes the secretaries of defense, education, commerce, and state, and the director of the CIA.[13]

The stated objectives of NSEP are:

1. To provide the necessary resources, accountability, and flexibility to meet the national security education needs of the United States, especially as such needs change over time,
2. To increase the quantity, diversity, and quality of the teaching and learning of subjects in the fields of foreign languages, area studies, and other international fields that are critical to the nation's interests,
3. To produce an increased pool of applicants for work in the departments and agencies of the United States government with national security responsibilities,
4. To expand, in conjunction with other federal programs, the international experience, knowledge base, and perspectives on which the United States citizenry, government employees, and leaders rely, and;
5. To permit the federal government to advocate the cause of international education.[14]

Creating the NSEP was only part of Boren's efforts in 1991 and 1992 to "rewire the CIA for the changing world." In February, 1992, he introduced Senate Bill 2198, the Intelligence Reorganization Act of 1992. In the House of Representatives, Congressman McCurdy introduced a companion bill. The bills contained the most comprehensive reforms of the American intelligence community since the CIA was created by the National Security Act of 1947.[15]

In announcing the goals for reorganization, Boren and Intelligence Committee co-chairman, and ranking Republican member, Senator Frank Murkowski of Alaska, called for an end to the tendency of intelligence agencies to produce "bland, hedged assessments that are watered down by bureaucratic battles."[16]

The reorganization affected the CIA, the National Security Agency, which monitors international communications, the Defense Intelligence Agency, which provides military intelligence, and the National Reconnaissance Office, which is responsible for developing and launching spy satellites.

Among other things, the bill would have created a new Director of National Intelligence to coordinate American intelligence activities. Under existing law, the CIA director was also the director of national intelligence. That situation often created turf battles within the various agencies contributing to the gathering of intelligence for the United States.[17]

In an interview with *The New York Times,* Boren said the sweeping changes were necessary "to renew an espionage apparatus whose leadership is spread throughout the government, whose duties often overlap, and whose overwhelming concern—the Soviet military threat—is rapidly becoming ancient history."[18]

Writing in the *Defense Intelligence Journal,* Boren said reorganization of United States intelligence should be a bipartisan effort:

> Both sides should see this as an opportunity to strengthen the management of the Intelligence Community to better cope with the challenging times that lie ahead. Just as many private businesses in the U.S. are restructuring to produce a better product at lower cost, so must the U.S. Intelligence

Community streamline. To fail to change our thinking to coincide with all the changes in the world around us would constitute an intolerable threat to our national security.[19]

In his writings of the time, Boren clearly saw the hazards that lay ahead for America. It was nearly a decade before the tragic events of September 11, 2001, yet Boren laid out the problems that the American intelligence community would have if it depended primarily on technological means, rather than old-fashioned infiltration of terrorist and enemy groups—human source intelligence. As a guest writer in *Foreign Affairs,* a publication of the Council on Foreign Relations, Inc., Boren wrote:

> A major priority of the new intelligence community will be its emphasis on human source intelligence. With a small American military force positioned around the world, earlier warnings of hostile intentions of potential adversaries will be essential. While satellite photographs and other technical data can reveal military movements before an attack, they cannot provide early warning of an enemy's intention…
>
> Had President Bush known the intentions of Saddam Hussein months before, instead of only days before the Iraqi invasion of Kuwait, he might have had the opportunity to consider other options that might have prevented the war altogether.[20]

Boren also was aware of the growing threat of individual terrorism. He said, "Human sources are critically important to the penetration of terrorist organizations and drug rings. A satellite photograph cannot detect the actions of a terrorist making explosive devices in an abandoned building."[21]

While parts of the bill ultimately were put into place, comprehensive reform was not approved by Congress until after the tragic terrorist attacks of September 11, 2001. Boren's earlier concern about the damage that could result from the acts of individual terrorists was correct.

In the November, 1992 general election, President Bush was defeated by Democrat William Jefferson "Bill" Clinton. In the closing months of the Bush administration, American troops were engaged in what began as humanitarian efforts in Somalia, in the horn of Africa. A civil war in the already poor country disrupted agriculture and food distribution. A famine caused the United Nations Security Council to authorize a limited peacekeeping force that, unfortunately, was disregarded by the warring factions.

In December, 1992, the United States organized an international military coalition with the purpose of securing southern Somalia so that food distribution could be made to alleviate the starvation of hundreds of thousands of people. Just three days after American troops arrived, Boren visited the country. Wearing a bullet-proof vest and riding in jeeps with machine guns mounted on them, Boren and his party saw what a difficult job was ahead. He was concerned about United States soldiers operating under the control of a United Nations leader who had no real authority over troops from separate nations and often lacked the ability to communicate with them by radio. Boren also thought the fierce turf battle among the three war lords spelled potential disaster.[22]

Only a few months after Boren's visit, the humanitarian mission of the United Nations coalition evolved into a military escalation. The violence spiraled out of control until 18 American soldiers and more than 1,000 Somalis were killed in fighting in the capital city of Mogadishu. The American public was incensed as the body of an American soldier was dragged through the streets of the city and American flags were burned on every corner.

Boren was critical of the military's "loss of sense of mission," taking sides with one faction rather than simply assuring the distribution of food and medical supplies to the hungry and starving people. Boren said, "We had no business getting involved in a civil war over which we had no control."[23]

Congress was so upset by the images of the hate demonstrated against American soldiers, resolutions were prepared to prevent any future deployment of American troops in a multinational force. Boren and Senator Nunn led the effort to stop the passage of such legislation. Nunn pointed out that the United States might not have won the Revolutionary War had not colonial soldiers fought under the command of French General Lafayette, and World War II may have been more difficult had not American military forces been allowed to fight under the command of British Field Marshal Montgomery in North Africa. Boren said, "It would have been foolish for Congress to make some kind of iron-clad rule to prevent participation in a multinational force."[24]

Instead, Boren, joined by President Bush, urged that units from other countries train together more often and develop communication capability that would allow them to work together more effectively when deployed in emergency situations. Bush and Boren even advocated that this "world police force" could train at Fort Dix, New Jersey, which had been scheduled for closure. Unfortunately, with the change in administrations, the proposal fell between the cracks and was never adopted.

Boren was part of a high-level mission to China immediately after the 1992 general election. Senators Pell, Levin, and Boren made up the first congressional delegation to visit China after the Tiananmen Square Massacre in 1989. In June of that year, a military crackdown on demonstrators in the square in the center of Beijing left nearly 1,000 civilians and soldiers dead, although Chinese Red Cross officials believed the toll to be closer to 3,000.

Following the violence, the Chinese government conducted widespread arrests to suppress protestors, banned the foreign press from the country, and purged government leaders who had publicly sympathized with labor activists, students, and intellectuals who had demonstrated against the authoritarianism and economic policies of the ruling Chinese Communist party.

Boren looked forward to the trip to China even though four years had passed with no high-level congressional delegation visiting the country. Boren believed it was critical for the United States to build a working relationship with China. He said, "It was obvious that China was indeed a new world power. Its economy was growing and its military influence was great." To Boren, an alliance with China in the twenty first century could encourage stability and bring about a period of unparalleled peace in the world.[25]

Boren and other senators conducted a series of confidential conversations with a number of Chinese officials who were concerned about what the next American administration might mean for them. As part of his campaign for the presidency, Clinton had argued that China should not be granted "most favorable nation" status, affecting American-Chinese trade policies. Boren assured Chinese leaders that America wanted to peacefully co-exist with the rest of the world and that the new President would surely listen to reason.[26]

After he returned to the United States, Boren visited with the President-Elect in Little Rock, Arkansas. After Boren relayed his private conversations with the Chinese, Clinton made it clear that it would be a mistake to isolate China. Clinton asked Boren to work with incoming Secretary of State Warren Christopher to draft a half dozen goals of the Clinton administration in dealing with the Chinese. In essence, Clinton was seeking justification for changing his campaign position on trade with China. It was agreed that Boren would meet secretly with Liu Huaqiu, the national security advisor to the Chinese president, and pass along Clinton's desires.

Two days before Clinton was inaugurated, Liu was a guest in Boren's home in Arlington, Virginia. It was a pleasant meeting in which the high Chinese official was reassured that the new administration and the Congress would seek a stable relationship with China.

The list of objectives worked out by Boren and Liu ultimately allowed the new President to change his positions about China. When China took actions to free religious or political prisoners, President Clinton publicly praised the move. One by one other Chinese actions were noted by Clinton as they occurred. Boren felt satisfaction in helping put the relationship between China and the United States on a better footing as a new President took office.

The meetings with the Chinese produced dividends later for Boren when he became president of OU. He was given wide access to Chinese education officials who made possible expansive exchange programs in China and a Confucius Institute at OU. After he had been at OU for ten years, the Chinese ambassador came to speak on the OU campus and greeted Boren warmly, remembering that he had been the interpreter for the secret talks between Mr. Liu and Boren at Boren's home in Virginia.[27]

Boren played a major role in a battle between Congress and President Clinton over the federal budget in 1993. At play was Clinton's huge, $343 billion package of taxes and spending cuts that was the heart of Clinton's economic plan.

The original budget offered by Clinton sought to reduce the budget deficit by raising taxes twice as much as it cut spending. Boren warned Clinton that such a budget contradicted his campaign promise of being a new kind of centrist leader and not an old-fashioned tax and spend politician. Boren opposed a new energy tax known as the BTU tax which not only disproportionately hurt energy producing states such as Oklahoma, but also would raise the price of all American products and disadvantage America in world trade.

Clinton could not pass the package in the House without the support of the more liberal wing of the party, but he asked Boren to get together a group of moderate Democrats and Republicans to offer an alternative plan. The President told Boren that once the alternative plan was introduced, he would use it as a reason to start bipartisan budget negotiations.[28]

Among those working with Boren were Senator Bob Kerry of Nebraska, Bennett Johnston of Louisiana, John Danforth of Missouri, William Cohen of Maine, and John Chaffee of Rhode Island. Boren regularly checked with Clinton's chief of staff to make sure the President still approved of the approach and would use the announcement of the bipartisan plan which balanced tax increases with spending cuts and removed the BTU tax as a good step and a reason to have White House talks on a new budget.

At the last minute, only one hour before the scheduled press conference to present the bipartisan plan, Clinton's legislative director informed high-level staff members and a strong supporter of the House liberal Democratic wing that the President had changed his mind and would stick with a Democratic-only liberal budget. Clinton called Boren to see if the press conference could be postponed. It could not because the senators already had briefed key reporters and were ready to walk to the room where the press conference was scheduled.[29]

Boren still expected Clinton to embrace the plan as a constructive move toward a new budget with support from both parties. Instead, Clinton, who was scheduled to speak at a ceremony at the Liberty Bell in Philadelphia, immediately denounced the proposal for having too many spending cuts. The President personally attacked Boren as caring more about oil than about people.[30]

Boren and the entire group of moderates were furious and felt they had been double-crossed. The entire epic was featured in a book by Bob Woodward which gave a blow-by-blow description of events. Boren spoke on every major television news show, pointing out that Clinton was wrong and that the country needed a non-partisan budget to stop growing federal deficits. Boren believed such a budget could remain in effect for years if it had the endorsement of both major political parties.

Boren forced most of the changes advocated by the group to be added to the budget bill before he would vote to allow the bill out of committee and onto the Senate floor. His vote was necessary because there were 11 Democrats and 9 Republicans on the committee. Boren refused to cast the deciding vote in the Senate Finance Committee until major changes were made and the BTU tax removed.

House Democrats, in conference committee later, reduced most of the spending cuts and added more tax increases. The bill, vigorously opposed by Boren, passed the House by only one vote and the Senate only by Vice President Al Gore's tie-breaking vote. Not a single Republican voted for the budget.[31]

The BTU tax remained out of the bill. Boren's independent effort on the budget bill at least won that battle that spared all American consumers and producers of all products from higher energy costs and lower competitiveness in world markets. Clinton, Gore, and some Democratic leaders continued to denounce Boren as a disloyal Democrat who was just out to protect Oklahoma's interest.[32]

Later, in a speech in Houston after Democrats lost control of Congress and Republican Newt Gingrich became Speaker of the House, Clinton said Boren had been right and that the party-line budget set up the administration for the argument that they were big spenders.[33]

After the budget fight, Boren's relationship with Clinton was never the same. Boren later declined to offer an alternative to bail out the Clinton health care plan because he feared that he would be undercut again if he offered a bipartisan approach.[34]

Daniel Boone is leaving Tinker with the party supplies for the Fall Festival. Secret code for "Senator Boren is leaving Oklahoma for Baghdad to rescue Ken Beaty."

TWENTY NINE

Mission of Mercy

N 1993, BOREN USED HIS POSITION as a United States Senator to help gain the freedom of an Oklahoma oil field worker who had been captured by the Iraqi Army and unjustly sentenced to eight years in an Iraqi prison.

Kenneth "Ken" Beaty had arrived in the Middle East in 1991 when he was hired by the Kuwait Oil Company to supervise its team of firefighters to extinguish thousands of oil well fires that had been set by retreating Iraqi soldiers after the Gulf War. Beaty, whose home was in Mustang, Oklahoma, was no stranger to foreign lands. He had worked all over the world for oil and gas companies for many years.[1]

On April 25, 1993, Beaty was headed to check a drilling rig somewhere in the northern Kuwaiti desert for the Santa Fe Oil Company based in Dallas, Texas. At a checkpoint manned by Iraqi soldiers, he was taken into custody and driven to Basra, Iraq. He was formally charged with espionage and trespassing into Iraqi territory and transferred to a prison in Baghdad where he was thrown into solitary confinement. His wife, Robin, and their two daughters, living in Kuwait, were concerned when Beaty's company could not contact him.

It was five days before Beaty's wife and his company were notified that he was being held captive. Beaty was housed in a cold and filthy Baghdad prison. The only food he was given was a daily bowl of rice and a cup of water that were slipped through a tiny slit in the door of his cell. Iraqi guards kept telling him that it was only a matter of time before he would be released. However, when a non-English speaking lady attorney was appointed to represent him in court proceedings, Beaty was worried.

Beaty was transported from the Iraqi Foreign Affairs Detention Center to the Iraqi Hall of Justice in downtown Baghdad for a trial before three judges. When the judges found him innocent of espionage, he believed he would be freed. But the next day, he was taken again to the Hall of Justice and the same three-judge panel caught Beaty by surprise and found him guilty of illegally entering Iraq. An even worse blow was that he was sentenced to eight years in prison.

Beaty was transferred to the infamous Abu Ghraib Prison 20 miles west of Baghdad. It was known as the place where Saddam Hussein's government had tortured and executed dissidents. Abu Ghraib also is known in history for American soldiers being accused of torturing Iraqi detainees, based upon a series of photographs published in the worldwide news media after the Gulf War.[2]

Robin Beaty was able to establish a line of communication with her husband through the Polish Embassy and Jan Piekarski, a Polish diplomat, who was charged with seeing to American interests in Iraq. Because the United States had no formal relations with Iraq, there was no American Embassy in Baghdad to negotiate with the Iraqi government.

Robin and her daughters returned to Oklahoma as Beaty asked the Iraqi government to overturn his harsh punishment for mistakenly wandering into Iraqi territory. He was granted a June 27th court date in Baghdad. Unfortunately, in the early morning hours before his court appearance, 23 American Tomahawk missiles fell on downtown Baghdad in retaliation for a failed assassination attempt on former President George H.W. Bush. Beaty's court appearance was canceled.

Meanwhile, Robin and her family began looking for a political solution. Iraqi officials were not willing to work with Republican Oklahoma United States Senator Don Nickles because it was a Republican president, Bush, who caused their humiliating defeat. The only Oklahoma politician the Beaty family believed they could turn to for help was Boren.[3]

To make matters worse, Beaty had a heart condition and needed medicine and other treatment. He was seen by volunteer workers from Medicines for Peace who reported his well being to his wife and family. In August, Robin was allowed to travel to Baghdad to visit her husband in prison. Polish diplomats also had made it possible for her to meet with Iraqi Deputy Prime Minister Tariq Aziz to plead for her husband's release. At the last minute, Aziz decided not to meet with Robin and instead sent rude and intolerant subordinates. With no hope, Robin went to a back room of the restaurant where the meeting had been planned and knelt in prayer.

When Robin visited with her husband, she mentioned that she might try to get help from Boren. He knew Boren by reputation and wholeheartedly endorsed the idea. Back home in Oklahoma, Robin contacted Boren's office. After a few intense days of gathering information about Beaty's capture, imprisonment, and sentencing, Boren had his staff work with Medicines for Peace that had reported success of trading millions of dollars in medical supplies for the release of Swedish prisoners from Iraqi prisons.[4]

Boren kept his involvement in the project secret. By October, 1993, Boren and his staff had finalized a plan using the supplies generated by several charitable organizations, including the

Methodist church, intent on freeing Beaty. Foods, medicines, water purification equipment, and other supplies valued at $5 million were transported to Tinker Air Force Base in Midwest City, Oklahoma, to await disposition.

Because of the secret status of the project, it was necessary for military and state department officials to use code words to communicate with Beaty in prison. Boren became known as "Daniel Boone," the supplies were called "party supplies," and the delivery date for the supplies was known as the "Fall Festival."

As final details of the rescue plan fell into place, Boren went to the highest levels of the American government to seek permission. He took his plan to Secretary of State Warren Christopher and President Clinton. The President was at first wary of the idea because one misstep on Iraqi soil could cause an international incident. In the end, both Clinton and Christopher trusted Boren and believed if anyone could bring about Beaty's release, it was him.[5]

Before he left Washington, D.C., Boren spoke at length with Ambassador Nazir Hamdoon, the Iraqi representative to the United Nations. Boren wanted the Iraqi government to know he was willing to personally travel to Baghdad to seek Beaty's release. He also wanted Iraq to know that he was coming on a personal mission to help a constituent—he was not an official representative of the American government.[6]

Back in Oklahoma, Boren received a call from Ambassador Hamdoon who told him that President Saddam Hussein would release Beaty only if Boren personally came to Iraq to get him and meet with Iraqi officials. Despite concerns by the CIA and Senate Intelligence Committee staff that Boren might be taken hostage, Boren still wanted to go to Iraq to win Beaty's release. The White House agreed to provide the transportation.

Boren put together a small team to accompany him on the secret mission to Iraq. His press secretary, Dan Webber, could handle press relations. Chris Straub, a member of the Senate Intelligence Committee staff and foreign relations specialist, spoke fluent Arabic. To treat Beaty's heart problem, Boren added his own physician and heart specialist Dr. Ronald White of Oklahoma City. White was a longtime friend who had grown up with Boren in Seminole.

With the team assembled and President Clinton's approval, the coded message was faxed to Beaty, "Daniel Boone is leaving Tinker with the party supplies for the Fall Festival." Boren excused himself early from a law school class reunion and met Robin Beaty and other team members at Tinker Air Force Base. At 11:00 p.m., the mission was ready to be launched. Boren, members of the Iraqi delivery team, Beaty's wife and daughters, and Boren's wife, Molly, said a quick prayer. Boren remembered, "It was an important prayer. Heading into an enemy country to negotiate for a man's life was a tall order, and any help we could get from above was appreciated."[7]

Boren's team boarded a Gulfstream jet, part of the 89th Air Wing stationed at Tinker, and headed for Amman, Jordan, the closest point that an American military plane could get to Baghdad. Upon landing in Amman, Boren's group was invited to stay in the official palace of King Hussein of Jordan. The next morning, November 14, Boren was up early and again led his team members in a short prayer.

The team was whisked into King Hussein's personal helicopter and flown to the Jordanian border with Iraq. There they climbed into a caravan of three cars. The first car was an escort car. Senator Boren and Straub were in the second vehicle and the third was occupied by Dr. White and Webber. They drove at 110 miles per hour for the 425-mile trip to Baghdad. Even though there was little traffic, the highway was dangerous, strewn with blown-out tires carelessly left in the roadway. The car in which Boren rode had slick tires with virtually no tread. Boren later said he was more frightened by the road trip than by what Saddam Hussein might do to him once he reached Baghdad.[8]

Arriving in Baghdad at 7:00 p.m., Boren met with Prime Minister Aziz in the luxurious offices of the Iraqi Prime Ministry located on the banks of the Euphrates River. It was a cordial meeting in a comfortable environment. Boren and Aziz talked about agriculture and the need for more water for Iraqi farmers. It was clear that Aziz wanted to prolong his conversation with Boren. He obviously enjoyed exchanging ideas with someone outside his region of the world. He talked of former times when the United States and Iraq were on friendlier terms. Aziz predictably blamed the Bush administration for the crisis between the two nations. He said, "Iraq does not want to be the enemy of the United States."[9]

Aziz also insisted that Beaty would have been released earlier, but that airstrikes by American fighter jets had "ruined everything." Boren assured Aziz that, if Beaty was released, he would communicate to the American people the circumstances of the humanitarian gesture. However, Boren told Aziz, "You must understand that even though I will make a statement that expresses gratitude for the actions of your president, I speak as only one man, and not as an official representative of the United States government." Aziz understood and gave Boren hope that the trip to rescue Beaty would have a happy ending. Aziz said, "It is not the way of the Arabs or the Iraqis to invite people all this way and then disappoint them."[10]

When the conversation turned to sanctions imposed upon Iraq by the United Nations, Aziz insisted that his country was fully compliant. Boren told Aziz that he had known President Clinton and Secretary of State Christopher for many years, and that they expected full compliance. "They have no hidden agenda," Boren said to the Iraqi official.[11]

The general tone of the conversation between Boren and Aziz was positive and businesslike. However, Aziz became emotional when he talked of the inability of his government to have private, meaningful talks with the United States government. Aziz said, "Why won't the American government talk to us. We can't communicate just through the press. This is important because each additional day of sanctions means the death of 100 more children."[12]

The room had mirrors on every wall so Boren knew they were being taped. Even in casual conversation, Aziz, one of the top officials of the Iraqi government, tried to get Boren and his team to say anything negative about the American government. Boren emphasized to Aziz that he was on a private mission of mercy and did not speak officially for the United States government or President Clinton.[13]

The meeting with Aziz lasted more than three hours. Boren wanted to complete the rescue of Beaty quickly. He had been told by the CIA that it was dangerous for him to stay very long in Baghdad, and that he should "get in and out as quickly as possible." However, Aziz said the final decision on Beaty's release had to come from President Hussein himself, and that he could not speak with him until later that night. Aziz said he would call Boren the following morning at 10:00 a.m. Boren reminded him that Ambassador Hamdoon had promised Beaty's release and that the promise must be kept.[14]

The Americans were sent to the Al Mansour Hotel where they and Iraqi intelligence agents were the only guests. Boren and Dr. White took one room while Straub and Webber slept in another. They knew the rooms were bugged so any conversation had to be completed on the balcony. They also suspected their every movement would be monitored by hidden cameras.

The following morning, as promised, Aziz called and set up another meeting for an hour later. In the brief encounter, Aziz said he had spoken to President Hussein who had decided to grant the request to release Beaty. Boren and Aziz made small talk while waiting for Beaty to be brought to the office and to be handed over to Boren. During the conversation, Aziz said Boren had an open invitation to return to Baghdad at any time.[15]

At the last minute, an Iraqi bureaucrat said that Beaty had to have his passport stamped before he left. The problem was that Beaty did not have his passport with him. However, the alert young Polish diplomat, Piekarski, who had developed an escape plan in the event Boren was taken hostage, made up a sheet of paper with Polish government stamps that could serve as a special passport for Beaty. The Iraqis accepted the makeshift document and stamped it, clearing the way for Beaty's release. Later, Boren arranged to have Piekarski honored at a reception at the United States State Department in Washington, D.C.

When Beaty arrived in the room where Boren waited, Boren handed him an American flag that had been flown over the United States Capitol. Beaty began crying—all the Americans began embracing and weeping. Boren, aware of the need to leave Iraq as soon as possible, urged the group back to their cars. On their way, Boren's car began belching an ominous cloud of black smoke. He was moved to another vehicle and the disabled car was left beside the road as the trek to Amman continued.

In Amman, Boren called a news conference to explain the mission and to prevent any misstating of the facts by the Iraqis. Beaty stood proudly by Boren before the television cameras. Beaty clutched the American flag he had carried with him from Iraq. To a small group of reporters, Beaty said, "I am just happy to be going home!"[16]

King Hussein asked Boren, Beaty, and the rescue team to stay at the Royal Palace again. But Beaty wanted to go home. While the aircraft was being readied for the trip back to the United States,

King Hussein requested that Boren visit him at the palace. When Boren pulled up to the palace, the king was standing at the curb to personally open the door where a visit ensued. During the conversation, King Hussein expressed sensitive views about events in the Middle East and asked Boren to convey a private message to President Clinton.[17]

Back at the Amman airport, the Americans headed home. Beaty could hardly maintain his composure when he saw the United States seal on the side of the military aircraft. On board, Boren and his team relaxed. Boren slipped into more comfortable clothing and called his wife and mother to let them know he was safe. He then called President Clinton and reported on the success of the mission. The President congratulated Boren and then asked to talk to Beaty.[18]

It was daylight when the Air Force jet neared the east coast of the United States. As a special gift for Beaty, the pilot arranged for the airspace above the National Mall to be cleared. Beaty still held the American flag as he looked down on the Washington Monument, the Lincoln Memorial, and the Capitol. All he could say was, "It's good to be home."[19] Minutes later, the jet set down at Andrews Air Force Base where Beaty was met by his wife.

*While at Oxford, I wrote in my diary that someday
I hoped to be president of the University of Oklahoma.
When the opportunity came to impact the next generation,
I grasped it with all the enthusiasm I could muster.*

David L. Boren

THIRTY

Coming Home

B Y 1994, BOREN HAD SERVED in the United States Senate for 15 years, longer than the legendary Robert S. Kerr. Boren had become increasingly frustrated with the partisanship he experienced in Congress. However, he believed that he had made a difference. After his six-year term as chairman of the Senate Intelligence Committee ended, he was a champion for campaign finance reform and co-chairman of the Joint Committee on the Organization of Congress. He was considered one of the most powerful members of the Senate and perhaps the senator with the most working knowledge of America's intelligence community.

In late 1993, University of Oklahoma Regent Steve Bentley visited the senator in Washington and asked Boren if he had any interest in becoming president of OU. President Richard Van Horn had told regents he would be leaving the following year. Several regents, Bentley said, hoped that Boren would succeed him.

The wheels began turning in Boren's mind. Was he interested? Was it time to leave Washington, D.C.? Did he want to follow in the footsteps of his mentor, Dr. George L. Cross? The questions were many—but answers would take awhile.

For most of his life, Boren had thought he someday wanted to be a university president. His roots were deep in Oklahoma—his entire life had revolved around the Sooner State. He always had said he wanted not just to be a United States Senator, but a United States Senator from Oklahoma. Concerning his goal to be a university president, there could be only one choice—the University of Oklahoma.[1]

Being president of OU was a natural progression of Boren's career. His family was filled with educators. He had enjoyed his teaching time at Oklahoma Baptist University. He often thought of his great mentors during his education in Seminole public schools and at Yale, at Oxford, and at the OU College of Law. His interest in education had dominated much of his agenda as governor of Oklahoma and resulted later in the establishment of the Oklahoma Foundation for Excellence.

While in the Senate, Boren's interest in higher education became even stronger when he served as a trustee for Yale University, and reengaged himself in challenges facing higher education.

Being invited to become president of OU was nothing new. Five years earlier, he had been asked to apply for the position. However, at that time, he was in the middle of his term as chairman of the Senate Intelligence Committee and did not feel the timing was right. Boren also had been approached by some in the early 1990s to consider becoming the president of Yale University.

This time, he and wife, Molly, began discussing the possibility over meals and before bedtime. Molly played the devil's advocate, asking him if he really wanted to give up his political career in the Senate. She wanted to make certain he thought of every angle and aspect of the new job and what part of his legacy he would be leaving behind in the nation's capital. She strongly hoped that he would decide to come home to Oklahoma permanently, but she did not want him to later regret leaving the Senate.[2]

Boren struggled with the decision. The polarization of the two political parties made it harder for a moderate bipartisan senator to make a difference. He said in a speech that he wished that he could have moved his desk into the central aisle of the Senate between the two parties and work to bring people together. However, if he had just been given an opportunity to practice law or enter the private sector at much higher compensation, he would have stayed in the Senate. He was in a meaningful position as one of the Senate's most senior members.[3]

The main attraction of the OU presidency for Boren was that it would allow him to come home and serve in such a special way. In February, 1994, he was a guest in the home of longtime family friend Fred Gipson, OU's chief legal counsel. Gipson had invited a select group of faculty members to talk to Boren about leading the university. Boren was not a traditional academic and wanted to know how the faculty would feel if he became president.

Boren was impressed with the enthusiasm and sincerity with which he was received by the faculty representatives. He was deeply moved by comments from two faculty members. One said, "We just want a president that will be a part of the university family and love this place as much as we do." Another person said, "We really need you." Boren's mentor, Dr. George Cross, called him and pleaded with him to come home. Cross spoke of his own lifetime investment in the university and told Boren, "The university is at a critical crossroads." The call from Cross was extremely influential in Boren's final decision.[4]

Boren also began hearing from political friends. One of the first to advise him to accept the OU presidency was Denzil Garrison who had served as Boren's legislative liaison in the governor's office. Garrison remembered, "I called him and told him I thought his true place was as president of OU. I knew he would make his most meaningful and lasting mark in education."[5]

In March, Boren was invited to meet with the OU Board of Regents in Norman. Members of the press began hearing about the meeting and staked out Oklahoma Memorial Union where the regents normally met. Boren was able to slip into the building unobserved and even escaped notice from a television news helicopter hovering overhead.

Newspapers and other media outlets had been saying for days that Boren might resign the Senate and take the OU president's job. He had refused to comment on such reports.

In a frank discussion with regents, Boren opened his heart about always wanting to be president of OU, how he struggled with the idea of leaving his senior status in the Senate, and how he would expect his presidency at OU to proceed. He was aware that the university had become splintered with the athletic department and other departments operating nearly independently. Boren told regents that if he was offered the job, he would need to be in charge. Every department would be required to report to him, and he in turn would report to the regents.[6]

At the end of the meeting, regents unanimously asked Boren to succeed Dr. Van Horn as president. Boren told the regents that he would give them a decision quickly. As he left the building with the assistance of Regents Secretary Dr. Chris Purcell, a television news crew was spotted at the end of the hallway. Boren and Purcell took a back stairway and headed for the parking lot where Boren's car was parked. When they saw two more news crews, they hid behind a hedge until the reporters and cameramen passed.[7]

"It was an amusing moment," Boren remembered. He had known Dr. Purcell since she was a high school student in Wewoka and he spoke to her government class as a young member of the state legislature. Boren said, "It would have been dramatic footage for the evening news had the cameras looked behind the hedge and saw us crouching there."[8]

Boren had other options. He was approached by a well-known national trade association and offered a salary of nearly $2 million annually, about seven times more than he could earn as OU's 13th president. Boren told the person making the offer that he would not even meet to discuss it. He had decided that the only way he would leave the Senate would be to go home as president of OU.[9]

Boren talked to many friends about his impending decision. Upon the suggestion of Dr. Cross, Boren visited with former OU Press Director Savoie Lottinville, who had served with Cross on the selection committee that had chosen Boren for a Rhodes scholarship many years before. Lottinville also was very encouraging and asked Boren to take the job. Lottinville told Boren that the high standards of the university were slipping and that he was needed to provide a vision of leadership for the future.[10]

Boren also discussed his future with banker H. E. "Gene" Rainbolt and Helen Walton, wife of Wal-Mart founder and native Oklahoman Sam Walton. Mrs. Walton was co-chair of the committee searching for a new OU president.

Rainbolt challenged Boren to think of OU as the major engine for progress in the state, and of the impact that education would have on economic development. Rainbolt said that if Boren really wanted to make a difference, his best chance was to help mold the lives of future leaders. Rainbolt also pointed out that the OU position would allow Boren and his wife to serve as a team. In the Senate, it was impossible for the spouse of a senator to play a great role in service. However, at OU, Boren could team with Molly and work with students, alumni, and faculty to change the face of the campuses of the university.[11]

Boren called Terry Sanford, whose path was similar to his. Sanford had been governor of North Carolina, a member of the United States Senate, and became president of Duke University.

Boren posed the question, "Terry, what do you think I should do?" Sanford quickly answered, "You get to Norman as quick as you can and accept before they change their minds!" Sanford said that if you truly love a state and want to be a part of the fabric of that place, you should invest your life in the next generation.[12]

Boren sought advice from his family and staff. Senate aide Tripp Hall asked his boss why Boren was favoring a move to Norman. Boren said, "Oklahoma has given me every opportunity. This is one way I can pay back the debt."[13]

Boren found in his files a letter written by Federal Judge Alfred P. Murrah in 1970 when Boren was a 29-year-old feisty Oklahoma legislator and professor at Oklahoma Baptist University. Murrah had suggested even then that Boren would make a good president for OU and had forwarded his recommendation to the OU Regents.

In the quietness of the night, Boren pondered his choices. He thought back to the great political leaders of Oklahoma such as Carl Albert, Robert S. Kerr, and Mike Monroney—men who reached the pinnacle of power in Congress. He then considered the impact of great Oklahoma educators, OU presidents Cross and William Bennett Bizzell, and Henry Bennett at Oklahoma A & M. He said, "I was hard pressed to say that any political figure left a more lasting impact on the quality of life in the state as those educators did."[14]

On mornings when he rushed to work at the United States Capitol, he sometimes paused and reflected on the time he had served there and realized the friendships that had developed. He had never lost a sense of awe when entering the Senate chamber. It was, for him, a great privilege to be part of the Senate's history.

Yet, at the end of the day, his heart led him toward Oklahoma and OU. His love for family time also led him toward home. He pointed out in a guest editorial in *The New York Times* that there were only three weekends during the previous year that he had not been airborne between Oklahoma and Washington or at meetings elsewhere. One month it had taken 27 days before he and Molly could have dinner together and an unscheduled evening at home. At the end of many 16-hour days of running to committee meetings, appearing in photographs with visitors, lunching just off the Senate floor waiting for an amendment to come up for vote, returning phone calls, and answering dozens of letters, he asked himself what he really had done that day to help solve the major problems facing the nation. His honest answer was often, "Not as much as I had hoped."[15]

With his decision made to become president of OU, Boren and his staff worked out a transition to his new post in Norman. It was decided that the public announcement would be made in Holmberg Hall on April 27, 1994. He chose Holmberg Hall because he had played in the All-State Band and spoken in debate competitions there. It had sentimental meaning to him and reminded him how much Oklahoma history had been made there by guest speakers in the past.

With a cast of campus notables appearing with him on stage, Boren laid out his reasons for leaving a job in which he had, by latest polls, a 91 percent approval rating. He said he and Molly wanted to make a difference in their home state, that "public service is not about power, it is about where you can do the most good." Second, he quoted former OU President Joseph Brandt that "no state can become truly great without having a truly great university within its borders."[16]

"There are seasons in your life," Boren said, "and for Molly and for me this is the season in our lives for going back to our state which has given so much to us by investing our lives in the next generation. Both of us have OU degrees, and our state's flagship university is the right place to serve."[17]

In the Op-Ed section of *The New York Times,* Boren tried to explain why he was leaving the Senate. He was direct and honest:

Today's Senate is not the body I joined 16 years ago. Partisanship is much stronger. Today, senators of different parties go into one another's states and campaign against one another, violating an old tradition and making it almost impossible to put party politics aside to work together in the national interest.

Too much time has to be spent raising money for campaigns instead of working on critical problems. The Senate has become a fragmented set of individual empires and political fiefdoms, with almost 300 committees and subcommittees. The average senator serves on 12 different panels. No wonder there is so much reliance on a cumbersome bureaucracy…

If America gets everything else right but fails to provide for the education of the next generation, we will lose our strength as a society. A reporter asked me, "Why would you give up power and influence to become a university president?" My answer, "At this point, I feel I can do more good at the university."[18]

Boren wrote a final letter to his fellow senators. He said, "I leave with the strong conviction that there is no more noble calling than public service and no greater satisfaction than the feeling that you have tried to make a difference on important issues." Boren continued, "I would not subtract one day from the time that I have been privileged to spend in public office or in the Senate with you."[19]

Boren left members of the Senate with a personal admonition to work together and move beyond the partisanship that had hindered progress in solving national problems. He wrote, "Reinstitute bipartisan social gatherings for new members and continuing ones. When the class elected in 1978 first came to the Senate, new members of both parties had potluck dinners together which included our spouses. We built strong personal friendships across party lines that helped us work together. Too often now, it seems to me that new senators only get to know the members of their own party."[20]

After saying personal good-byes to many of his closest friends in the Senate, Boren and his wife packed their belongings, sold their Virginia home, and moved their lives to the presidential home in Norman.

*The university is not here merely to amass information;
it is here to advance knowledge and to teach students
how to think and how to seek knowledge for themselves.*

DAVID L. BOREN

THIRTY ONE

President Boren

A S WITH HIS PAST ENDEAVORS, Boren began his presidency at OU with a flurry of meetings with students, faculty, staff, and administrators. His new job was different than his previous assignments. All at once he was chief executive officer of a huge concern, a university that had thousands of support staff, museums, hospitals, its own police department, food service, and hotel system. However, he did not have the tools at his disposal that a CEO of a major corporation would have. He also did not have absolute authority to mandate every action which he considered in the best interest of the university.

Instead, he had to lead by persuasion and cooperation. He had the help of General Counsel Joe Harroz, Alumni Director Tripp Hall, Executive Assistant Ann Dubler, Administrative Vice President Nick Hathaway, Press Secretary Josh Galper, and office assistant Marolyn Sauls, all of whom had come to OU from Boren's Senate staff.[1]

Others who later joined Boren's personal office staff were Sherry Evans, who suceeded Dubler as executive assistant; Shad Satterthwaite, an academic assistant and team teacher with Boren in the classroom; and recent OU graduates who became assistants and press secretaries, Jeff Hickman, Kim Hefty, Jabar Shumate, Blake Rambo, and Jay Doyle. Boren and Hickman worked with Boren for three years. Shumate and Hickman later became members of the Oklahoma legislature—one a Democrat, the other a Republican.

In his first weeks on campus in November, 1994, Boren developed a working plan of first-year goals. He wanted to work with a faculty committee to evaluate the undergraduate experience, establish an endowment for Bizzell Memorial Library, and open a presidential helpline to promote a more user-friendly university. He also wanted to promote student volunteerism, begin work on the student center at the OU Health Sciences Center campus in Oklahoma City, emphasize international studies, and raise money. In his first two years, he also brought new leaders into 80 percent of the top 35 administrative positions on the campus.[2]

Boren recognized that raising money might be the key to improving OU. He wanted to raise $200 million quickly to create professorships to attract gifted and talented instructors and to stop other universities from raiding the OU faculty. Higher salaries were the most important elements of his plan to keep quality professors. OU's faculty salaries languished at the bottom of the Big Twelve Conference schools and top professors were being lured to other universities.

Boren also wanted to change the mindset that OU was perceived as a state-funded institution. He said, "As long as people think that the state funds all our programs, we will have trouble raising private dollars from alumni and other sources." Boren noted that 91 percent of Yale alumni donated to their school, while less than 15 percent of OU alumni contributed.[3]

Before long, Boren was working harder than he ever had in his life. As governor and United States Senator, he had often spent 14 to 16 hours a day on the job, but usually had Saturdays and Sundays off. In promoting OU, he found he was working the same number of hours, but seven days a week. Many Saturdays were filled with athletic events that he felt he needed to attend, and Sunday afternoons were excellent times for fund raisers or speeches to groups of alumni that could be counted on to contribute private funds to make possible Boren's dreams of excellence for OU.[4]

Boren greatly enjoyed interaction with students. He began teaching the freshman government class two days a week. It was on those days that he was in the best mood of the week. He said, "I truly enjoy that personal interchange with students. There is nothing more special than the relationship existing between teacher and student, the intellectual energy from the two generations coming together." Boren believed he gained as much from the interaction as the students did. He shared his experiences, but he got back from them the energy, enthusiasm, and idealism that came from seeing things through new eyes. By 2008, Boren had taught freshman political science classes for 27 consecutive semesters.[5]

Other differences about his new job came from dealing with alumni who wanted his influence on every issue from getting their children admitted to the university or improving their seating assignments for home football games. He also was under constant scrutiny by the press. As a member of the Senate, he had some control over what issues were on the table, what he could be quizzed about on any given day. However, at OU, his dealings with the state legislature on appropriations, proposed tuition increases, or drinking policies for fraternities and sororities were all issues in which the local and state press had an interest.[6]

Boren had been on the job at OU for a year before his official inauguration took place on September 15, 1995. More than 6,000 guests gathered under umbrellas on a rain-soaked Parrington Oval on the Norman campus. Boren was dressed in academic robes of red and black and held a jeweled mace. With all the trappings of a coronation, OU students placed the presidential collar around Boren.

After his formal investiture, conducted by OU Regents Chairman G.T. Blankenship, Boren said no institution in the state is more important to the economic, educational, and political future of Oklahoma than OU. He called it a special place, "because you will meet people here who will change your life."[7]

Boren challenged OU's faculty and staff to return to old-fashioned values that had been lost. He said:

> Today, more and more of our students come to us without the strong support of traditional families or sheltering communities. They desperately need the mentoring which only our faculty can give in the classroom, in the laboratory, and above all, on the park bench or at the dinner table outside the formal education environment.
>
> No students should ever leave this campus without having had a chance to share their hopes and dreams with faculty members who know them by name and care about them as individuals.[8]

Boren called for OU to become a centerpiece of cultural diversity. He said, "If we cannot create a true community with our own diverse racial and ethnic groups…how can we ever hope to build the spirit of community in the nation and world around us?" Boren concluded that OU would fail in its duty to society if "we do not pass on to the next generation the ability to create communities."[9]

Boren set out to fulfill his dreams he so ably communicated in his inaugural address. He began raising private donations at a record pace. On the steps of Evans Hall, he unveiled the "Reach for Excellence" program, a five-year, $200 million fund raising effort. The goal was to work harder than any previous private fund-raising effort in the state.

Additional scholarships generated from the program attracted highly gifted students and endowments helped keep the brightest professors and entice new ones to the campus. Boren set up a model honors program mostly funded by private money that would produce an intense learning experience a student would normally have only in a small, highly-endowed university.

Boren and his wife began a series of programs to rebuild a sense of family and community, restoring the values of teaching and mentoring outside the classroom. Molly took on the daunting task of beautifying all OU campuses—the main campus in Norman, the campus in Tulsa, and the sprawling campus of the OU Health Sciences Center in Oklahoma City.

Boren valued scholarly university research, but saw OU as providing so much more for its students. He said, "We should never undervalue great teaching and mentoring." He brought back 50 retired professors to reach first and second-year students. Because the older professors did not have the pressure of "publish or perish," they had time to spend with students and become mentors for them.[10] In OU residence halls, each floor "adopted" a professor and periodically hosted the professor for dinner, the perfect kind of interaction between student and teacher Boren was striving for.

Molly undertook the restoration of Boyd House, the original home of the president across Boyd Street from the campus. The primary idea behind the restoration was to allow the Borens to be visible on campus. It also gave Boren the chance to walk to work so he had the chance to talk to students and faculty. It made him approachable in the same manner that Dr. Cross was available to Boren in his formative years.[11]

Boyd House had not been used as the presidential home for 27 years. A privately-funded renovation greatly enlarged the home that was built in 1905 for OU's first president, David Ross Boyd. In addition to adding the presidential master suite and the 1,000-square-foot entertainment area named for the late former first lady, Cleo Cross, at the back of the house, architect Hugh Newell Jacobsen reconfigured the upstairs to add three guest bedrooms. Three types of gardens were constructed in the backyard for entertaining. More than 10,000 people, mostly students, attend events at Boyd House each year. [12]

Boren's passion for teachers becoming mentors was not an idle, politically-correct vision. In his office was a photograph of Dr. Cross and Ruth Robinson, Boren's first grade teacher, who he talked with every month of his adult years until she died shortly after he became president of OU. He also had constant communications with other mentors from high school and college. He believed his life had been so positively affected by mentors—he should do everything in his power as the leader of OU to give students the opportunity to develop their own mentors. Boren felt he was "paying back" the huge debt he owed his educational mentors in life.[13]

In Boren's first five years of OU, the university was transformed in a whirlwind of activity. Twenty major new programs were unveiled, including the establishment of the Honors College, the Charles M. Russell Center for the Study of Art of the American West, the Artist-in-Residence Program, the International Programs Center, and the Faculty-in-Residence Program, putting faculty family apartments in residence halls to promote intergenerational friendships.[14]

The Office of Student Volunteerism and the OU Women's Center were opened. Presidential Study Abroad Scholarships were funded along with a number of new scholarships in a variety of colleges throughout the university. Alumni Association executive director Tripp Hall began an aggressive class reunion program. The Presidential Professors Program rewarded outstanding professors with stipends. At the OU Health Sciences Center, a public-private joint venture was launched to keep the teaching hospitals strong.

There was a revitalizing energy evident on the Norman campus in the form of massive construction. A $16 million renovation of Oklahoma Memorial Union was underway. The $16 million Catlett Music Center was opened. The Jimmie Austin OU Golf Course was opened. The Sam Noble Oklahoma Museum of Natural History, the largest university-based natural history museum in the world, opened in the spring of 2001.

The Barry Switzer Center and Siegfried Family Strength and Conditioning Complex supplemented OU's athletic facilities. The Health Sciences Center had a new student union and the $24 million Stanton L. Young Biomedical Research Center. OU opened a new softball stadium, a wing was added to the Nielsen Physics Building, and ground was broken for a $17 million addition to the OU College of Law.

Under Molly's leadership, OU's campuses were more beautiful. Many parks were added, including Burr Park, with its gazebo, in a student residential area; the Harold Powell Garden on the North Oval; the Evans Hall English Garden, a serene garden area between Evans Hall and the library; and the Canyon Garden below ground level in the library courtyard.

The Rose Sharp Rose Garden, named for the wife of former OU President Paul Sharp, a new park east of the football stadium, and another garden setting west of the Catlett Music Center, helped beautify the campus. A multi-million dollar private endowment assured that OU's gardens would be adequately maintained in the future.[15]

The First Lady is dedicated to placing sculpture, inspiring architecture, and beautiful gardens where students will be exposed to them. Shortly after the Allan Houser sculpture, "Homeward Bound," was located in the garden between the library and the College of Business, the Borens encountered a young Asian student standing by the sculpture. He told them that he had visited the sculpture four times that day. He knew nothing about the Native

American scene Houser so realistically portrayed, but there was something so universal about the piece of art that "it spoke to him."[16]

To give students a sense of their history as members of a university family, historical markers were placed in front of buildings, historic photographs lined hallways. Molly said, "It helps students understand the history and tradition and gives them a strong sense of place." Benches strategically set in convenient locations throughout the campus are named as memorials or to honor living persons. The benches are important to give people a place to sit on their journey across campus. Molly said, "If you can create places for people to sit and visit, you create community."[17]

Boren pushed for increased state funding and private giving to university research. Soon OU was leading the Big Twelve Conference schools in new research grants being awarded to its professors and researchers. The increases had a profound positive impact upon Oklahoma's economy.

However, there was no doubt that the OU student was the number one priority at the university. A walk across the campus with Boren meant stopping several times as he visited with students. When student protest groups gathered in front of Evans Hall, Boren did not barricade himself in his office and call campus police. Instead, he walked outside to visit with the students. Many times, protests turned into healthy dialogue.[18]

Boren sees the breakdown of a sense of community as one of the nation's most critical problems. "The community is a place where we must teach our future leaders how to create real communication," he said, "That happens when students get to know and respect those who have different backgrounds from their own. Our students come from different racial and religious backgrounds, from different countries, and from families with different economic means."[19]

Boren sees the university's challenge as forging students into a family. He said, "None of us grows unless we get to know people unlike ourselves." To help promote the spirit of community, Boren changed the old housing rules which allowed students to select their dormitories and suite mates and even large groups together on the same hallway. He wanted to break up social cliques and saw diversity in housing as one of the essential ways to create community. Changes in the housing rules have resulted in students' increased respect and tolerance of others.[20]

University development leaders had to work hard to keep up with Boren's vision. When Boren originally announced intentions to raise $200 million, vice president for development David Maloney, was worried, often spending sleepless nights planning how to raise even half that amount, a goal that far exceeded anything the university had raised in the past. A devoted Catholic, it was rumored that Maloney sat alone in Boren's office with his rosary in prayer.

However, Maloney shed his worries. When the Reach for Excellence campaign concluded in 2000, more than $514 million in gifts and pledges had been received. At that time, it was one of the largest fundraising drives ever at a public university.[21]

Boren took personal interest in raising funds for OU. He discovered that only eight individuals had ever given $1 million to the university in its first 105 years. In the Reach for Excellence campaign, OU received million-dollar gifts from 60 people. Maloney assessed Boren's skill as a fund-raiser, "He gave credit to the past and built upon it. He could make any potential donor feel proud of the university from which he or she graduated and completely buy into his dream of OU excellence. By the end of the conversation, everyone wanted to be part of the new era at OU."[22]

A veteran politician such as Boren could not just assume the presidency of OU and never think or act politically again. Boren remained in contact with many officials of the federal government. He twice turned aside overtures to run as a vice presidential candidate on the Reform Party ticket with Texan Ross Perot. Perot and

Boren were longtime friends. Each time Perot visited Norman or Boren visited with Perot in Texas, the press speculated that again Boren was being courted for either a presidential or vice presidential run on a third-party ticket. There were also occasional reports that Boren would return to Washington to take a cabinet post or be named ambassador to a major foreign country.

Each time, Boren responded that he was happy at OU and had a long-term commitment to the university. "To me," he said, "serving here is a personal calling." Boren saw his role as similar to that of a pastor, priest, or rabbi. The OU family is his congregation.[23]

Boren was a member of a special United States mission to China. The committee of American leaders spent several days in intense discussions with Chinese officials to consider the future of American-Chinese relations. While there, Boren renewed friendships with Chinese leaders and met with officials from Bejing University and Fudan University in Shanghai to discuss exchange programs for OU.[24]

Boren returned to Washington, D.C., to assist former Secretary of State James Baker win Senate ratification of the chemical-biological weapons treaty. At a rally in support of the treaty's approval, Boren was asked to introduce President Clinton on the south lawn of the White House beneath the Truman Balcony. [25]

When George W. Bush was elected President in 2000, he called Boren for advice on whether or not to retain George Tenet as director of the CIA. Boren told the President-Elect that it would be a good bipartisan signal to keep Tenet, who was appointed to the post by Democratic President Clinton. Boren believed intelligence gathering should be shielded from politics and that Tenet's staying at the CIA would be good for continuity.[26]

Boren also urged Bush to consider doing what Winston Churchill had done with the British government during World War II—in essence have a war cabinet with an equal number of Democrats and Republicans. Bush's election had been by the narrowest of margins and Boren thought he should try to be a President of national unity. Boren also suggested having bipartisan legislative working groups. The idea was to be able to produce legislation that was hammered out by leaders of both parties, thus minimizing the partisan squabbling that had sent Congress and the White House into deadlock. Bush did not heed Boren's recommendations. Boren was greatly disappointed and became concerned that others around the President, especially Karl Rove, wanted him to follow a partisan path and use emotional and divisive issues to build political power. Boren was deeply troubled by the change of direction of bipartisan efforts that Bush had followed as governor of Texas.[27]

On the morning of September 11, 2001, a day that changed America forever, Boren met CIA Director Tenet at 8:30 a.m. for breakfast at the St. Regis Hotel in Washington, D.C. President Bush was out of town so Tenet was available for a long breakfast to catch up on what was happening in Boren's life. In the middle of a conversation, Tenet was interrupted by Tim Ward, a member of his security detail. Normally a calm man, Ward's urgent tone caused Tenet to know something bad had happened. They stepped away from the table where Tenet learned that an airplane had flown into the World Trade Center's South Tower in New York City.[28]

Tenet remembered the moment, "Most people…assumed that the first crash was a tragic accident…That wasn't the case for me. We had been living too intimately with the possibility of a terrorist attack on the United States." Quickly, Tenet returned to the table and told Boren about events unfolding in New York City. He mentioned Osama Bin Ladin by name and wondered aloud if al-Qa'ida was involved. Tenet said a short goodbye to Boren and raced with his security detail back to CIA headquarters.[29]

After the terrorist attacks on New York City and Washington, D.C., many people called Boren with concerns about what would happen to the national economy in light of the attacks. Boren talked with former President George H.W. Bush and leaders of the Congress to suggest a public works program to provide jobs for out-of-work people in building roads, electrical grids, water transfer systems, airports, and other public works projects similar the Works Progress Administration (WPA) in the Great Depression.[30]

Former President Bush suggested that Boren take his idea to Andy Card, the President's chief of staff. Boren told Card that he had spoken with the Democratic leadership in Congress and that they were prepared to work on a quick public works program that could minimize the negative economic impact of the aftermath of the terrorist attacks. Card later called Boren and said President Bush liked the idea and would be in touch with him soon.

However, Bush never called. Instead, presidential aide Karl Rove called Boren and said, "This idea is under advisement." Boren was convinced that the President was never given full information on the chance to help the country with a strong show of bipartisanship. Boren said, "We missed a great chance. It was a time when opposites such as Senators Jesse Helms and Ted Kennedy were arm-in-arm and singing 'God Bless America' on the Capitol steps."[31]

When winds of war swept the nation's capitol for a new invasion of Iraq in 2003, Boren often talked with Tenet to express his opposition to the idea. He knew that the Bush administration was using CIA information about Saddam Hussein having weapons of mass destruction as the primary reason for the invasion. Boren had advised Tenet to resign his post the previous November after the congressional elections. Boren told Tenet, "Be careful, you are not one of the inner circle going back to the campaign. It doesn't matter how the president may feel; if it suits that group, they will throw you overboard."[32]

When it appeared that the Bush administration would launch the war, Boren advised Tenet to threaten to resign, hoping that the threat might prevent the invasion, an action Boren has called "a tragic mistake."[33]

After the 2003 invasion, Operation Iraqi Freedom, the security situation in Iraq began to deteriorate and, as Boren had predicted, the Bush administration laid the blame for the invasion at Tenet's doorstep. Vice President Dick Cheney pointed to statements by Tenet as the major reason for the administration deciding to invade Iraq and topple the Saddam Hussein government.[34]

It was not the last time Boren would advise Tenet to resign before he was made the scapegoat for the war in Iraq. In May, 2003, Tenet and his wife, Stephanie, came to Norman where Tenet was scheduled to give the commencement address at OU. President Boren and Molly took the Tenets out to the site where they planned to build a new home in the Norman countryside.

Tenet described the poignant moment of a conversation with Boren in the middle of a field, "David once again argued vehemently that it was time for me to resign. I had put in my time, served under two presidents, and weathered 9/11, David said. No one could ask for more…It was best to go out on a high note."[35]

Tenet listened carefully to Boren, who he considered an "astute observer of the ebb and flow of politics," and told the White House that he was considering stepping down as director of the CIA. But in a private conversation with President Bush in the Oval Office, the President said, "I really need you to stay." Tenet could not say no to the President and stayed in his job until blame for further problems in Iraq came his way, causing him to resign in 2004.[36]

If the Regents want me to, I would like to stay at OU until I stop having new ideas.

DAVID L. BOREN

THIRTY TWO

Seeking Excellence

AS PRESIDENT OF OU, Boren made himself available to students and faculty alike. He had taken the advice of former President Cross and his wife, Cleo, to fully interact with faculty groups, particularly the Faculty Senate. Every few weeks Boren met with the Faculty Senate Executive Committee to discuss recommended changes or proposed programs. "Helpful conversations" prevented a split between administration and faculty that plagued many institutions of higher learning.

Being president of OU involves being a football fan. Boren, at age four, began attending home football games with his father and continued to be a Sooner supporter during his years in college, law school, as governor, and as United States Senator. When he came to OU, he inherited a troubled athletic department, "King Football" was suffering, and fans were restless. Boren wanted to be number one in both academics and athletics, so he put into place a series of plans to improve the athletic department.

Boren's answer to improving both the administration of the athletic department and the winning record of the football team ultimately was the hiring of Joe Castiglione as athletic director. A $120 million fund-raising program for the athletic department allowed the construction of new facilities, an expansion of the Gaylord Family Oklahoma Memorial Stadium, and putting the department on a self-supporting basis. Because they believed in Boren's vision for OU, the family of publisher Edward L. Gaylord contributed in excess of $30 million for the expansion of the football stadium and building a new state-of-the-art journalism building to house the Gaylord School of Journalism and Mass Communication.[1]

The hiring of Castiglione came after Boren personally used his wit and influence to "seal the deal." Castiglione met with OU regents and was offered the athletic director's job. However, he asked to go home to Missouri, talk to his wife and family, and think about it over the weekend.[2]

By the time Castiglione arrived home, Boren already had talked to his wife several times and extolled the virtues of living in Oklahoma. There was no question Kristen Castiglione was impressed. Boren called Castiglione every night to talk about his dream of returning OU athletics to a position of supremacy, both in the classroom and on the playing field. Castiglione said, "I was impressed that a university president would take that level of interest in the hiring process and the overall welfare of intercollegiate athletics."[3]

When Castiglione and his wife visited Norman a few days later, they were "blown away" by the family atmosphere they felt on the campus. As they walked on a tour of the campus, several students would stop and say, "President Boren, how are you doing today?" or "Good morning, President Boren." There was such friendliness that Castiglione asked, "Is this a set-up?" He had never seen a campus leader so warmly received wherever they went.[4]

Boren convinced Castiglione to call the Missouri chancellor by telephone and tell him of his decision to come to OU. There was little time to waste because word of Castiglione's possible hiring had leaked to the press and television news crews were outside

Boren's office. Within an hour, Boren and Castiglione went to the steps of Evans Hall to meet reporters. It was obvious that Boren had been optimistic about Castiglione's decision. A platform had been built, adorned with about 500 red and white balloons. A pep band had been assembled and several dozen supporters of the university were present.[5]

Castiglione began reorganizing the athletic department and spent much time talking with Boren about the search for excellence in Sooner athletics. The new athletic director soon had to choose a new head football coach. Rather than appoint a cumbersome committee, Boren trusted Castiglione to consider a very small, but highly skilled pool of candidates. Boren said, "We have hired a professional athletic director and we are going to let him do his job." Through an intense process, and in a close consultation with Boren, Castiglione narrowed the field to two candidates. One was Bob Stoops, a University of Iowa graduate, who was at the time defensive coordinator at the University of Florida.[6]

Boren arranged a meeting at DFW Airport in Texas with Stoops, several of the OU regents, alumni leaders, and former OU athletic greats. The group agreed that Stoops was the right choice and the second candidate would not be interviewed. He gave a final "yes" to the offer after spending about an hour with Boren in a small private room while the others waited for the answer. When Boren announced to them that Stoops had accepted the OU job, there was a great round of applause.[7] Castiglione remembered, "With his usual energy, President Boren made both Coach Stoops and me feel like it was the greatest day in the history of the university."[8]

Stoops, who pleased OU fans enormously, won a national football championship in only his second season at the helm of the Sooners. He said, "I had not been at OU long before I saw the tremendous impact that President and Molly Boren had on OU, not only in bricks and mortar, but I could sense it in the energy I felt and in the caliber of students, faculty, and staff we attract. There is no doubt OU has been transformed by their great leadership." Both Stoops and Castiglione have often commented that there is no university at which there is a closer communication between the president, coaches, and athletes.[9]

Longtime higher education supporter and university regent John Massey believes Boren is rare as a university president who recognizes that excellence in athletics goes hand in hand with excellence in academics. Massey said, "Many potential large donors come to a campus to sporting events, but may never visit the history department or the school of business. They want excellence in major sports that create positive national publicity for the school. Boren knows how important OU's winning tradition is, and he uses it to his advantage of raising money for the university." By 2008, OU was one of the only universities in the nation with a totally self-funded athletic department which receives no university subsidy. In fact, the OU athletic department contributed more than $4 million to the OU library and academic programs between 2004 and 2008.[10]

During Boren's presidency, graduation rates for student athletes have increased dramatically and OU ranks first in the nation in the number of athletes who returned to the university to complete degrees after leaving to play professionally.

There is no doubt there is a "Boren Factor" that has enveloped OU and its worldwide presence since 1994. Longtime District Judge William Hetherington of Norman described the Boren Factor as has having its own energy and momentum. He said, "People trust President Boren so much that they respond quickly to his suggestions and accept his challenge when other leaders could not convince them. Boren has an uncanny ability to turn a vision, a seed, into something real. The Boren Factor rolls on."[11]

Other astute observers recognize what a transformation has occurred at OU since the Borens arrived. DeVier Pierson said, "The Boren years are unlikely to be matched. OU has flourished in every aspect that makes an educational institution great—the explosive growth of its physical plant, a dedicated and enthusiastic faculty, a beautiful campus, and most of all, a student body of academic excellence who could compete well at any university in the land."[12]

Noble Foundation President Michael Cawley marvels at how Boren has successfully pleased all constituencies of the university—students, faculty, alumni, Board of Regents, and the state legislature.[13] Libby Blankenship said, "David and Molly have literally changed the face of OU. They have done it with style and grace."[14] Former Oklahoma House Speaker and current Chancellor of Higher Education Glen Johnson believes Boren's best quality is the ability to "get right to the heart of an issue." Johnson said, "He analyzes an individual's strengths and weaknesses and determines rather quickly whether or not he or she will fit into the picture to accomplish the goals and objectives he has on his plate." Johnson says Boren is the most persuasive person he has ever known, to be able to take an agenda and turn it into a course of action. Johnson said, "His enthusiasm is contagious."[15]

Federal Judge Lee West is convinced that Boren "is even more able at his present position than he was in any of his previous ones—and that is no small statement."[16] OU Vice President Nick Hathaway said Boren truly knows what a great university ought to be and "everything he does is a planned step in that direction."[17] Marolyn Sauls, Boren's assistant as United States Senator and as president of OU, said, "He views as vitally important his role as caretaker of the university."[18]

Energy magnate Harold Hamm, whose generosity to OU is well known, is glad Boren is at OU. Hamm said, "His vision of a greater state and nation is reflected in the many facets of this great institution's programs, campus, student body, and intellectual and cultural development which reach all parts of the world as a shining example of the highest quality standards in education. I cannot imagine Oklahoma without its favorite son."[19] Larry Nichols, co-founder of Devon Energy Corporation, the state's largest company, simply called Boren "the best thing that has ever happened to OU."[20]

Boren has had to use his persuasive powers to deal with the state legislature that annually tackles the challenge of appropriating money for higher education. Danny Hilliard, a former member of the legislature and OU's vice president for government relations, often accompanies Boren on visits to the State Capitol. Hilliard said, "He's at home there. He speaks to the maintenance workers, the security guards, and the tourists. He has served in so many positions, it is interesting to see how people address him differently, as 'governor,' 'senator,' or 'president.'" Hilliard marvels at how Boren treats each person differently and uniquely. Even if the president is running his usual ten minutes behind schedule, he "shakes every outstretched hand as if he had all the time in the world." Hilliard said, "But unlike a rock star, with David Boren there is no huge ego to deal with, only a huge servant spirit."[21]

Boren raised more than $1.5 billion in private donations in his first 14 years at OU. The donor base has increased from 17,000 to more than 108,000. By 2008, private endowment increased from $204 million to more than $1.2 billion, ranking OU in the nation's top 25 public universities. The number of endowed faculty positions at OU, at 94 when he arrived, rose to 538 by 2008. Private scholarship funds tripled. The student-faculty ratio has been reduced from 23-to-1 to 17-to-1 as Boren has increased the size of the faculty.

Boren was constantly concerned about keeping OU affordable for students from low and middle income families. In addition to increased scholarship funding, he worked with Dave Annis, director of food services, to develop a plan to give students who worked in dining halls free room and board. Boren designated funds in the libraries budget to buy a pool of course textbooks to be placed in reserve at the library for use by students who could not readily afford the expensive textbooks.

Boren has worked with OU administrators to try to find jobs for students who needed them to be able to work their way through college. Administrators were never surprised to get personal phone calls from Boren asking for their help to find a job for a student. Matt Hamilton, Director of Financial Aid, said never more than a week has passed without Boren calling him for assistance for a student in financial need. Growing up in a small town and knowing many worthy students who came from economically deprived families has had a marked impact on the intensity of Boren's concern for meeting the needs of students.

Paul Massad, who has worked for seven of OU's 13 presidents, says it is easy to raise money with Boren at the helm, "He instills a confidence in people that is rare. His fierce pride in Oklahoma and OU shows. He gets so excited about the opportunities to shape the future by investing in OU that alumni and interested citizens naturally want to get on board. Many times, I have seen potential donors become so enthralled with President Boren's enthusiasm about a particular project that they end up giving more than they ever intended. He makes believers out of them!"[22]

In his first 14 years at OU, the Borens' accomplishments are many. OU is number one in the nation per capita among public universities in the number of National Merit Scholars and in the top five in graduation of Rhodes Scholars. The *Princeton Review* has rated OU as a "Best Value" in higher education. *U.S. News & World Report* gave OU a higher ranking than any public university in Oklahoma history.[23]

Boren has often said, "It is very simple. To have a great university, it takes great faculty interacting with great students in adequate facilities. Since Boren came to OU, its freshman class has increased by 60 percent in size. Average ACT test scores have been raised three points and SAT scores have increased 150 points, making OU's student body the highest ranked at a public university in Oklahoma history.[24]

OU has increased its lead in National Merit Scholars enrolled, ranking first in the nation on a per capita basis among public universities. It has ranked in the top ten public and private universities in the United States in Goldwater Scholars in math and science. Boren and the OU regents have raised academic performance standards at OU twice in ten years.

OU ranks first in the Big Twelve and at the top in the nation in international exchange agreements with countries around the world. OU has 150 student exchange agreements with universities in 60 countries, emphasizing Boren's strong belief that students must be part of the larger international community in the future. More than 1,500 students from nearly 100 countries are enrolled at OU. OU partners with local programs to host several summer programs at Oxford University, in Italy and China, and in other locations.[25]

Research spending at OU has dramatically risen, from $90 million in 1994 to nearly $300 million in 2008. The increased research spending and development of new external programs impact Oklahoma's economy more than $1.5 billion annually.[26]

New student-oriented programs include The President's Trophy, an annual $5,000 prize to the best housing unit, fraternity, and sorority, based upon academic performance, volunteer service, campus leadership, and multicultural activities; the Cousins program, putting American student volunteers into a role as honorary cousins to international students; an intensive writing and editing program based on a freshman composition course at Harvard; reviving the publication of the yearbook after 25 years of silence; reduction in class size in all freshman English courses to no more than 19 students; and a major effort to fund Study Abroad Scholarships to help students experience the opportunity of studying overseas. In addition, the college debate team has been reinstituted at OU, following the long line of great debaters who left OU and became state and national leaders. In only its third year after its revival, the OU debate team won the national inter-collegiate debate championship.[27]

A new Religious Studies Program, one of few at public universities, offers a non-denominational interdisciplinary program that focuses on the history, social, and political landscapes, and doctrines of the world's major religions. The Institute for the Community Excellence is an interdisciplinary program in community planning. It reaches out to cities and towns of all sizes in Oklahoma to help them plan for the future and to create a real sense of community. The Center for the Creation of Economic Wealth teaches entrepreneurial skills and provides assistance to those seeking to utilize intellectual property to create new businesses and commercial enterprises.[28]

The new OU Cancer Institute is a comprehensive cancer research and treatment center that serves the state and region. The Harold Hamm Oklahoma Diabetes Center is becoming a world-class regional diabetes research and treatment center. Boren pushed for the cancer and diabetes centers because he does not want people to have to leave the state for treatment, leaving their family and support groups behind to fight severe illness. He also recognizes that many citizens cannot afford the extra expense of going to other states for prolonged medical treatment.

Boren's emphasis on medical research has helped diversify Oklahoma's economy with major facilities in both Oklahoma City and Tulsa. Forty thousand new jobs were created within a decade, at a time when other states were losing them.

In addition to the national success of OU's athletic teams, including the football team playing in the national championship game three times since the beginning of the new century and five more national championships in men's gymnastics in seven years, many other areas of the university have excelled. The Norman campus is home to the university's academic programs, except for health-related fields. The OU Health Sciences Center in Oklahoma City is one of only four comprehensive academic health centers in the nation with seven professional colleges. Both the Norman and Oklahoma City campuses offer programs at the Schusterman Center, the site of OU-Tulsa. OU has more than 30,000 students and more than 2,000 full-time faculty members. The annual operating budget in 2008 was more than $1.3 billion, but with the percentage of administration overhead more than 50 percent lower than when Boren became president.[29]

Since 1994, more than $1 billion in construction projects have been completed on the three campuses. The largest was the $67 million National Weather Center. A new wing of the Fred Jones Jr. Museum of Art houses the Weitzenhoffer Collection of French Impressionism, a gift of OU alumnus Max Weitzenhoffer. It was the single most important gift of art ever given to an American public university.[30]

OU's new 271-acre Research Campus is anchored by the Charles and Peggy Stephenson Research and Technology Center, where cutting-edge research in a variety of fields from robotics to genomic studies is taking place. Created in 1998, the OU Office of Technology Development has created two dozen companies that have generated nearly $100 million in capital and provided high-paying jobs for Oklahomans. OU's College of Education continues to be ranked in the top graduate colleges of education by *U.S. News & World Report*.[31]

Part of Boren's goal as president of OU has been to expose students to the world's leaders in government, business, the arts, and world affairs. The list of national and international scholars and policy makers is impressive. Boren has brought special guests to the campus that include former President George Bush; former Soviet President Mikhail Gorbachev; former United States Secretaries of State Henry Kissinger, Lawrence Eagleburger, Colin Powell, James A. Baker, III, and Madeleine Albright; "NewsHour" anchor Jim Lehrer; presidential historians David McCullough and Doris Kearns Goodwin; NBC's Washington Bureau Chief Tim Russert; former British Prime Minister Margaret Thatcher; Nobel Peace Prize winner Archbishop Desmond Tutu; investigative reporter Bob Woodward; and award-winning broadcast journalists Katie Couric and Tom Brokaw.[32]

Other famous guests who have shared their experiences with OU students and alumni include actor James Garner; former CIA directors George Tenet, Richard Helms, William Webster, Robert Gates, and James Woolsey; former Vice President Al Gore; presidential adviser David Gergen; world-renowned pianist Van Cliburn; former Joint Chiefs Chairman Admiral William Crowe; and former or present United States Senators Sam Nunn, Robert Dole, George Mitchell, John McCain, Paul Tsongas, Jon Corzine, Daniel Inouye, and Joe Lieberman; Queen Noor of Jordan; Lord Christopher Patten, the last British governor of Hong Kong; former New York City Mayor Rudy Giuliani; former Mexican President Vincente Fox, and Ellen Johnson-Sirleaf, President of the Republic of Liberia.[33]

Boren's presence is felt daily at OU. Even though he turned 67 in April, 2008, he keeps the same intense schedule which has guided his life since his days as governor of Oklahoma. He often skips the chain of command and goes directly to the person per-forming a job to get information. He shows up unannounced at offices, classes, and even in lobbies of dormitories late at night. His gift of communication is well known, whether with an American president, world leader, or a freshman returning from a date. As OU historian David Levy said, "One of President Boren's great gifts is his eloquence, his unparalleled ability to put his thoughts into words."[34]

THIRTY THREE

A Letter to America

I N 2008, BOREN WROTE *A LETTER TO AMERICA*, a powerful wake-up call to Americans. The best-selling book was published by the University of Oklahoma Press.[1]

Boren began his book with an alarming salutation, "Dear American, this letter is to you. If I were mailing it to you in an envelope, it would be marked URGENT. The country we love is in trouble. In truth we are in grave danger of declining as a nation. If we do not act quickly, that decline will become dramatic."[2]

With skill and passion, Boren explained his deep concerns that American citizens are not focused on the future, that we assume we will always be a superpower. But, he said, with only six percent of the world's population and with the economy of other countries growing faster than ours, our stature is not guaranteed. He is alarmed that even the attitudes of some of our longtime allies have grown negative. Polls show that most citizens of the world regard America as arrogant and incapable of listening to the needs of other nations and peoples.[3]

A Letter to America, released in the midst of a presidential campaign, was a scathing indictment of the lack of campaign finance reform in the country. Boren wrote:

It is time to quit wringing our hands about too much money distorting politics and do something about it. It is time to start a national movement to draft a constitutional amendment to limit and regulate campaign spending, followed by an unstoppable effort to ratify the amendment. We may try to rationalize what is going on, but the right word for it is "corruption." If it is not stopped, it will destroy our political system.[4]

Boren criticized the American educational system for de-emphasizing the teaching of history. He said, "A nation cannot remain great unless it understands how it became great in the first place. We cannot preserve our freedom and democracy and our own basic rights unless we know how they evolved."[5]

In his book, not only does Boren analyze the elements of a national crisis in America, he offers a bold and ambitious plan to get the nation back on track. He lays out specific ways to re-direct foreign policy and reduce the federal deficit. He also issues a plan to make higher education more affordable and how to structure the tax codes to strengthen the middle class.

After the book was released in early 2008, Pulitzer-Prize winning historian David McCullough said, "This is a book that should be read, re-read, and passed along to all who care about our country and its future." Jim Lehrer said, "Here now is the letter to us all, the one we have been waiting for—and sorely need." Brown University President Ruth Simmons called the book "a summons to action" and Yale University President Howard R. Lamar said Boren's suggestions were "a powerful, compelling analysis of the major crises facing the United States."[6]

Boren's life of public service has been recognized by many people, from presidents to the men and women along main streets in Oklahoma. Former President George H.W. Bush said, "He is one of the people that gives public service a noble name."[7] Oklahoma City business leader Clayton I. Bennett said Boren's "love for public service" comes through loud and clear in every speech he gives. Bennett said, "From every speech I come away inspired, thinking how I can improve myself to accomplish things on the same order as David Boren."[8] State civic leader Lee Allan Smith said if any Oklahoman ever deserved to be inducted into the Oklahoma Hall of Fame a second time, it is Boren.[9]

Former CIA Director James Woolsey said Boren is a superb leader because of the combination of his judgment and his easygoing style. Woolsey said, "It allows him to get things done without ordering people around or throwing his weight around. He simply convinces them his position is the right one."[10] William Paul, an Oklahoma lawyer who served as president of the American Bar Association, said, "With the possible exception of Will Rogers, Boren is the most remarkable Oklahoman, ever."[11] Judge Tom Cornish said Boren's epitaph might read, "The Lord put me here to help those most in need."[12]

"Boren's loyalty, brilliance, and magnificent ability to understand complex situations makes him one of the greatest statesmen of our time," said Andy Coats, Dean of the OU College of Law. Federal District Court Judge Frank Seay also believes that Boren's loyalty is near the top of his outstanding attributes. "Once you are his friend," Seay said, "he stands beside you for life."[13] Federal Appeals Court Judge Robert Henry said Boren is a leader because of his teaching skills. Henry said, "The reason he is who he is today is first and foremost because of what he is, a superb teacher."[14]

Loyalty is perhaps one of Boren's best-known qualities—loyalty to friends, associates, employees, and supporters. An example is help given Oklahoma Supreme Court Justice Steven Taylor at critical junctures of his life. As a district judge in McAlester, Taylor was assigned the heavy burden of presiding over the state trial of Oklahoma

City Murrah Building bombing perpetrator Terry Nichols. In the days before the trial, Taylor received an unexpected telephone call from Boren. Taylor said, "He just called to tell me he was thinking about me as I began the trial. He said the Supreme Court has chosen the right man to give Nichols a fair trial. It was an incredible boost of morale for me."[15]

When Taylor applied for a vacant position on the Oklahoma Supreme Court, he asked Boren for a letter of support. Boren said, "No." But after a long pause, Boren said, "I won't write you a letter. I will personally go to the governor's office and speak to him about my support for your appointment." True to his promise, Boren appeared a few days later at the office of Governor Brad Henry and told of his support for Taylor's appointment.[16]

Boren's daughter Carrie said, "My Dad is a true public servant. Throughout my life, he has modeled for me the importance of giving back. He does that not just in speeches, but in the privacy of the home. I have seen the side of him that often remains secret. After a long day on the campaign trail, his late night talking to a family who has lost their farm, his changing light bulbs on the OU campus, picking up trash in parks and gardens, advising a young person about his or her future, sitting at his desk thinking of ways to better our education system, thanking his first grade teacher through a personal phone call, or telling his family around the dinner table how important it is to make a difference, one life at a time."[17]

Congressman Dan Boren, Boren's son, described Boren's public service as constant encouragement. He said, "Dad always has a way of convincing you that it was your idea to do something. In reality, he has planted the seed without you knowing. He does this with senators, governors, legislators, and even his own children."[18]

Boren's wife, Molly, has suggested that three qualities have made possible her husband's stellar career as a public servant—tenacity, a keen sense of timing, and being able to be both a visionary and implementer at the same time. Molly said, "He never gives up on a good idea. Even if there is strong opposition, he is stubborn in his support for a cause in which he believes. Often he has been successful because his opponents know he will not give up."

Boren's sense of timing has demonstrated itself at critical times in his career. He correctly chose the right year to run for governor of Oklahoma and the perfect occasion to become a United States Senator. Molly said, "That superb sense of timing also was present when David came to OU. He left a position as a popular United States Senator, and some questioned his move. History has proven it was the right time for him to be able to accomplish the most good for OU."

Some leaders are visionaries—others are implementers or "doers." Molly believes her husband is both. She said, "He sees both the big and long range picture in a particular project, while at the same time recognizing the little things that are necessary to make the project successful. He can be a good macro manager and micro manager at the same time." Molly often quotes former OU vice president Russell Driver who said Boren's management style was so unique that he made others feel like partners in a project. Boren gave them a sense of ownership.

Extraordinary leadership sometimes results in unexpected consequences. OU Historian David Levy said Boren, as much as any other person in the state's history, has made intellectual excellence "respectable." Because of Oklahoma's frontier heritage, Levy believes that many Oklahomans have been suspicious of intellect as a threat to informality and neighborliness. "One of President Boren's greatest contributions," Levy said, "has been to break down that barrier between intellectual distinction and the citizenry of the state." Levy theorizes that the barrier no longer exists in the mainstream because Boren has spent his enormous credibility and popularity to bring together all people in the state, encompassing within the community men and women of special talents and intelligence.[19]

Boren has no plans to leave his post at the University of Oklahoma. He will continue to speak out on state and national issues without regard to their popularity.

The final chapters of David Boren's life are yet to be written. Even though his remarkable career already has left the largest footprints of anyone in state history, he surely has much more to accomplish.

Boren's influence is unmatched in Oklahoma history. It spreads across political party lines in the executive, legislative, and judicial branches of both the state and national governments. The *Tulsa World* called him an "Oklahoma legend." In a special feature, reporter Randy Krehbiel, wrote:

> David Boren is the Bruce Springsteen of Oklahoma. He doesn't play the guitar or sing, but to two generations of former interns, staffers, campaign volunteers, and protégés, he will always be called The Boss.[20]

Notes

Two/The Letter

1. Interviews with David Lyle Boren and transcripts of private recollections of Boren, August, 2006, to June, 2007, Archives, Oklahoma Heritage Association, Oklahoma City, Oklahoma, hereafter referred to as David Boren interview.
2. Interview with Howard Baker, January 15, 2007, hereafter referred to as Howard Baker interview.
3. Tower Commission Report, February 26, 1987, Library of Congress, hereafter referred to as Tower Commission Report.
4. David Boren interview.
5. Ibid.
6. Ibid.
7. *The Daily Oklahoman* (Oklahoma City, Oklahoma), March 1, 1987.
8. Tower Commission report.
9. David Boren interview.
10. Ibid.
11. Letter from David Boren to President Ronald Reagan, August 2, 1987, Archives, Ronald Reagan Presidential Library, Simi Valley, California.
12. Ibid.
13. Ibid.
14. Ibid.
15. Ibid.
16. David Boren interview.
17. Ibid.
18. Ibid.
19. Ibid.
20. Presidential speech by Ronald Reagan, August 12, 1987, Archives, Ronald Reagan Presidential Library.
21. Ibid.

Three/A Proud Heritage

1. www.clarelibrary.ie
2. Bob Burke and Von Creel, *Rebel Congressman,* (Oklahoma City: Oklahoma Heritage Association, 1991), p. 5.
3. Ibid.
4. Ibid., p. 6.
5. www.ennistexas.com
6. *Rebel Congressman,* p. 7.
7. *Rebel Congressman,* p. 10.
8. Ibid., p. 18.
9. Interview with Lyle Boren, January 8, 1988, and April 15, 1988, Archives, Oklahoma Heritage Association, Oklahoma City, Oklahoma, hereafter referred to as Lyle Boren interview.
10. Ibid.
11. Ibid.
12. Ibid.
13. *Rebel Congressman,* p. 32.
14. Lyle Boren interview.

Four/Childhood
1. Lyle Boren interview.
2. Ibid.
3. Ibid.
4. Ibid.
5. Interview with Victor Wickersham, December 15, 1991.
6. Lyle Boren interview.
7. *The Daily Oklahoman,* January 8, 1975.
8. Lyle Boren interview.
9. David Boren interview.
10. Ibid.
11. Ibid.
12. Ibid.
13. Ibid.
14. Ibid.
15. Ibid.
16. Ibid.
17. Ibid.
18. Ibid.
19. Ibid.
20. Interview with Lucille Dacus, December 8, 2006, Heritage Archives.
21. Interview with Alex Adwan, December 28, 2006, hereafter referred to as Alex Adwan interview.
22. Interview with Linda Sue Gipson Stone, December 15, 2006, hereafter referred to as Linda Sue Gipson Stone interview.
23. Ibid.
24. Ibid.
25. Ibid.
26. Linda Sue Gipson Stone interview.
27. Ibid.
28 Interview with Mike Knowles, December

1, 2006, Heritage Archives.
29. David Boren interview.

Five/Preparing For the Future
1. David L. Boren interview.
2. Ibid.
3. Ibid.
4. Linda Sue Gipson Stone interview.
5. David Boren interview.
6. Ibid.
7. Ibid.
8. Ibid.
9. Ibid.
10. Linda Sue Gipson Stone interview.
11. David Boren interview.
12. Ibid.
13. Ibid.
14. Ibid.
15. Ibid.
16. Ibid.
17. Ibid.
18. Ibid.
19. Ibid.
20. Ibid.
21. Lyle Boren interview.
22. David Boren interview.

Six/The Yale Experience
1. www.yale.edu/about/history
2. Ibid.
3. Ibid.
4. Ibid.
5. David Boren interview.
6. Ibid.
7. Ibid.
8. Ibid.
9. Ibid.

10. Ibid.
11. Ibid.
12. Ibid.
13. Ibid.
14. Ibid.
15. Ibid.
16. Ibid.
17. Ibid.
18. Ibid.
19. Ibid.
20. Ibid.
21. www.en.wikipedia.org/wiki/Prescott_Bush
22. David Boren interview.
23. Ibid.
24 Ibid.
25. Ibid.
26. www.en.wikipedia.org/wiki/John_Stuart_Mill
27. Ibid.
28. Ibid.
29. Ibid.
30. Ibid.

Seven/Rhodes Scholar
1. David Boren interview.
2. Rhodesscholar.org
3. David Boren interview.
4. Interview with James Woolsey, Jr., December 21, 2006, hereafter referred to as James Woolsey, Jr., interview.
5. David Boren interview.
6. Ibid.
7. Ibid.
8. www.ox.ac.uk, the official Website of Oxford University.
9. *Smithsonian* Magazine, January, 2008, p. 24.

10. www.ox.ac.uk, the official Website of Oxford University.
11. www.balliol.ox.ac.uk
12. David Boren interview.
13. Ibid.
14. Ibid.
15. Ibid.
16 .Ibid.
17. James Woolsey, Jr., interview.
18. David Boren interview.
19. Ibid.
20. Ibid.
21. Ibid.
22. Ibid.
23. Ibid.
24. Ibid.
25. Ibid.
26. Ibid.
27. Ibid.
28. Ibid.

Eight/Law School and Race for the House

1. www.law.ou.edu, the official Website of the OU College of Law.
2. David Boren interview.
3. Ibid.
4. Ibid.
5. Ibid.
6. Ibid.
7. Ibid.
8. Ibid.
9. Ibid.
10. Ibid.
11. David Boren interview.
12. Ibid.
13. Ibid.
14. Ibid.
15. Ibid.
16. *The Seminole Producer,* May 1,

1966.
17. Ibid. May 4, 1966.
18. Ibid., May 25, 1966.
19. Letter from Lee West to Bob Burke, September 17, 2007, Heritage Archives, hereafter referred to as Lee West letter.
20 .*The Seminole Producer,* November 9, 1966.
21. Timothy D. Darr, unpublished dissertation, Oklahoma Baptist University, 2004, hereafter referred to as Timothy Darr dissertation.
22. David Boren interview.

Nine/Maverick Legislator

1. Letter from Earl Sneed to Lyle Boren, July 31, 1966, Heritage Archives.
2. David Boren interview.
3. Ibid.
4. Ibid.
5. Ibid.
6. Ibid.
7. Letter from Frank Elkouri to Bob Burke, November 4, 2006, Heritage Archives, hereafter referred to as Frank Elkouri letter.
8. Letter from Daniel G. Gibbens to Bob Burke, January 6, 2007, Heritage Archives, hereafter referred to as Daniel Gibbens letter.
9. Ibid.

10. Letter from Tom Cornish to Von Creel, December 5, 2006, Heritage Archives.
11. Timothy Darr dissertation.
12. David Boren interview.
13. Ibid.
14. Interview with Elizabeth Ann "Liz" Robertson, July 18, 2007, Heritage Archives, hereafter referred to as Liz Robertson interview.
15. David Boren interview.
16. Ibid.
17. Ibid.
18. Ibid.
19. Ibid.

Ten/Professor Boren

1. www.okbu.edu, the official Website of Oklahoma Baptist University.
2. Ibid.
3. Timothy Darr dissertation.
4. Letter from John W. Parrish to Bob Burke, October 5, 2006.
5. Ibid.
6. Interview with Rudolph Hargrave, January 22, 2007, Heritage Archives.
7. David Boren interview.
8. Letter from David Smith to Bob Burke, June 30, 2006, Heritage Archives.
9. Ibid.
10. Ibid.

11. Interview with Sam Hammons, January 12, 2007, Heritage Archives.

12. Interview with David Cox, January 27, 2007, Heritage Archives.

13. Interview with David Berrong, November 27, 2006, Heritage Archives.

14. David Boren interview.

15. Address by David Boren to OBU Assembly, May 12, 1970, Archives of Oklahoma Baptist University.

16. Ibid.

17. Interview with Robert Henry, January 3, 2007, Heritage Archives, hereafter referred to as Robert Henry interview.

18. Undated essay by David Boren, Archives of Oklahoma Baptist University.

19. Ibid.

20. *Baptist Messenger,* August 13, 1973.

21. Ibid.

22. Letter from Steven Taylor to Bob Burke, November 3, 2006, Heritage Archives, hereafter referred to as Steven Taylor letter.

23. David Boren interview.

24. Ibid.

25. Ibid.
26. Ibid.
27. Ibid.
28. Ibid.
29. Ibid.
30. Ibid.

Eleven/Loss of Trust
1. Ibid., March 8, 1972.
2. Ibid., January 3, 1974.
3. Ibid., January 8, 1974.
4. David Boren interview.
5. Ibid.
6. Ibid.
7. Ibid.
8. Interview with Sven Holmes, December 15, 2006, Heritage Archives, hereafter referred to as Sven Holmes interview.
9. David Boren interview.
10. Ibid.
11. Ibid.
12.. Liz Robertson interview.
13. David Boren interview.
14. Sven Holmes interview.
15. Ibid.
16. David Boren interview.
17. Interview with Mike Wofford, November 15, 2006, Heritage Archives, hereafter referred to as Mike Wofford interview.
18. Ibid.
19. David Boren interview.

Twelve/The Broom Brigade
1. Sven Holmes interview.

2. David Boren interview.
3. Sven Holmes interview.
4. David Boren interview.
5. Sven Holmes interview.
6. Ibid.
7. Ibid.
8. Ibid.
9. *The Daily Oklahoman,* July 21, 1974.
10. Ibid.
11. Ibid.
12. Mike Wofford interview.
13. Ibid.
14. Ibid.
15. David Boren interview.
16 Ibid.
17. Ibid.
18. Ibid.
19. Ibid.
20. Ibid.
21. Ibid.
22 Ibid.
23. Ibid.

Thirteen/The Final Push
1. *The Daily Oklahoman,* January 12, 1974.
2. Ibid., January 5, 1974.
3. Ibid., March 29, 1974.
4. Mike Wofford interview.
5. Ibid.
6. Ibid.
7. Interview with Charlie Morgan, January 15, 2007, Heritage Archives.
8. Newspaper advertisement, Heritage Archives.
9. David Boren interview.

10. Interview with Walter H. Helmerich, III, Heritage Archives, hereafter referred to as Walter Helmerich, III, interview.
11. From a Pottawatomie County Boren for Governor brochure, Heritage Archives.
12. Ibid.
13. Newspaper advertisement, Heritage Archives.
14. *The Daily Oklahoman,* July 25, 1974.
15. *The Daily Oklahoman,* August 25, 1974.
16. Ibid.
17. Ibid.
18. Ibid.
19. Ibid., August 29, 1974.
20. Ibid.

Fourteen/And the Broom Swept
1. *The Daily Oklahoman,* August 29, 1974.
2. Sven Holmes interview.
3. *The Daily Oklahoman,* August 29, 1974.
4. David Boren interview.
5. Ibid.
6. *The Daily Oklahoman,* January 8, 1975.
7. Ibid., August 30, 1974.
8. Ibid.
9. Ibid., September 5, 1974.
10. Ibid., January 8, 1975.
11. David Boren interview.

12. *The Daily Oklahoman,* September 15, 1974.
13. Ibid., August 18, 1974.
14. Ibid., November 3, 1974.
15. David Boren interview.
16. *The Daily Oklahoman,* October 27, 1974.
17. David Boren interview.
18. *The Daily Oklahoman,* September 22, 1974.
19. Sven Holmes interview.
20. Ibid.
21. Ibid., November 6, 1974.
22. Ibid.

Fifteen/Forming a Team
1. *The Daily Oklahoman,* November 7, 1974.
2. Ibid., December 8, 1974.
3. Ibid., November 13, 1974.
4. Ibid., November 14, 1974.
5. Ibid.
6. Ibid., November 20, 1974.
7. Ibid., December 10, 1974.
8. Ibid., December 12, 1974.
9. Ibid., November 21, 1974.
10. *Oklahoma Statehouse Reporter,* January 15, 1975.
11. *The Daily Oklahoman,* December 14, 1974.
12. David Boren interview.

13. *Oklahoma City Times,* June 13, 1975.

Sixteen/Governor Boren
1. *St. Louis Globe Democrat,* January 15, 1975.
2. Speech of David Boren, Heritage Archives.
3. From the inaugural address of Governor David L. Boren, January 13, 1975, Heritage Archives.
4. Ibid.
5. *The Daily Oklahoman,* January 14, 1975.
6. Ibid., January 15, 1975.
7. Ibid.
8. David Boren interview.
9. Letter from Denzil Garrison, November 30, 2006, Heritage Archives, hereafter referred to as Denzil Garrison letter.
10. *Time* Magazine, November 15, 1974.
11. *The Daily Oklahoman,* January 16, 1975.
12. Ibid., January 18, 1975.
13. Ibid.
14. Ibid., January 23, 1975.
15. Interview with Robert Mitchell, November 27, 2006, Heritage Archives.
16. David Boren interview.
17. *The Sunday Oklahoman,* February 9, 1975.
18. David Boren interview.

Seventeen/Tax Relief and Yes-All-8

1. *The Daily Oklahoman,* February 20, 1975.
2. David Boren interview.
3. *The Daily Oklahoman,* March 8, 1975.
4. Mike Wofford interview.
5. Ibid.
6. *The Daily Oklahoman,* April 15, .1975.
7. Ibid., June 8, 1975.
8. Ibid., July 18, 1975.
9. Ibid., July 20, 1975.
10. Ibid., July 25, 1975.
11. Interview with Denise Bode, February 26, 2007, Heritage Archives.
12. Interview with Jack McCarty, November 27, 2006, Heritage Archives.
13. *The Daily Oklahoman,* September 18, 1975.
14. Ibid., October 22, 1975.
15. David Boren interview.
16. *Tulsa Tribune,* October 25, 1975.
17. David Boren interview.
18. *The Daily Oklahoman,* October 28, 1975.
19 .Ibid., David Boren interview.
20. Ibid.
21. *Tulsa Tribune,* January 5, 1976.
22. Ibid., January 8, 1976.
23. David Boren interview.
24. *The Daily Oklahoman,* June 2, 1976.
25. Ibid., June 30, 1976.

26. Ibid., May 23, 1976.
27. Ibid., March 21, 1976.
28. Ibid., December 8, 1976.

Eighteen/Sunset Laws and Worker's Comp

1. David Boren interview.
2. Interview with Charles Cashion, November 27, 2006, Heritage Archives.
3. Interview with Marian Opala, January 29, 2007, Heritage Archives.
4. *The Daily Oklahoman,* April 16, 1977.
5. Ibid.
6. Ibid., April 17, 1977.
7. Ibid.
8. *Tulsa World,* April 27, 1977.
9. David Boren interview.
10. Ibid.
11. *Oklahoma Journal,* June 16, 1977.
12. Ibid.
13. David Boren interview.
14. www.okartinst.org the official Website of the Oklahoma Arts Institute.
15. Interview with Molly Shi Boren, May 21, 2007, Heritage Archives, hereafter referred to as Molly Boren interview.
16. Ibid.
17. Ibid.
18. Ibid.
19. *The Daily Oklahoman,* December 6, 1977.

Nineteen/A Crossroads

1. David Boren interview.
2. *The Daily Oklahoman,* December 15, 1977.
3. David Boren interview.
4. Bob Burke and Kenny Franks, *Dewey Bartlett: The Bartlett Legacy,* (Edmond: University of Central Oklahoma Press, 1996), p. 30.
5. *The Daily Oklahoman,* January 22, 1978.
6. Ibid.
7. Ibid., January 31, 1978.
8. *The Daily Oklahoman,* April 16, 1978.
9. Ronn Cupp and Bob Burke: *Mr. Water: Robert S. Kerr, Jr.,* (Oklahoma City: Oklahoma Heritage Association, 2005), p. 180.
10. Ibid., p. 182.
11. Ibid., p. 181.
12. Ibid.
13. David Boren interview.
14. Ibid.
15. Ibid.
16. Rob Pyron interview.

Twenty/Dirty Politics

1. *The Daily Oklahoman,* July 2, 1978.
2. Ibid., July 17, 1978.
3. David Boren interview.
4. *The Daily Oklahoman,* August 11, 1978.
5. David Boren interview.
6. *The Daily Oklahoman,* August 29, 1978; August 30, 1978; September 1, 1978; and September 6, 1978.

7. Ibid.
8. Ibid.
9. Ibid.
10. David Boren interview.
11. Ibid.
12. Ibid.
13. Ibid.
14. Ibid.
15. Ibid.
16. Ibid.
17. Molly Boren interview.
18. *The Daily Oklahoman,* September 20, 1978.
19. Ibid.
20. David Boren interview.

**Twenty One/
Senator Boren**
1. David Boren interview.
2. Ibid.
3. Ibid.
4. *The Daily Oklahoman,* January 4, 1979.
5. Molly Boren interview.
6. Ibid.
7. *Congressional Quarterly,* December 30, 1978.
8. David Boren interview.
9. Ibid.
10. Ibid.
11. Ibid.
12. Interview with Sam Nunn, January 26, 2007, Heritage Archives, hereafter referred to as Sam Nunn interview.
13. *Congressional Quarterly,* December 30, 1978.
14. David Boren interview.
15. Ibid.
16. Ibid.

**Twenty Two/Reform
at the National Level**
1. Bob Burke and David L. Russell, *Law and Laughter: The Life of Lee West,* (Oklahoma City: Oklahoma Heritage Association, 2002), p. 214, hereafter described as *Law and Laughter.*
2. *The Daily Oklahoman,* April 10, 1977.
3. *Law and Laughter,* p. 218.
4. David Boren interview.
5. *The Daily Oklahoman,* October 25, 1979.
6. Ibid., January 26, 1979.
7. Ibid.
8. Ibid., April 12, 1979.
9. Ibid., August 6, 1979.
10. Ibid., September 7, 1979.
11. Ibid., September 4, 1979.
12. David Boren interview.
13. Ibid., August 30, 1979.
14. David Boren interview.
15. *Congressional Quarterly,* January 12, 1980.
16. Ibid., February 9, 1980.
17. Ibid., March 29, 1980.
18. Ibid.
19. Molly Boren interview.
20. Ibid.
21. Ibid.
22. Ibid.
23. Ibid.

**Twenty Three/
Bridge Builder**
1. David Boren interview.
2. Ibid.
3. *Congressional Quarterly,* June 13, 1981.
4. Ibid.
5. Ibid.
6. Ibid.
7. Ibid.
8. Ibid.
9. Ibid.
10. Ibid.
11. Ibid., September 4, 1962.
12. David Boren interview.
13. Ibid.
14. "The David Boren Report," 1984 Edition, Heritage Archives.
15. Ibid.
16. Ibid.
17. Ibid.
18. Ibid.
19. Ibid.

**Twenty Four/Campaign
Finance Reform**
1. David Boren interview.
2. *Congressional Quarterly,* November 23, 1985.
3. Ibid.
4. Ibid.
5. David Boren interview.
6. Ibid.
7. *Congressional Quarterly,* August 16, 1986.
8. Ibid.
9. Ibid.
10. "Operation Bootstrap II" information sheet, Heritage Archives.
11. Ibid.
12. Ibid.
13. Ibid.
14. Robert Henry interview.

15. Ibid.
16. Ibid.
17. Ibid.
18. Ibid.
19. Ibid.
20. *Congressional Quarterly,* February 15, 1986.
21. Ibid.
22. David Boren interview.
23. Sam Nunn interview.

**Twenty Five/
The World of American Intelligence**
1. David Boren interview.
2. Ibid.
3. Ibid.
4. Ibid.
5. Ibid.
6. Ibid.
7. Ibid.
8. Ibid.
9. Ibid.
10. Ibid.
11. Ibid.
12. Ibid.
13. Ibid.
14. Ibid.
15. Ibid.
16. Ibid., Sam Nunn interview.
17. David Boren interview.
18. Ibid.
19. Ibid.
20. Ibid.
21. Ibid.
22. Ibid.
23. Ibid.

**Twenty Six/
World Traveler**
1. David Boren interview; Sam Nunn interview.
2. David Boren interview.

3. Ibid.
4. Ibid.
5. Ibid.
6. Ibid.
7. Ibid.
8. George Tenet, *At the Center of the Storm: My Years at the CIA,* New York:

**Twenty Seven/
Winds of War**
1. Letter from Robert Dick Bell to Bob Burke, March 26, 2008, Heritage Archives.
2. Letter from Dan Webber to Bob Burke, January 2, 2007, Heritage Archives, hereafter referred to as Dan Webber letter.
3. Ibid.
4. *The New York Times,* January 2, 1990.
5. Ibid.
6. David Boren interview.
7. Ibid.
8. Ibid.
9. Ibid.
10. Ibid.
11. Ibid.
12. Ibid.
13. Ibid.
14. Ibid.
15. *The Daily Oklahoman,* March 22, 1991.
16. David Boren interview.
17. *U.S. News & World Report,* June 3, 1991.
18. *The Daily Oklahoman,* April 26, 1991.
19. Interview with Dan Boren, February

12, 2007, Heritage Archives, hereafter referred to as Dan Boren interview.
20. David Boren interview.
21. *Oklahoma Gazette,* May 8, 1991.
22. *The Daily Oklahoman,* March 23, 1991.

Twenty Eight/In the Eye of the Storm
1. *The Daily Oklahoman,* March 29, 1991.
2. Ibid.
3. Ibid.
4. Ibid.
5. David Boren interview.
6. Ibid.
7. Ibid.
8. Ibid.
9. Ibid.; *The Daily Oklahoman,* April 6, 1991.
10. David Boren interview.
11. www.ndu.edu/nsep, the official Website of the National Security Education Program.
12. Ibid.
13. Ibid.
14. Ibid.
15. *The New York Times,* February 8, 1992.
16. Ibid.
17. *Defense Intelligence Journal,* Spring, 1992, p. 17.
18. *The New York Times,* February 7, 1992.
19. *Defense Intelligence Journal,* Spring, 1992, p. 29.
20. *Foreign Affairs,*

Summer, 1992, p. 55.
21. Ibid.
22. David Boren interview.
23. Ibid.
24. Ibid.
25. Ibid.
26. Ibid.
27. Ibid.
28. Ibid.
29. Ibid.
30. Ibid.
31. Ibid.
32. Ibid.
33. Ibid.

Twenty Nine/ Mission of Mercy
1. *The Daily Oklahoman,* November 17, 1993.
2. Ibid.
3. David Boren interview.
4. Ibid.
5. Ibid.
6. Ibid.
7. Ibid.
8. Ibid.
9. Memorandum of David L. Boren, November 18, 1993, a memoir of his visit with Deputy Prime Minister Tariq Aziz, Heritage Archives.
10. Ibid.
11. Ibid.
12. Ibid.
13. Ibid.
14. Ibid.
15. Ibid.
16. David Boren interview.
17. Ibid.
18. Ibid.
19. Ibid.

Thirty/Coming Home
1. David Boren interview.
2. Molly Boren interview.
3. David Boren interview.
4. *Norman Transcript,* October 27, 1994.
5. Denzil Garrison letter.
6. David Boren interview.
7. Ibid.
8. Ibid.
9. Ibid.
10. Ibid.
11. Ibid.
12. Ibid.
13. Interview with Tripp Hall, January 31, 2007, Heritage Archives.
14. David Boren interview.
15. *The New York Times,* May 13, 1994.
16. *The Daily Oklahoman,* April 28, 1994.
17. Ibid.
18. Ibid.
19. Letter from David L. Boren to members of the United States Senate, October 12, 1994, Heritage Archives.
20. Ibid.

Thirty One/ President Boren
1. David Boren interview.
2. *Norman Transcript,* October 27, 1994.
3. Ibid.
4. David Boren interview.
5. *The Rostrum,* May, 1996, p. 20.
6. David Boren interview.
7. Inaugural Address of David L. Boren,

September 15, 1995, Heritage Archives.
8. Ibid.
9. Ibid.
10. David Boren interview.
11. Ibid.
12. Molly Boren interview.
13. David Boren interview.
14. Ibid.
15. Molly Boren interview.
16. *Sooner Magazine,* Fall, 2004, p. 7.
17. Molly Boren interview.
18. David Boren interview.
19. Ibid.
20. Ibid.
21. Interview with David Maloney, November 14, 2006, Heritage Archives, hereafter referred to as David Maloney interview.
22. Ibid.
23. *The Daily Oklahoman,* September 5, 1996.
24. Ibid., July 4, 1996.
25. David Boren interview.
26. Ibid.
27. Ibid.
28. George Tenet, *At the Center of the Storm* (New York: HarperCollins Publishers, 2007), p. 161.
29. Ibid.
30. David Boren interview.
31. Ibid.

32. *At the Center of the Storm,* p. 364.
33. David Boren interview.
34. *At the Center of the Storm,* p. 365
35. Ibid., p. 477.
36. Ibid., p. 478.

**Thirty Two/
Seeking Excellence**
1. David Boren interview.
2. Interview with John Massey, January 15, 2007, Heritage Archives; Interview with Joe Castiglione, January 28, 2007, Heritage Archives, hereafter referred to as Joe Castiglione interview.
3. Joe Castiglione interview.
4. Ibid.
5. Ibid.
6. Ibid.
7. David Boren interview.
8. Joe Castligione interview.
9. Letter from Bob Stoops to Bob Burke, February 27, 2007, Heritage Archives.
10. John Massey interview.
11. Letter from William Hetherington, March 17, 2007, Heritage Archives.
12. *OU People,* Fall, 2005, p. 8.
13. Ibid., p. 11.
14. Ibid., p. 10.
15. Interview with Glen Johnson, December 15, 2006, Heritage Archives.

16. Lee West letter.
17. Interview with Nick Hathaway, March 28, 2007, Heritage Archives.
18. Interview with Marolyn Sauls, January 23, 2007, Heritage Archives.
19. Letter from Harold Hamm to Bob Burke, November 7, 2006, Heritage Archives.
20. Interview with Larry Nichols, November 18, 2006, Heritage Archives.
21. Letter from Danny Hilliard to Bob Burke, September 21, 2006, Heritage Archives.
22. Interview with Paul Massad, July 26, 2007, Heritage Archives.
23. University of Oklahoma Annual Report—2006-2007, hereafter referred to as OU Annual Report.
24. Ibid.
25. Ibid.
26. Ibid.
27. Ibid.
28. Ibid.
29. Ibid.
30. Ibid.
31. Ibid.
32. Ibid.
33. Ibid.
34. Interview with David Levy, January 4, 2007, Heritage Archives.

**Thirty Three/
A Letter to America**
1. David Boren, *A Letter to America,* (Norman: University of Oklahoma Press, 2008).
2. Ibid.
3. Ibid.
4. Ibid.
5. Ibid.
6. *The Daily Oklahoman,* March 18, 2008.
7. Letter from George H.W. Bush to Bob Burke, November 22, 2006, Heritage Archives.
8. Interview with Clay Bennett, December 15, 2006, Heritage Archives.
9. Interview with Lee Allan Smith, January 16, 2007, Heritage Archives.
10. James Woosley interview.
11. Letter from William Paul to Bob Burke, May 21, 2007, Heritage Archives.
12. Letter from Tom Cornish to Von Creel, December 5, 2006, Heritage Archives.
13. Interview with Frank Seay, January 15, 2007, Heritage Archives.
14. Robert Henry interview.
15. Steven Taylor Letter.
16. Ibid.
17. Comments of Carrie Boren at

the Oklahoma
Foundation for
Excellence banquet,
May 20, 2006,
Heritage Archives.

18. Dan Boren interview.
19. Comments of
David Levy at
the Oklahoma
Foundation for

Excellence banquet,
May 20, 2006,
Heritage Archives.
20. *Tulsa World,* Janurary
22, 2006.

Index